OXFORD ENGLISH MONOGRAPHS

Metaphors of Change in the Language of Nineteenth-Century Fiction

Scott, Gaskell, and Kingsley

MEGAN PERIGOE STITT

CLARENDON PRESS · OXFORD
1998

Oxford University Press, Great Clarendon Street, Oxford OX2 6DP

Oxford New York

Athens Auckland Bangkok Bogota Bombay
Buenos Aires Calcutta Cape Town Dar es Salaam
Delhi Florence Hong Kong Istanbul Karachi
Kuala Lumpur Madras Madrid Melbourne
Mexico City Nairobi Paris Singapore
Taipei Tokyo Toronto Warsaw

and associated companies in
Berlin Ibadan

Oxford is a registered trade mark of Oxford University Press

Published in the United States
by Oxford University Press Inc., New York

British Library Cataloguing in Publication Data
Data available

Library of Congress Cataloging in Publication Data
Data available
ISBN 0–19–818442–5

1 3 5 7 9 10 8 6 4 2

Typeset by Cambrian Typesetters, Frimley, Surrey
Printed in Great Britain on acid-free paper by
Bookcraft Ltd,
Midsomer Norton, Somerset

Acknowledgements

FUNDING for my research was generously provided by the following sources: the Overseas Research Students' Award Scheme (Committee of Vice-Chancellors and Principals of the Universities of the United Kingdom); the University of Oxford; Oriel College, Oxford; the Canadian Women's Club, London; and, by no means least, Dr David R. Holbrooke.

I would also like to thank the staff at the Bodleian Library, the Oriel Library, the English Faculty Library, Oxford; and the John Rylands University Library of Manchester.

I am indebted to my supervisor, Dr Stephen Gill (Lincoln College, Oxford), for his help and encouragement all along the way.

Finally, I want to express my gratitude to family and friends who gave many different kinds of support during my years at Oxford; to those who made nights short with talk, in a lovely mix of fact and enigma.

Contents

Introduction

All philology must end in history . . .[1]
(Bunsen)

IN the early decades of the nineteenth century, before Darwin began to form his ideas, some people were fixing language to a model of change: a line of progress or decay. The model was akin to biology. Friedrich von Schlegel in 1808 suggested that 'the discipline closest to the new science of "comparative grammar" was comparative anatomy', and Jacob Grimm announced the same in 1819.[2] Geology offered another metaphor.[3] In a letter home to his parents, from Ilfracombe, Charles Kingsley wrote: 'Mansfield and I go geologizing & shell-picking—but Ah!!! ther baint no shells!—Where be they gwan?'[4] He was gathering not just rocks and shells; he also put a few west coast words into his sack. Dialect was coming into favour. William Gaskell in the 1850s argued that 'instead of saying that the Lancashire dialect is a corruption of English, it would seem truer to say that English is very often a corruption of Anglo-Saxon'; Lancashire 'forms of speech and pronunciation' were not a corruption but rather 'bits of old granite, which have perhaps been polished into smoother forms, but lost in the process a good deal of their original strength'. His task was to learn whether his dialect 'retains any relics of the old British tongue'.[5] He implies that we must hold onto the earlier forms, while admitting their fall from usage, in the way that we view fragments of history in a museum, under glass.

---

[1] Christian Charles Josias Bunsen, *Outlines of the Philosophy of Universal History* (London, 1854), i. 61.
[2] Martyn Wakelin, *The Archaeology of English* (London, 1988), 175.
[3] Tony Crowley, *The Politics of Discourse* (Basingstoke, 1989), 58.
[4] Robert Bernard Martin, 'An Edition of the Correspondence and Private Papers of Charles Kingsley 1819–1856', D.Phil. thesis, Oxford, 1950, 140. The letter is dated Apr. 1849.
[5] William Gaskell, 'Two Lectures on the Lancashire Dialect', in *Mary Barton* (1854; Halifax, 1993), 383, 362, 371.

Richard Chenevix Trench elaborated upon the term 'fossil poetry'. He tried to shake people from a habit of reading on the surface for content, to get them to analyse the language itself: 'Many a single word is itself a concentrated poem, having stores of poetical thought and imagery laid up in it.'[6] The philologist became a sort of hero who rescued the feelings and ideas of the past. Trench, who helped move the focus towards English in particular, had a large impact on language theory in the 1850s.[7] He tapped into a Victorian fear, while attempting to soothe it away. Linda Dowling gives an account of how Trench used philology to help build 'an enduring vision of civilization'; of how he brought the fossils of language into a genre of homily that diminished fears of decay. Yet Trench's own value of 'scientific lexicography', lifted by a desire to bring his own country into eminence, also helped 'erode the foundations of the Victorian ideal of civilization and threaten its eventual collapse'.[8] Dennis Taylor, in his work on Thomas Hardy, explains: 'The philologists' belief, that the history of words illumined current usage, was also haunted by the fact that the ultimate history was lost beyond recall.' Deepening the concern were parallels made among the strata of the earth, the language, and the mind.[9] William Barnes, a linguist and poet of the Dorset dialect, saw the analogies and the fear they aroused when he chose for a title-page the biblical line: 'Look unto the rock whence ye are hewn, and to the quarry whence ye are digged.'[10] The very term 'diachronic'—linguistic jargon for 'lasting through time'—came into being in 1857 in a book called *Creation*, by Philip Gosse, with the subtitle *Omphalos: an Attempt to Untie the Geological Knot*.[11] 'Omphalos' is the Greek word for navel.

The use of dialect in literature had been going on for centuries.

---

[6] Richard Chenevix Trench, *On the Study of Words* (London, 1851), 5.

[7] Crowley, *The Politics of Discourse*, 52.

[8] Linda Dowling, *Language and Decadence in the Victorian* Fin de Siècle (Princeton, 1986), 49, 60.

[9] Dennis Taylor, *Hardy's Literary Language and Victorian Philology* (Oxford, 1993), 11.

[10] William Barnes, *Early England and the Saxon-English* (London, 1869), title-page. The quotation is from Isa. 51: 1.

[11] Taylor, *Hardy's Literary Language and Victorian Philology*, 13.

Chaucer is one of the better-known early examples. The study of dialect in Britain began to take a more scholarly tone in the seventeenth century. Improvements in travel, rising sharply in the early nineteenth century, gave people a wider sense of the variants in their own country.[12] In 1855 John Davies wrote an article 'On the Races of Lancashire' for the Philological Society, and in it he made no 'apology' for his study of dialect: 'for all philologists are now well aware of the importance of such forms of a language, both in determining historical questions, and in the examination of the structure and progress to which they belong'. Words of a past race (Celtic, in this instance), remaining in a dialect of English, filled a gap left by other historical inquiries. Davies could argue, as William Gaskell had done in the previous year, that 'a large Celtic element' had gone into the formation of England's power. The value of the study of dialect, to our knowledge of progress, had not yet been 'sufficiently acknowledged in England, though well understood by the scholars of France and Germany'.

Davies saw philology as a way of understanding the inner life of a nation; for the English, as a means of self-knowledge. No real distinction is made, in Davies's work, between history and the individual mind, as a focus through which the study of language could illuminate our knowledge of the past. It was the only way to interpret the 'early literature' of the nation.[13] In other words, dialect became recognized, not only as a kind of archive, but also as a factor in our understanding of what an author meant. When an author has gone to the trouble of marking out dialect (with different spelling, or quotation marks, or translation) we can infer that the 'strangeness' is meant to stand for something in itself, apart from the content of what is said. The word 'dialect' in the nineteenth century hovered among the sciences of earth, history, and the mind; it moved amid ideas of form and intention in the genres of fiction.

I use the term 'dialect' loosely. A more rigid definition would

---

[12] Valerie Shepherd, *Language Variety and the Art of the Everyday* (London, 1990), 34–5.
[13] John Davies, 'On the Races of Lancashire', *Transactions of the Philological Society*, no. 13 (1855), 210, 242, 283.

mislead, in the context, because the writers treated here did not
have a fixed idea. Dialect may be a subspecies of language in
some books, but others see language as an abstract idea, with
dialect as the speech or writing in use. When people in
nineteenth-century Britain wrote about dialect, they tended to
mean a particular accent and vocabulary (more often than
grammatical uniqueness) of a region. The works of a 'dialect
writer' would be examined for accuracy of representation (did
the verses *sound* like a Lancashire ploughman?) and read as an
attempt either to challenge the standard or, by raillery, to
reinforce its value. Essays into the topic did not give a clear
definition; they made examples of words that could in isolation
be both standard and non-standard; and terms of the workplace,
or religion, or a field of study could signify as much difference as
a 'provincial' (geographically located) example. Also, the more
general notion of *varieties* of language resonates with the model
of the origin and variety of species that can be found in many of
the writings on language in the novelists' circle.

The novel took an interesting part, growing as a vehicle of
realism, where not only the subject but also the style was
individual; yet it also contributed to the ideal of a standard
English. Few nineteenth-century novels (in English) adopted
dialect (by which I mean obvious marks of difference) as the
narrating voice. Mark Twain's *Huckleberry Finn* came late in
the century, and was American. Most novels of the period
inserted fragments of non-standard speech (as speech) in a
matrix of standard writing.

The basic structure reflects, in both crude and subtle ways,
ideas about language; ideas that do not always interlock. The
fifth (1854) edition of Elizabeth Gaskell's *Mary Barton* is a good
example. The novel 'records' the speech of the Manchester
working class; footnotes guide the reader to the meaning and
etymology of certain words and phrases. They give the work a
scholarly tone. At the end of the book are two lectures by
Gaskell's husband, William, on the origin and nature of the
Lancashire dialect. William was one of many philologists of his
time claiming that dialects meant something about the origin of
a part of society, and hence about its role in the forming of the
nation. In the novels, too, different voices were placed to invoke
a scale of progress. Yet the genre is equivocal in another sense:

as a ground on which the artful use of language (a deliberate mingling of variants) had a less than snug fit into the model of non-standard forms as relics of the past, and clues to immanent change. There are moments, often, when it is unclear if a speech is meant to be a mark of progress (or decay), or a tool that a character may take up or set down at will.

Mary Barton is a key to the structure of my own book. Some time after Gaskell came out with the first edition (1848) she and William thought to add the non-fiction account of language. The two genres do not compete; they say different things. The idea, here, is to look at fiction in dialogue with other, scientific works. It may not be fair to lump all non-fiction into one category; nor do I think it invariably wise to set fiction apart from other artefacts. Gillian Beer has written a valuable book on the interplay between Darwin and literature, in which she shows a likeness between science and art, where both use metaphor to alter our perceptions. It was no accident that Darwin read the novels of Dickens: 'Because of its preoccupation with time and with change evolutionary theory has inherent affinities with the problems and processes of narrative.'[14] There is a structural sameness. And yet, to make the claim that fiction was more than just a mirror of nineteenth-century language studies, I divide each chapter into three parts. The first is a look at the scholarly treatment of ideas. In the second, the ideas form a backdrop to a closer analysis of the fiction, and to the genre's uniqueness. The final part is a summary of the questions that were being tried.

To merge discussions of history, patterns of change, and language, I draw upon the works of three novelists who wrote from different parts of Britain, who shared some key influences, and who took different lines. Walter Scott tended to focus on issues of a nation within a nation; Elizabeth Gaskell, on how personal bonds (often more social than biological) interplay with language; Kingsley, on the links between national and racial inheritance. Gaskell (1810–65) and Kingsley (1819–75) were closer in time and space to each other than to Scott (1771–1832). They read his novels, but they lived in a circle of influence (including Trench, Davies, and Max Müller) unknown

---

[14] Gillian Beer, *Darwin's Plots* (London, 1983), 7.

to Scott. Yet all three came in contact with images (in contemporary works) that linked geology, human development, and the study of language.[15] The links were often threaded with nationalism. The novels transform basic metaphors of language— of its origin and process of change—into the politics of standardization; yet the genre itself, helping to create an audience for non-standard varieties, allows tension to remain between ideas of nature and accident in history. The deliberate use of non-standard speech threaded by the 'proper' language of the narrator offers a fascinating insight into how authors created—with their own nuances—a belief in gradual progress and human will; into how they dealt with the voices (quietly) implying chance.

Judith Wilt describes the novelist as 'a deployer of languages as well as a recounter of deeds'. She finds this to be most strikingly the case with the historical novelist, whose language may differ greatly from the speech of the characters. The author's awareness of the difference builds a stronger parallel between the plot and 'linguistic change'. Scott's adoption of the genre reveals a 'wish to play with the recognition that language has a history. Language, like other actions, has a dialectical process; languages, like other characters, have their dramas of competition and mating.'[16]

The three novelists, here, set at least part of their fiction in the past. It gives us a chance to compare the effects of historical and modern contexts upon the use of language. How far back does meaning go? What moments of change, linguistic and historical, are chosen to matter? Obscurity, in the merging of disciplines that sketch the distant past, may be seen as a device in the novelists' art. The first three chapters of my book explore the belief (growing popular in the nineteenth century) that universal laws can be drawn from observable processes. Most of the scientific references, here, are to the fields of geology and evolution—sciences of idiosyncrasy, where each new oddity

---

[15] Brigitte Nerlich writes about the influence of biology, palaeontology, and zoology upon 19th-century linguistics, in 'The Evolution of the Concept of "Linguistic Evolution" in the Nineteenth and Twentieth Century', *Lingua*, 77/2 (1989), 102.

[16] Judith Wilt, *Secret Leaves* (Chicago, 1985), 80.

(like the 'harsh sounds' of a dialect) was expected to add proof of steady progress, once the past function was known. The fourth chapter, treating the 'modern' works of the three, will show that even the non-historical novels unfurl a preoccupation with laws of change. A different sort of obscurity is invoked: one that is seated in the mind of a character. The notion of psychology, as analogous to other forms of development, was often blended (in the novels) with commentary on art—on the willed use of language. The use of blind spots in time is one way of distinguishing fiction from science.

The link between language variation and art got even tighter in the later part of the century. William Axon, writing about George Eliot, noted the accuracy of the dialect in her novels, but argued that her 'use of dialect was distinctly artistic'. She did not use dialect merely to mark out a stereotype; rather, she used it more subtly as a way of telling apart one character from another. Men in the shop in *Adam Bede* speak the same dialect, but each in his own style.[17] A character's speech, then, could be seen to proclaim individuality, while placing him or her into a 'drama' of changing language.

Eliot appears in Chapter 4 as a kind of foil—a background move away from dialect as a static sign. In *The Mill on the Floss* speech changes as the Tulliver children grow up, through stages of social integration. Other novelists made characters speak in alternative forms, at interesting moments in the plot, but not with the same sense of gradual, or accumulative, change. Eliot gives us a parallel between individual, linguistic development and social 'progress'; yet, her novel questions the axiom that the world will ever break away from its struggles. Her awareness of individual responses to language erodes the confidence that philology can somehow look back to and predict sweeping trends of benefit to the nation. The Edgeworths, earlier, had written that the 'ambition of a gentleman . . . [was] to know whence the terms of most sciences are derived, and to be able, in some degree, to trace the progress of mankind in knowledge and refinement, by examining the extent and combination of their

---

[17] William E. A. Axon, 'George Eliot's Use of Dialect', in Gordon S. Haight (ed.), *A Century of George Eliot Criticism* (1880; London, 1966), 132.

different vocabularies'.[18] Eliot operates, in my thesis, as a counterpoint to such an idea; to Kingsley, for example, who tended to use characters (and commentary on their speech) to dramatize the rise and decay of nation and race. Chapter 4 looks at how each author deals with the conflict between the idea of character (individual and national) as a fixed identity and pattern of speech, and the plots of growth and change.

Nationalism enters the picture, not as an aside, but as part of the framework. Others have written on the effect of German thought upon British philology, both as a model of research and as a competitive drive. Here, the attempt is to show how beliefs in the future of Britain got worked into some basic metaphors of language: dialect-as-fossil, for example, or a cycle of growth and decay. Images often got conflated, not only in the novels, but in other writings of the period. Charles Lyell, for example, talked about geology and variations of speech in the same breath. Alexander Bain, known to Eliot and (if fleetingly) to Kingsley, drew together psychology, language, and etymology. He also wrote *An English Grammar*, and followed it with a book on how to teach the language. An excerpt from the former gives a useful sense of how the mid-Victorians understood the development of standard English:

The Anglo-Saxon compositions that have come down to us exemplify one dialect,—the dialect of the western counties; and it is now generally believed that modern English partakes more of a different dialect, spoken in the midland counties. Thus, although the Anglo-Saxon writings are valuable as illustrating an early Saxon tongue not far removed from ours, we do not reckon it as the immediate parent of the English language. This circumstance does not prevent us from using the name Saxon, or Anglo-Saxon, as describing the basis or foundation of English.[19]

The quotation reveals a number of key points. Victorians did not equate themselves with their Saxon ancestors. History had given them room to grow—by the injection of a different culture at the time of the Norman invasion. Bain's recognition of a multiple parentage works against the stultifying image of mere

---

[18] Maria and R. L. Edgeworth, *Essays on Practical Education* (London, 1815), ii. 2.

[19] Alexander Bain, *An English Grammar* (London, 1863), 120.

repetition. Bain also performs a neat trick: he admits that even the modern standard of English is just one of several dialects, and not even the Saxon one at that, giving it the mutability of speech over the fixity of a written dialect; yet he then slides the name 'Saxon, or Anglo-Saxon' onto what he now calls 'the English language' (rather than dialect). In other words, he does not allow that English must be trapped by old writings, but he wants to maintain (against his own sense of the importance of other dialects and languages) the association between the earliest 'English' (German) ancestors and the present living tongue.

The novels, here, are rife with values that would seem to conflict; values that are brought together, often, by metaphor. The notion of speciation, at the core of the evolutionary process, in some cases will merge with the belief that God knew what he was doing when he divided people by walls of speech. An image used by some (Kingsley, for example) is of Babel—referring to the point in time when God divided people by language. It may be simply a way of describing a cacophony of voices; but at times it is taken further to suggest that the effect of linguistic barriers was the rise of nations, and that the struggle among languages created a better England. Hybridization becomes an image central to the belief in a superior race. Kingsley takes furthest the idea that a 'universal' language corrupts; that a national language, legitimized by a long history of success, is the most useful tool; that God gave England (in particular) not only the skill but also the authority to use it.

The three novelists shared an attempt to solve the dilemma of a standard language: how can it be open to all, and yet provide the nation with a means of sorting out the wheat from the chaff; how can it be both a tool (arbitrarily formed) and evidence of necessary stages of progress? A letter from the linguist Max Müller to Gaskell is apt. He writes: 'I enclose a little poem in the Schleswig Holstein Dialect with all the marks of the printer's fingers on it.' The poem expresses a desire to be young again. It appears in parallel text—English and the German dialect. Inky fingerprints show that Müller meant the last statement literally.[20] Here, we see Gaskell in a circle of German influence, at the

[20] John Rylands University Library of Manchester, Eng. MS 731/71.

centre of which is a poem of wistful regeneration and the trust in attempts at translation, notwithstanding the particularity of dialect. Kingsley, more blatantly, wished to create a 'plain English' out of the findings of scholarship, rather than trust the clumsier 'machinery' of the people to find the language that will best evoke their needs.[21] What the fiction offers, in every case, is a way of combining structure and theme to look at the role of individual speech (or writing) in the formation of plot.

I took a risk in my focus. Excellent books have been written about a given author's use of language. Two of great use to me were Dennis Taylor's study of Hardy, and Graham Tulloch's of Scott. They combine close readings of the novels with a social context. Taylor in particular shows Hardy in the thick of debates on linguistic and natural history; enough of Hardy's own writing is treated to make it seem a creative (rather than imitative) act. My own idea was to show how the novelists added to the debates a medium that altered what seem to be parallel arguments in more straightforward (single-voiced) prose. This would require many references to the fiction, and lines of interpretation leading from them. It would be impossible to cover all the works of any one writer, much less of three, and the risk is that the examples may seem haphazard, or too disembodied from their plots. What I hope to have gained from the choice, however, is a sense of the novelists interacting not only with linguists, historians, and scientists, but also with writers of their own genre, who use a cluster of images in different ways.

Finally, a word by Linda Dowling, who brought to her analysis of Victorian *fin de siècle* literature an enviable knowledge of Romantic and Victorian philology. She warns:

[21] Charles Kingsley, *Two Years Ago* (London, 1893), 210, 213. The novel leans towards a belief that central government, using the tools of plain English, can raise the mental standard of its people to a style that will reflect the nation more accurately, in spite of losses on a smaller scale. It implies that 'locals' can hardly represent themselves as they are. We are prompted to listen in on 'The charming machinery of local governments', where 'One man has "summat to say,"—utterly irrelevant', and the rest chatter and quarrel, with outbursts of 'Hear 'mun out!' and so on. The spread of cholera in the village is attributed to 'that "local government" which signifies, in plain English, the leaving the few to destroy themselves and the many by the unchecked exercise of the virtues of pride and ignorance, stupidity and stinginess'.

'the emergent study of language, particularly as it developed in Germany and England, combined a number of disparate and even antagonistic motives'.[22] The novels held a unique place in the mêlée.

---

[22] Dowling, *Language and Decadence in the Victorian* Fin de Siècle, 49.

The Fossil and the Germ:
Rhetorics of Etymology

THE image of words in a course of change did not arise in the nineteenth century. It had been a topic and·allusion in much earlier writings. The difference is rather one of emphasis, and metaphor. In the eighteenth century we see a trend of building 'typologies of order', where the place of a verb in a sentence was noted more keenly than the genealogy of the language.[1] Time, as a way of organizing languages, had more to do with syntax than with the location of words in history. Yet there was no exclusive scheme; the nineteenth century did not inherit a fixed method. Language could be studied in two ways: simple observation, from which laws could be derived, and the application of laws (or tables) to 'other' languages in order to see how they had formed, and why they were unique. A problem troubling Victorian philologists, using either approach, was the origin of uniqueness: if languages grew from a single 'germ', why were they different? They seemed to have basic laws in common. If differences were the result of natural mistakes, where did that leave human initiative, and the vigour of diverse speech?

In Hegel (1770–1831) we find a clue to the thought behind early to mid-nineteenth-century linguistics: 'The principle of *Development* involves also the existence of a latent germ of being—a capacity or potentiality striving to realise itself. This formal conception finds actual existence in Spirit; which has the History of the World for its theatre, its possession, and the sphere of its realization.'[2]

The image of history as an inner force—pushing words from acorn to oak—is found in many Victorian analyses of language. On the one hand, dialects could be arranged by their parts (as in

---

[1] Michel Foucault, *The Order of Things* (1970; New York, 1994), 90.
[2] Andrew Sanders, *The Victorian Historical Novel* (London, 1978), 1.

Latin or Greek), and were available to the linguist as a whole system. They were not just fragments that time had shaken off. On the other hand, they were warehouses of old language, coexisting with the more evolved, standard version, making feasible both temporal and atemporal comparison. Not just accidents of nature—the mistakes of natural selection—they gave evidence that could refine history. Dialectology, or 'comparative philology', became a *method* as well as a compilation of facts, with a built-in assumption that ignorance, only, put a veneer of disorder on history; that a closer look at language revealed a higher level of complexity. By filling in the gaps, the study of dialects could make history look more highly organized.

Trench made a case for the etymological approach; for the axiom that the 'flaws' of language were part of a deeper order. In 1855 (and sounding like Carlyle) he remarks that 'the present is only intelligible in the light of the past'; it is not enough to study language in the present, or, indeed, at any one point in time: 'There are anomalies out of number now existing in our language, which the pure logic of grammar is quite incapable of explaining . . .'. Knowledge of the evolution of words is the basis of our advance 'in the unfolding of the latent capabilities of the language, without the danger of some barbarous violation of its very primary laws'. Just as with our understanding of a man, we must know a word's 'antecedents': 'we must know, if possible, the date and place of their birth, the successive stages of their subsequent history, the company which they have kept, all the road which they have travelled, and what has brought them to the point at which now we find them'.[3]

The important thing, it seems, is to tally up events in the past, as we would the episodes in a man's life, in order to decide how best to use the word in the future—if at all. We may point to another development in Victorian culture: the increasing use of the novel to analyse the cause, or motive, behind an act. Trench invoked the idea of latency—of order in gestation. But he also turned it backwards. He saw the present as a half-dumb testament to order in past ages. As in the novel, Trench saw the

---

[3] Richard Chenevix Trench, *English: Past and Present* (London, 1855), 5, 159–60.

bivalent potential of time: either to lead up to an event, or to hint of past and causal moments. We can see the novel as a metaphor of the philologist's dilemma. Even the hidden details needed a container and a plot. And 'characters'—whether caught in, or influencing, the flow of the story—were not to change beyond recognition from one page to the next, or they lost the reader.

Davies (quoted in the Introduction) objected to the belief that 'a common element in two classes of languages necessarily implies an absolute oneness in nature and origin'.[4] John Stuart Mill tried to bring to the problem (of linguistic development) a clearer way of discussing it. He saw the need for very precise definitions; scientific investigation suffered from the blurred edges around its terms. We should fix connotations. At the same time, it is important to hold on to all of the past meanings of a word; otherwise, language loses its value as 'the conservator of ancient experience'. Somehow, then, we are to create a clear system of language that none the less carries with it the shadow of past, blurrier meanings. It is our only way of keeping in touch with former, alien times.[5]

Mill (hardly alone) deemed historical knowledge basic to an improvement of the present—whether it be linguistic or social. If modern times were to be enriched, 'new' energies were to be drawn from the strata of the ground below one's feet, rather than from places distant in mere space. It was safer, it seems, to keep things in the 'family', even if most of it was dead. Scott, Gaskell, and Kingsley each wrote modern and historical novels: reading the past through the present, and the present through both. Each drew upon old languages in order to dramatize realities beyond the ken of standard English. The murkiness of origin that surrounded each dialect gave the authors a flexibility that other, living dialects would have denied them. While mimicking a neutral, investigative approach to language varia-tion, they 'edited' each fragment, picking out moments of change in the history of language best suited to their purposes.

---

[4] John Davies, 'On the Connexion of the Keltic With the Teutonic Languages', *Transactions of the Philological Society* (1857), 40.

[5] John Stuart Mill, *A System of Logic* (1843; Toronto, 1974), books IV–VI, pp. 679–80.

The science of language—as we see in Mill—was no less an ambiguous framework.

Chevalier Bunsen, a theologian admired by Gaskell and Kingsley, wrote in 1854 a *Philosophy of Universal History*. His model may well have been Leibniz, who in the seventeenth century 'was both the author of the comparative philosophy of language, and the first successful classifier of the languages then known'. Given the title of Bunsen's work, one might be surprised at the detail in his comparison of many languages. And yet, his idea was to harmonize, while showing that the study of language provides us with source material; that language *is* history: 'For beyond all other documents, there is preserved in language that sacred tradition of primeval thought and art which connects all the historical families of mankind, not only as brethren by descent, but each as the depository of a phasis of one and the same development.'[6] The model of languages as 'brethren' involves two, not always consistent possibilities. One implication is that languages share the same parent; another, that all languages go through the same stages. William Barnes suggested at the time that etymological studies could lead us to mistake sisterhood for motherhood.[7] The metaphor of family will be treated at more length in Chapter 4. It is enough, now, to point to the confusion of images—of likeness (ontogenetic) and descent.

Some of Bunsen's attempt—to paint a family tree—may be seen as a racial bias. In a letter to her eldest daughter, Gaskell mentions that Bunsen had recommended that a mutual friend 'study the Anglo-Saxon basis of our language & laws'.[8] In other parts of England, mid-century, non-standard speakers were claiming for their own dialects the 'greatest amount of Anglo-Saxon'.[9] Not everyone agreed. Bunsen's protégé Max Müller told an audience that 'Anglo-Saxon is not an original or

---

[6] Christian Charles Josias Bunsen, *Outlines of the Philosophy of Universal History* (London, 1854), i. 44, ii. 126.

[7] William Barnes, *Tiw* (London, 1862), p. xx.

[8] From a letter dated 19 Oct. 1858, in Elizabeth Gaskell, *The Letters* (Manchester, 1966), 520.

[9] R. G. Latham (1862) quoted in Raymond Chapman, *Forms of Speech in Victoria Fiction* (London, 1994), 41–2.

aboriginal language'; also, that Leibniz had pointed out the importance of dialects for 'elucidating the etymological structure of languages'.[10]

Müller influenced many with his popularization of language theory; the Chair of Comparative Philology at Oxford was founded on his behalf in 1868.[11] His importance, here, derives from a close tie with Kingsley, and infrequent but friendly exchanges with Gaskell. In a series of lectures on language given at the Royal Institution in 1861 and 1863 he elaborated upon his view that languages ought to be the object of neutral and close observation. He used Dugald Stewart to make his point. Stewart, one of Scott's professors at the University of Edinburgh, lectured on moral philosophy; he gave Scott a sense of how people both affected and were shaped by their worlds; he 'convinced him that there is a core of human nature which for all its variety of forms is fundamentally unchanged', a view that Scott tempered with readings and lectures that impressed upon him the great variety of social forms.[12]

Müller did not complain of Stewart's universalist approach. On the contrary, he cites him as an example of one so prejudiced by his education that he would do anything 'to escape from the unpleasant conclusion that Greek and Latin were of the same kith and kin as the language of the black inhabitants of India'. (It caused Stewart to deny the existence of Sanskrit, rather than associate the classical languages with the 'jargon of mere savages'; he thus blinded himself to the key that unlocked for many eighteenth-century linguists the door to a true genealogy of tongues.) Müller distinguishes the true linguist from the scholar who studies a language in order to understand 'bygone ages' or the 'best society' of modern Europe; to whom 'grammars and vocabularies' are just a means to an end. The true linguist has no object beyond the language:

In the science of language, languages are not treated as a means; language itself becomes the sole object of scientific inquiry. Dialects

---

[10] Max Müller, *Lectures on the Science of Language* (1861; London, 1871), i. 133, 152.

[11] Robert Bernard Martin, 'An Edition of the Correspondence and Private Papers of Charles Kingsley 1819–1856', D.Phil thesis, Oxford, 1950, 355.

[12] Edgar Johnson, *Sir Walter Scott* (London, 1970), i. 72, 521–2.

which have never produced any literature at all, the jargons of savage tribes, the clicks of the Hottentots, and the vocal modulations of the Indo-Chinese are as important, nay, for the solution of some of our problems, more important, than the poetry of Homer, or the prose of Cicero.

Ironically, Müller, like Stewart, was not interested in diversity for its own sake; rather, he studied the many dialects in order to find out the origin, nature, and laws common to all.[13]

Müller used metaphors of geology and botany, but did not see language as a subspecies of Darwinian evolution. Language separated humans from all other life forms. E. B. Tylor, a fellow linguist, was unsympathetic to Müller's 'rejection of the uniformitarian principle of geology as applied to linguistics'—a principle which stated 'that the *same forces* in all periods (though not necessarily acting at the same rate once the bulk of a language had been created) effected linguistic change'. Nor did Tylor accept Müller's belief that the roots of a language 'had been formed for all time in the prehistoric past'. He, like a critic of Bunsen, 'discouraged mystical interpretations of the origin and development of language'.

Opposed to Müller were the ideas of Darwin, who, with Dugald Stewart and Hensleigh Wedgwood, 'held that certain facial expressions, gestures, tones of voice and onomatopoeic words were natural signs, based upon and recognized from instinct, inherited habit or wilful imitation of nature'.[14] This was the 'ourang-outang' theory that Trench deplored, countering it with the idea of the modern savage as a decayed branch, instead of a relic of an earlier stage.[15] Wedgwood (cousin of both Elizabeth Gaskell and Darwin, whose sister he married) argued in his *Dictionary of English Etymology* that the common forms of speech among languages could be explained by the human urge to imitate. Thus, if a person wants to speak of an animal (a dog, for example) in its absence, and has no word in common to raise the thought 'in the mind of another', he or she

---

[13] Müller, *Lectures on the Science of Language*, i. 189, 188, 24–5.
[14] Joan Leopold, 'Anthropological Perspectives on the Origin of Language Debate in the Nineteenth Century', in Joachim Gessinger and Wolfert von Rahden (eds.), *Theorien vom Ursprung der Sprache* (Berlin, 1989), ii. 154–7, 167–8.
[15] Trench, *On the Study of Words* (London, 1851), 13, 15–16.

will imitate the animal, and will be understood. The 'bow-wow theory' (so dubbed by such critics as Müller) was part of Wedgwood's belief that languages arose from the basic needs that can be observed in an infant; that more complex forms evolved. The roots of all modern languages are the 'remains' of an older period that has escaped our inquiry.[16]

Once again, the origin of words is pushed into a murky past; the philologist need not (indeed cannot) point to a moment when nature put the germ of language into humanity, determining its future development; or to a pre-Babel speech; or to the first abstract sentence. Taylor notes the modest historicism of Victorian philologists, and their assumption 'that the history of words, in recent centuries, offered a key to unlock the significance of current words'.[17] By keeping to the near past, one could avoid the question of whether or not the laws of language bend to human will. When August Schleicher applied Darwinism to the science of language, he concluded that 'Languages are organisms of nature; they have never been directed by the will of man ...'.[18] Müller disagreed, but recognized that the 'history of language' begins at a moment long after the 'period of youth and growth', making it rather a 'history of decay'.[19] Müller saw that the amazing diversity of tongues made it hard to equate laws of language with the laws that had formed a flower. The flower 'was as perfect from the beginning as it is today'. By contrast, language keeps changing: 'if we watch this stream of language rolling on through centuries in three mighty arms, which, before they disappear from our sight in the far distance, clearly show a convergence towards one common source: it would seem, indeed, as if there were an historical life inherent in language, and as if both the will of man and the power of time could tell, if not on its substance, at least on its form'.

---

[16] Hensleigh Wedgwood, *A Dictionary of English Etymology* (London, 1859), vol. i, pp. xviii, v, iii.

[17] Dennis Taylor, *Hardy's Literary Language and Victorian Philology* (Oxford, 1993), 233.

[18] August Schleicher, *Darwinism Tested by the Science of Language*, trans. Alex V. W. Bikkers (London, 1869), 20–1.

[19] Letter to the Duke of Argyll dated 28 Feb. 1868, in *The Life and Letters of the Right Honourable Friedrich Max Müller*, 2 vols. (London, 1902), i. 349.

Müller contends, however, that the *look* of human history does not deny language the status of a natural science; in fact, man is as subject to the laws of speech as he is to the circulation of his blood. '*History* applies to the actions of free agents; *growth* to the natural unfolding of organic beings.' He thus implies that language, a product of growth, is not changed by free agents. What he wants to make clear, though, is that the *science* of language is outside political history—to the linguist any dialect is a complete system regardless of who speaks it, or of how few. He elsewhere suggests that the growth of language allows room for individual effort. It is possible for the poet and philosopher to become 'the lords of language' if they obey its laws. He by no means wants to claim that history is irrelevant.[20]

Müller's claim—that language is a science as well as an artefact—sums up much of the dilemma that Victorians were facing. It is visible in the science and fictions of time. Müller, Bunsen, Mill, and others saw language as both method and source for historical inquiry. The effort to promote philology as a science (and not just the toy of dotty old men, as in Scott's *The Antiquary*) took shape, often, as a growing lexicon of clear terms. Yet, as a science that tries to reach the past through a transparent lens, it opened up the possibility that language is part of the strata (of human development) and may never in fact let us see the whole, vertical slice of rock. Our 'new species' of terminology may bar us from understanding the trilobites.

Gillian Beer dates the first use of the word 'evolution', 'to describe the development of the *species* rather than of the individual', from the 1830s. She adds: 'The blurring of the distinction between ontogeny—individual development—and phylogeny—species development—in the single term "evolution" proved to be one of the most fruitful disturbances of meaning in the literature of the ensuing hundred years, and is a striking example of the multivalency of evolutionary concepts.'[21] The three novelists, here, share not only a scholarly frame with the historians of language; they also wonder about how the past, like bundles of peat, can be used to fuel and illuminate the

---

[20] Müller, *Lectures on the Science of Language*, i. 34–6, 80, 40.
[21] Gillian Beer, *Darwin's Plots* (London, 1983), 15.

present. They share the ambivalent hope of being able to see the past by analogy with their own life-span. They measure success by one's ability to use language, as a tool, and not solely to be fixed by it into a particular age. A voice is wanted outside the loop of recapitulation. In other words, the bid for a science of language, in many genres, had much to do with the hope that development was not just a cycle of birth and death.

A paradox, unique to the fiction, was that our dim sight of long ago could be taken as proof of the improved art of the observer. The novel adds to the debate. Not only does it conflate time periods (the past, the characters' age, the novel's publication date, the author's memory, the reader's present), as other genres do; it also *revels* in the act, or art, of selection without the gloominess of historians (and linguists) who see the ever-vanishing past as unmitigated loss. Regret, in the fiction, is transposed often into a key of simplicity that does not give order to chaos; rather, it puts into relief the author's ability to use, meaningfully, the variety of tongues in a more complex present. The form of the novel (and short story), rather than a 'simple' past, affords a sense of hope. The historical fiction, in particular, paints the past as an *environment* shaping the individual; while, in the present, the art of language allows for greater control of the narrative. In other words, the writer takes hold of the selective process—even with matter long gone. The nation, in the germ of its development, is held up as a latent unfolding, parallel to the writing of a story; it is almost an alternative to the rougher hands of nature.

THE FICTION

Gerald Newman outlines two aspects of nationalist movements: (1) nostalgia for a natural ('uncorrupted') community; 2) an 'academic, scholarly component' (including philological research) to give it legitimacy.[22] Both aspects can be found in the works of the three novelists. In fact, the novels may be pictured as a meeting-ground of scholars and people less embedded in the culture of literacy. Dialect-speaking characters range from

[22] Gerald Newman, *The Rise of English Nationalism* (London, 1987), 111.

completely illiterate to well-read, but the novels tend to locate them within a predominantly oral community, in spite of the availability of printed dialect literature in urban centres of northern England.[23] Parallels are drawn in the novels between illiteracy, ignorance, and strong emotional bonds, while standard English is *usually* the voice of control—narrative and political. The ideal seems to be a hybrid of vigour and detached analysis. The former draws upon the 'nativity' of language (word as a given), the latter upon its use-value (word as a tool) in a complex society. The greater a nation becomes, the more demand it puts upon language; the Victorians were not the last to equate greatness with linguistic sophistication, by which a tradition of writing was implied.

The three novelists make it clear, in a modern setting, that a primal cry is not their end; it no longer works. *Mary Barton* has been characterized as a book that 'constantly returns to the difficulty of speaking'.[24] Failure to articulate, in the novels, is often a sign of primitive, dangerous emotion. Descriptions of workers, in moments of passion or secret anger, take an inhuman form—a shadow moving past a window, the roar of a crowd. When the press-gang captures Monkhaven sailors in *Sylvia's Lovers*, the 'dense mass' of villagers emits a 'low, deep growl . . . now and then going up, as a lion's growl goes up, into a shriek of rage'.[25] When a mob comes to Thornton's mill in *North and South*, the workers are at first 'voiceless, wordless, needing all their breath for their hard-labouring efforts to break down the gates'; then Thornton's 'commanding voice' sets up in them 'a fierce unearthly groan'.[26] It is as if the strain of violence precludes breath for speech; while Thornton is capable of a cool articulation of reason.

Scott (and his characters) often compare the voices of Highlanders to animal cries: Andrew Fairservice tells Captain Thornton (as cool in the face of 'ruffians' as Gaskell's man) that the Aberfoil women 'are like the scarts and sea-maws at the Cumries, there's aye foul weather follows their skirling'.[27]

[23] David Vincent, *Literacy and Popular Culture* (Cambridge, 1989), 207.
[24] Jenny Uglow, *Elizabeth Gaskell* (London, 1994), 202.
[25] Elizabeth Gaskell, *Sylvia's Lovers*, (1863; Oxford, 1982), 29.
[26] Elizabeth Gaskell, *North and South* (1854–5; Oxford, 1982), 174.
[27] Walter Scott, *Rob Roy* (1817; London, 1995), 280.

Kingsley did the same, with greater thematic result. Lancelot
Smith, the wealthy young hero in *Yeast*, asks Tregarva to lead
him among the villagers. He goes in disguise as a labourer, so as
not to bias the experiment, but he is muffled by his own
breeding: 'Sadder and sadder, Lancelot tried to listen to the
conversation of the men around him. To his astonishment he
hardly understood a word of it. It was half articulate, nasal,
guttural, made up almost entirely of vowels, like the speech of
savages.' These 'coarse, half-formed growls' remind him 'of a
company of seals'; the sound 'connected itself with many of his
physiological fancies'.[28] Gaskell's characters, if speechless with
rage, at other times are capable of a 'rough Lancashire
eloquence'.[29] The villagers in *Yeast*, when Lancelot looks on,
are not deeply moved by fear or hatred; they are going about
their daily lives. Calmness will not change their dialect; it then
may be called 'physiological'—a sign of a different race, not of a
fleeting, turbulent mood.

Gaskell did not promote the 'innocence' of primitive culture;
she disagreed with educators who made their pupils imitate the
'ideal savage', avowing it a poor training for civilized life.[30]
More to the point, her novel *North and South* shows how
society perpetuates, while it seems to deplore, the bestiality of
the mostly illiterate workers. Mrs Thornton, when asked if she
does not mind living close to the mill, remarks: 'and as for the
continual murmur of the work-people, it disturbs me no more
than the humming of a hive of bees'.[31] It is Tennyson's murmur,
but with a different angle of intention. The workers' voices are
inhuman, but they represent the infrastructure (the hive) of a
literate culture of 'masters', who use a knowledge of the classics
to validate economic gains. Industrialists of the period also took
lessons in standard English to secure their newly won status.[32]
The Thorntons are not intrinsically 'other than', except in so far
as they can *use* a style of speech to mark, and effect, control.

---

[28] Charles Kingsley, *Yeast* (1848; Dover, 1994), 126–7.
[29] Elizabeth Gaskell, *Mary Barton* (1848; Harmondsworth, 1976), 220.
[30] Elizabeth Gaskell, *The Life of Charlotte Brontë* (1857; London, 1985), 88.
[31] *North and South*, 161.
[32] Dick Leith, *A Social History of English* (London, 1992), 56.

Once, in an argument, Mrs Thornton 'set her teeth; she showed them like a dog for the whole length of her mouth'. Then the tone of the dialogue shifted, and she and her son 'fell back into their usual mode of talk,—about facts, not opinions, far less feelings. Their voices and tones were calm and cold . . . .'.[33] The unread books lying about their house suggest that the literate 'mode' of thinking and speaking can be taken up or set down; it is, none the less, a mode.

Gaskell, then, does not 'agree' with Kingsley's model of races apart. Nor does Scott, entirely. Their differences (as we find them in the novels) are perhaps most visible in fiction that sets out to retell the beginning of a nation.

Scott's *Ivanhoe* is set in the twelfth century; its source, we are told, is an Anglo-Norman manuscript kept by Sir Arthur Wardour, who figures in *The Antiquary* as Oldbuck's friend and rival. The novel's language, of course, belies its source. Tulloch notices that much of Scott's period speech is not genuinely old, and that few of his Middle English words are specific to that period alone; he might have pulled them from later sources.[34] What matters here, though, is not Scott's historical accuracy so much as the attitude to language that comes through the different speakers—the 'unconscious' utterances of characters and the more integrative comments in the narrator's voice.

Most noticeable in *Ivanhoe* is a tension between French and 'plain [or Saxon] English'; it works into a complicated polemic over 'natural' language, and the difficulty of separating what is natural from what is imposed (by war, commerce, or whatever). A good illustration is the dialogue between Cedric and the Templar. Cedric 'the Saxon' argues that French terms are not necessary; that Saxon terms work just as well: 'I can wind my horn, though I call not the blast either a *recheate* or a *morte*—I can cheer my dogs on the prey, and I can flay and quarter the animal when it is brought down, without using the newfangled jargon of *curée*, *arbor*, *nombles*, and all the babble of the fabulous Sir Tristrem.' French words, to him, may be synonymous, but are inessential. The Templar objects: French, he

---

[33] *North and South*, 211–12.
[34] Graham Tulloch, *The Language of Walter Scott* (London, 1980), 16, 22.

claims, 'is not only the natural language of the chase, but that of love and of war'. Words are inseparable from the acts.

Underlying the argument are contradictory positions of time. The Templar implies that French words gave rise to, or arose in concert with, hunting, love, and war. Cedric pushes the French language into the 'fabulous' period of Sir Tristrem—into the realm of fairy-tale and incredulity. He looks back instead 'some thirty years to tell you another [far more recent] tale. As Cedric the Saxon then was, his plain English tale needed no garnish from French troubadours . . .'. By collapsing the time-frame he makes English anterior to French, while maintaining its current value. He does not speak with the times like a serf to linguistic motion.

Cedric's character was influenced by, and no doubt fed into, the stereotype of Saxon pride, force, and stubbornness. The narrator's occasional use of French words works against a total sympathy towards the Saxon element. He comments on the trouble of blending the two cultures, and on its hierarchical nature: 'In short, French was the language of honour, of chivalry, and even of justice, while the far more manly and expressive Anglo-Saxon was abandoned to the use of rustics and hinds, who knew no other'. It seems very close to the Templar's avowal. What the narrator adds to the equation is politics, locating the linguistic change in political time. He describes the 'gradual formation of a dialect, compounded betwixt the French and the Anglo-Saxon'. The dialect is 'necessary', but for practical rather than natural reasons: 'and from this necessity arose by degrees the structure of our present English language, in which the speech of the victors and the vanquished have been so happily blended together; and which has since been so richly improved by importations from the classical languages, and from those spoken by the southern nations of Europe'.

In the author's notes at the end of the novel he clarifies his approach. He values the antiquaries for their attempt 'to trace the progress of society' by its efforts either to improve a thing to the point of excellence, or to discard it. He refers to 'new and fundamental discoveries, which supersede both the earlier and ruder system, and the improvements which have been ingrafted upon it'. Now that gas produces the light in our homes, it is possible to imagine 'the heads of a whole Society of Antiquaries half turned by the discovery of a pair of patent snuffers'.[35] Scott, here, could as well be speaking of language. The image of the Antiquaries, looking back to all of the failed experiments and trying to make sense of alien forms, exists parallel to Scott as amateur philologist, turning to look at outmoded tongues. He gives credit to 'inventors', but places their efforts in a time-scheme ('line' is too simple) that mitigates the appearance of their agency.

Graham Tulloch tells us of two attempts Scott made 'to reproduce the language of the past in all its detail'; neither took the form of a novel. One was a 'Continuation' in Middle English of the poem *Sir Tristrem*; the other a batch of fake seventeenth-century letters that he and his friends hoped to publish as genuine.[36] In his fiction, Scott was no true archivist of words. When Oldbuck quotes from Chaucer in *The Antiquary*, we *see* little trace of Middle English. We are simply told that he gave 'each guttural the true Anglo-Saxon enunciation, which is now forgotten in the southern parts of this realm' (Scots being closer than modern English to Chaucer's speech).[37] Scott may well be following the example of Bishop Percy, whose *Reliques of Ancient English Poetry* he had read many times. Percy admits in his preface to taking some 'considerable liberties . . . with the old copies', but adds that he has retained in the margins any word or phrase that is 'antique, obsolete, unusual, or peculiar' in order to convince the reader of an 'undoubted antiquity'. He wanted to 'please both the judicious Antiquary, and the Reader of Taste; and he hath endeavoured to gratify both without offending either'.[38]

The relegation of old words to the status of proof implies that Percy saw the old and new 'copies' as parallel, but not radically different, texts. In *Ivanhoe* we are told that Gurth and Wamba speak in Anglo-Saxon: 'But to give their conversation in the original would convey but little information to the modern reader . . .'. In the letter that Scott added to the front of *Ivanhoe*

---

[35] Walter Scott, *Ivanhoe* (1819; London, 1904), 58–9, 4, 665.
[36] Tulloch, *The Language of Walter Scott*, 13–14.
[37] Walter Scott, *The Antiquary* (1816; Edinburgh, 1995), 23.
[38] Thomas Percy, *Reliques of Ancient English Poetry* (1764; London, 1794), vol. i, pp. xvi–xvii.

(it did not appear in the 1819 edition) Chaucer is said to intimidate the novice reader with 'obsolete spelling, multiplied consonants, and antiquated appearance of the language'; but the difference is 'more in appearance than reality'. A modern translation will enable the reader 'to approach the "well of English undefiled" ', and to partake of 'the humour and the pathos' of a past age.[39] The quotation from Spenser links the 'editor' of *Ivanhoe* with another writer who drew upon obsolescent vocabulary. Samuel Johnson had used the same excerpt to illustrate his own belief that words taken from great literature of the past give us a working definition. Johnson made it clear that all words were not equal. He chose, for his dictionary, the 'genuine diction' of pre-Restoration writers, by which he meant an English that kept 'its original *Teutonick* character' before it began to lean toward '*Gallick* structure and phraseology'.[40]

Scott was writing out of a tradition of accepted preferences— for words that were not necessarily the oldest, but that stemmed from a period 'typically' English. Tulloch refers to *Ivanhoe* as a 'turning point' for Scott, wherein the matter and speech change from Scotland and Scots to England and 'a language reinforcing not locale but period, not Scottish but old'.[41] If the novel lacks some of the subtlety that Scott brings to the use of language in other works, it may be that *Ivanhoe*'s motif (the triumph of Saxon values in spite of Norman conquest) inherits too many stereotypes of '*Teutonick*' descent. What Scott adds, though, is a tongue-in-cheek awareness of linguistic pride, and in contrast, a display of very pragmatic reasons for verbal change. If French was the language of law and chivalry, it was also the speech of hunting, love, and war; and not so very far from the passions ordinarily given to speakers of a more 'Saxon' dialect.

In *Past and Present* (a book that parleys with *Ivanhoe*) Carlyle mocks Dryasdust, who researches the origin of the word 'Beodric's-worth'; he shows how 'our erudite Friend' gathers

---

[39] *Ivanhoe*, pp. 9, xlviii–ix.
[40] Samuel Johnson, 'Preface to a Dictionary of the English Language' (1755), in W. F. Bolton (ed.), *The English Language* (London, 1973), 145.
[41] Tulloch, *The Language of Walter Scott*, 13.

facts from a sort of potted etymology, gathered from old Saxon and present 'North-Country dialects'. Carlyle's 'editor', in his own revival of a seven-centuries-old manuscript, distinguishes between two approaches: 'our antiquarian interest in poor Jocelin and his Convent', whose 'whole dialect, of thought, of speech, of activity, is so obsolete, strange, long-vanished'; and the 'mild glow of human interest for Abbot Samson', who seems a man of flesh and blood—who spoke not only Monk-Latin but also a Norfolk dialect. Jocelin's Monk-Latin 'lies across not the British Channel, but the ninefold Stygian Marshes, Stream of Lethe, and one knows not where!' Consequently, Jocelin's whole mind is 'covered deeper than Pompeii with the lava-ashes and inarticulate wreck of seven hundred years!' Jocelin's speech is too old to comprehend; the Abbot's (because English, if just as old) is not.

A single period, then, could contain a wide gulf of years in the history of language. Empathy cannot reach across the widest part; understanding is determined by events that formed the present. Carlyle uses Old English and Latin words (' "Lord or *Law-ward*", "*Hlaf dig*", Benefactress, "*Loaf-giveress*", "*Presbyter*" or "Priest" ') to imply the rightness of feudal communities; his choice of words implies an acceptance of the Norman influence on English. He defends the feudal aristocracy: 'To a respectable degree, its *Jarls*, what we now call Earls, were *Strong-Ones* in fact as well as etymology. . . . It is, in many senses, the Law of Nature, this same Law of Feudalism . . .'. Poor Dryasdust, we are told, 'talks lamentably about Hereward and the Fen Counties', regretting the Norman Conquest; but did not the Normans come by nature's call to revive the Saxons? Even Dryasdust admits that William's leadership created a safer England: 'My erudite friend, it is a fact which outweighs a thousand!' *Ivanhoe*'s Gurth may have been a slave, but he *belonged*. Carlyle uses etymology to show that historical facts move according to nature; indeed, he uses such facts to select his etymology, and deems impenetrable the dialects that might have led to another outcome—the Monk-Latin, for example, that might have outbalanced English.[42] Taylor sums it up neatly:

[42] Thomas Carlyle, *Past and Present* (1843; Oxford, 1918), 190, 220, 192, 220, 36.

'Carlyle is famous for his rhetoric of etymology. His cultural prophecies are laced with etymologies, mostly false (*Lord* from '*Law-ward*, maintainer and *keeper* of Heaven's *Laws*') which parallel Trench's notion that spiritual realities can be recalled through the etymological reinterpretation of words.[43] Crowley writes in more general terms of how the science of language in the nineteenth century 'imposed historical order and constructed a history'.[44] It is a sort of reading backward: the present determines the selection of 'old copies' on the basis of dialect (or language), which in turn make the present look inevitable.

Charles Kingsley, in his own novel of the Norman Conquest, beckons Scott's muse. He opens *Hereward the Wake* by announcing his wish to bring heroes of the English lowlands and fens into the tradition of Highland tales. He faces a problem: 'There is in the lowland none of that background of the unknown, fantastic, magical, terrible, perpetually feeding curiosity and wonder, which still remains in the Scottish highlands; and which, when it disappears from thence, will remain embalmed for ever in the pages of Walter Scott.' The vision of Scott as undertaker, and of the Scottish past as 'unknown', is an echo (if not deliberate) in Carlyle, who in 1830 wrote an article, 'On History', for *Fraser's Magazine*—a journal that later published Kingsley's essays. Carlyle includes 'feather-pictures' and 'monumental stone-heaps' in a list of ways in which history has been written—as if linguistics and archaeology share a pursuit. All people, he says, live 'between two eternities' and try to unite with them 'in clear conscious relation' with signs. The goal always eludes us; the most important part of history 'is lost without recovery'. We can at best 'look with reverence into the dark untenanted places of the Past, where, in formless oblivion, our chief benefactors, with all their sedulous endeavours, but not with the fruit of these, lie entombed'.[45]

Kingsley seems to regret the *lack* of mystery in the fens; he suggests that in order to find mystery there, one must go further back in time. His mentor and friend F. D. Maurice wrote to him

---

[43] Taylor, *Hardy's Literary Language and Victorian Philology*, 224.
[44] Tony Crowley, *The Politics of Discourse* (Basingstoke, 1989), 19.
[45] Thomas Carlyle, 'On History', in *English and Other Critical Essays* (London, 1967), 80, 83.

in 1844 about the importance of the study of words.[46] Later, in the 1860s, Maurice gave a series of lectures on language at Cambridge, praising the 'old languages' that express the vitality of nations. These languages 'enable us to think more of the mystery of words than we are apt to do when we are merely using them for the occasions of every-day life'. It was important to hold on to words of the past, feeding their strangeness into the present, to renew its vigour. Borrowing from other, contemporary nations is no sound alternative. Language grows, and sends out 'new shoots', but it is perilous to graft: 'we shall generally adopt what least deserves to be adopted'. The old language from our own land, however different from modern English, can be counted on for 'veracity' because of internal properties. J. S. Mill had implied the same. Maurice warns against the 'lust of Imperialism' that makes people look to other countries (France, for example) for new qualities. He claims, tentatively, that the 'diffusion of French' throughout Europe led 'to the death of the continental nations', and that renovation began when the Germans revived their own literature.[47]

Hereward the Wake takes us back to the dawn of the Norman impact on the Anglo-Saxon language. Kingsley wants us to imagine a confusion of tongues—not just a battle of two. Hereward gets into trouble with a 'red-bearded giant, who spoke in a broken tongue, part Scotch, part Cornish, part Danish, which Hereward could hardly understand'. His own army shouts in 'half-a-dozen barbarous dialects'.[48] Kingsley knew very well that eleventh-century England did not have a uniform language; he even *seems* to contradict Maurice by judging cross-national tongues a good thing—if confusing. To a friend, J. M. Ludlow, he puts blame on his own 'plain English' for his lack of a Tennysonian 'mythic grandeur'.[49] He gives an epic voice to Hereward, who sings a Viking song in accord with the narrator's bias. The Vikings are held superior to the Picts, for they 'had become Christianized, and civilized also—owing

---

[46] Letter quoted in *Charles Kingsley: Letters and Memories of His Life* (London, 1877), i. 129.
[47] F. D. Maurice, *Social Morality* (London, 1893), 149–51.
[48] Charles Kingsley, *Hereward the Wake* (1866; London, 1881), 73, 326.
[49] Letter dated 1852, in Martin, 'Correspondence of Kingsley', 365.

to their continual intercourse with foreign nations—more highly than the Irish whom they had overcome'.[50] Mythic grandeur is not sung by the insular. In *Hereward* the narrator takes civilization to mean two things: a higher standard of dialogue, and inevitable decay. The more civil people become, the less likely they are to kill off the weak, allowing them to spread their weakness into future generations. But encounters with other nations can effect a 'natural' selection. The Darwinian term is valid: Kingsley met Darwin in 1854;[51] he did not hesitate to accept Darwin's *Origin of Species*.[52] Rome fell because of inbreeding; the Anglo-Saxon race was once in danger of it. He wrote of plans for a lecture: 'The rotting of the Anglo-Saxon system—inability of Saxon mind to originate—Anglo-Saxon, (a female race) required impregnation by the great male race,—the Norse introduction of Northmen by Edward paving the way for the Conquest, &c'.[53]

Maurice warned of cross-fertilization. It eroded national boundaries, making them weak. Kingsley recommended it. Beneath the contradiction, however, is a more essential agreement. After all, Kingsley does not embrace just any intercourse. His locations in time put into dialogue very particular blends. Bunsen, writing to Müller, calls him 'the genius of our country'; Kingsley's mission, as he saw it, was to place next to Shakespeare's historical dramas 'another series from Edward VI to the landing of William of Orange. This is the only historical development of Europe which unites in itself all vital elements, and which we might look upon without overpowering pain.'[54] While Kingsley did not exactly fulfil the plan, he adopted its approach to history: to select from the past the most 'vital' moments—and also the least offensive to the present.

His degree of selection is clearer when we compare his model of the history of language to Thomas De Quincey's. In 1839 De Quincey wrote an article for *Blackwood's* calling for a 'History of the English Language' from beginning to end. He, too, uses a

[50] *Hereward the Wake*, 85–6, 91.
[51] *Charles Kingsley: Letters*, i. 427.
[52] Robert Bernard Martin, *Dust of Combat* (London, 1959), 223.
[53] Letters dated 1846 and 1849, in *Charles Kingsley: Letters*, i. 140, 201.
[54] Bunsen's letter is quoted in *Charles Kingsley: Letters*, i. 151.

metaphor of fertility. English 'has a special dowry of power in its double-headed origin'—Saxon and Latin. Before the Latin influence, Anglo-Saxon was 'rude' and 'barren' with only a few hundred words, mostly about war. The hybridization made English multiform, able 'to reflect the thoughts of myriad-minded Shakespeare' while retaining 'old forest stamina for imparting a masculine depth'.[55] The two men shared not only metaphors, but also a need to fill the gaps of history.

But Kingsley's bias did not take quite the same path as De Quincey's. He looked to another 'double-headed origin'. In a letter to Gerald Massey he takes up the need for a 'People's Songs' on the model of German 'song-literature' (just as Alton asks for a People's Commentary on Shakespeare, and a People's History of England). 'But to do it', he tells Gerald, 'you must learn to write in the very simplest & severest style, with the plainest Saxon words. You must avoid all recondite & high flown thoughts & images, all long dictionary words derived from the Latin . . .'.[56] It was not just a bid for historical accuracy—a belief that the People used an older form of English. Probably most of the songs in question had been written long after 1066, and felt the Latin influence through Norman French. An interesting change happens in *Hereward the Wake*. Early in the novel the narrator shows a great keenness for the Scandinavian entry. The 'men of Wessex' are more Danish than French. They 'never really bent their necks to the Norman yoke'; rather, they held on to the 'proud spirit of personal independence' they had brought from Denmark, and kept alive 'those free institutions which were without a doubt the germs of our British liberty'. A footnote in the text refers us to Isaac Taylor's book *Words and Places*, to convince us of just how many names north of the 'Danelagh' are derived from Danish, Norwegian, and Anglo-Saxon words. The Danes, the Angles, and the Saxons had blended perfectly. Modern English dialects and traits seem to have grown naturally from their union.

In contrast, we meet someone like Lady Godiva, who 'as the constant associate of clerks and monks—spoke after an artifical

---

[55] Thomas De Quincey, 'The English Language', in W. F. Bolton (ed.), *The English Language* (1839; London, 1973), 201, 209, 203.
[56] Letter dated 25 Dec. 1851, in Martin, 'Correspondence of Kingsley', 281.

and Latinized fashion'.[57] The Latin does not belong. The Norman French, too, appears to be superimposed, unnatural, in accord with the views of some philologists. William Gaskell, for instance, declares that Northumbria was Danish, and that half of the 600 Lancashire names seem to be of Scandinavian origin. He gives another proof: 'Another verb in Lancashire, which, I imagine, cannot be referred to the Anglo-Saxon, is to "baist," to beat; from which the substantive "baistin" comes. In Icelandic, "beysta" is to strike'.[58] The dialect gets its strength from the mixture; and it is a particular blend—without a French aroma. Davies, a year later, insisted that dialects are the only source to determine who once populated the country, and that the Lancashire dialect in particular shows that there was less of a Norman element in Lancashire than in other parts of England.[59] *Hereward the Wake* provides rich soil for anti-Norman seeds. Hereward refers to a 'kempery-man—knight-errant, as those Norman puppies call it'. Their language is inessential, and part of their weakness.

Even so, Hereward must feel some need to use it. By the end of the novel there is a decided swing towards an acceptance of the Norman invasion; before the middle we are told of Queen Victoria's German *and* French ancestry. Half-way through, the narrator is grateful that England did not become 'a mere appanage of the Scandinavian kings'. The same 'spirit of personal independence' that grew into British liberty also, in the eleventh century, 'made every battle degenerate into a confusion of single combats'.[60]

Andrew Sanders helps to make sense of the novel's apparent hypocrisy. Many Victorians, it seems, felt that the Normans had restored vigour to the land, if temporarily holding it under subjugation. They gave new life to 'ineradicable English institutions'. Kingsley saw 1066 as 'the last phase in the long process of the transformation of England from a Roman-British culture to an emphatically Teutonic one and the Normans

[57] *Hereward the Wake*, 4–5, 28.
[58] William Gaskell, 'Two Lectures on the Lancashire Dialect', in *Mary Barton*, (1854; Halifax, 1993), 387–9.
[59] John Davies, 'On the Races of Lancashire', in *Transactions of the Philological Society*, no. 13 (1855), 247, 281.
[60] *Hereward the Wake*, 31, 130, 274, 286.

themselves are to be seen as descendants of the same Vikings who had already remade Northern and Eastern Britain'.[61] Towards the end of *Hereward* the Norman influence feels not only inevitable but good. Hereward is 'as able to play the Englishman which he was by rearing, as the Frenchman which he was by education'. Hereward's conduct towards Torfrida is compared with Napoleon's towards Josephine. Finally, Hereward is succeeded by Richard de Rulos, who, in spite of his French-sounding name, is the first of the New English, and 'who, by the inspiration of God, began to drain the Fens'[62]—the same fens that now lack mystery, if they are the better for it.

In a preface to one of his Cambridge lectures, Kingsley reminds us that the southward migrations of the Teutonic tribes began 'long before the time of Tacitus'; this being the case, 'may they not have commenced before the different Teutonic dialects were as distinct as they were in the historic period?' His question puts the most crucial moment of linguistic growth into a time that can never be clear to us, because it had no Tacitus to write it down. Etymology may bring to the surface what is (or was) shared; yet Kingsley puts the huge influence of the Teutons— their many and varied conquests—down to a strangeness that begs finer detail. They conquered so many nations because they were strange: 'and we may therefore expect them to have done strange things even in their infancy'.[63] Trench, less than a decade before, had made the strangeness a verbal one:

Of course the period when absolutely new roots are generated will have past away, long before men begin to take any notice by a reflective act of processes going forward in the language which they speak. This pure productive, or creative energy, as we might call it, belongs only to the earliest periods of a nation's existence,—to periods quite out of the ken of history. It is only from materials already existing either in its own bosom, or in the bosom of other languages, that it can enrich itself in the later, or historical stages of its life.[64]

By the time of *Ivanhoe* (the twelfth century) and *Hereward* (the eleventh) the nation was well beyond the stage of

---

[61] Sanders, *The Victorian Historical Novel*, 152.
[62] *Hereward the Wake*, 361, 496, 518.
[63] Charles Kingsley, *The Roman and the Teuton* (Cambridge, 1864), 58–60.
[64] Trench, *English: Past and Present*, 49–50.

unconscious fertility. In both novels there are deliberate mixes of language. Scott depicts the change as gradual. Only if you look closely do you see crises, where the speech reflects a tension of circumstance and will. The narrator also stretches time to show that the merging of languages is itself a natural process; the changes are not due to the intrinsic superiority of one word over another, so much as to the pragmatics of adapting to shifts in power. In Kingsley's work one finds a positioning of virility in the language itself. The root of a word is a force that affects the growth of a nation. Language is given the rhetoric of nature (growth, inevitability) which implies a kinship between the very thoughts of people and the development of a nation. In Scott there is a greater divide. Mystery, in *Ivanhoe*, is a past that cannot be fully recovered; and a moment of history that points to the use of materials at hand. In *Hereward* we are led to imagine a mysterious past in which the origin of thought and the germ of the nation were closely bound.

None of Gaskell's novels is set in the murky past; her historical works (*Sylvia's Lovers* is the best example) seldom go back further than the late eighteenth century. One of her short stories, however, puts much of what I have been saying into a different light. 'The Doom of the Griffiths' moves across nine generations of a Welsh family, though only the first and the last are treated in detail. It is a strange tale of fatalism. The past does not illuminate the present; it just makes it unavoidable. It is a sort of anomaly among Gaskell's writing, because its characters twitch and struggle against fate but do not have much life beyond the doom that had sprung from a single act a long time ago. The story fits in, here, by virtue of its mysterious past. There is also the inexorability one finds in Carlyle, who compares the present to a tree that 'has its roots down deep in the Death-kingdoms, among the oldest dead dust of men, and with its boughs reaches always beyond the stars; and in all times and places is one and the same Life-tree!'[65] Gaskell tends in other works to be un-Carlylean in her focus on the differences that ordinary people (not the Luthers and Cromwells) make in the world.

But the extraordinary quality of 'The Doom of the Griffiths'

[65] Carlyle, *Past and Present*, 34.

does not lessen its value, or its relevance. As in *Ivanhoe* and
Hereward the Wake, we are not thrown directly into an alien
time. Its narrator is a collector of tales, with an editor's attention
to barriers (and curiosities) of language, and begins: 'I have
always been much interested by the traditions which are
scattered up and down North Wales relating to Owen
Glendower (Owain Glendwr is the national spelling of the
name) . . .'.[66] Bishop Percy had mentioned him too; it was
resentment towards 'Owen Glendour', and the rebellious words
of the Welsh Bards, that provoked the English government to
make severe laws against them.[67]

In Gaskell's circle, however, one finds a more generous
attitude. It came in the form of dialect research. In her novel
Ruth Mr Benson gives the etymology for the English word
'foxglove'; he derives it from the Welsh, 'Maneg Ellyllyn—the
good people's glove; and hence, I imagine, our folk's-glove or
fox-glove'.[68] William Gaskell referred to the Welsh language as
the 'nearest representative we have of the old British'. He
surmised that the Saxons took 200 years to separate North
Britons from the Welsh, by conquering Lancashire; the length of
the struggle accounts for the traces of 'the old tongue' in the
Lancashire dialect.[69] Davies believed that a study of the
Lancashire dialect and local names proved not only that Celts
('of the Welsh or Cymraic race') once inhabited the county, but
that they 'survived the great torrent of Saxon invasion' and
remained. 'History does not offer a decisive testimony on the
subject, but the language of the Lancashire peasantry gives
unexceptionable and sufficient evidence by which we may
determine the question'. In fact, traces of the Celts in standard
English and in every other dialect of England show a Celtic
element in the force that raised England 'to so marvellous a
height'.[70]

'The Doom of the Griffiths', though, does not slip neatly into
the discourse on language that surrounded it. The studies of

---

[66] Elizabeth Gaskell, 'The Doom of the Griffiths', in *My Lady Ludlow* (Oxford, 1989), 229.
[67] Percy, *Reliques*, vol. i, pp. xciii, xliii.
[68] Elizabeth Gaskell, *Ruth* (1853; Oxford, 1985), 69.
[69] William Gaskell, 'Two Lectures on the Lancashire Dialect', 363.
[70] Davies, 'On the Races of Lancashire', 218, 225, 242.

dialect suggest a virile past that fed into the present (linguistically *and* economically; note William Gaskell's metaphors of coinage); the distance between now and then accounts for dialect gaps and shows just how much progress was made. Gaskell's story holds another, darker shape.

It also contains elements found in *Ivanhoe* and *Hereward*. The past is shrouded in mystery. Robert (from the eighth generation) collects 'Cambrian antiquities of every description, till his stock of Welsh MSS. would have excited the envy of Dr. Pugh himself [a Welsh antiquary], had he been alive at the time of which I write.' His wife understands none of it. His son Owen sits with him in 'the dim room, surrounded by wizard-like antiquities'. The original Owain Glendwr 'is, even in the present days of enlightenment, as famous among his illiterate country-men for his magical powers as for his patriotism'. Magic obscures him.

Magic also invades the present, and not just among the 'lower orders'. It climbs as high as Shakespeare, whose voice is 'much the same thing' as Owain's. It climbs as high as Oxford. Obscurity, in the fiction here, allowed for a violent growth in language—a blend of lateral tongues—that gave modern English its strength and virtue. In contrast, the 'scientific' realism of the present was associated with studies that could draw from the past for vitality, without looking to other present nations or races. The same antiquarian motif occurs in 'The Doom of the Griffiths', but with a different effect. It has to do with the narrator's use of translation; the etymology that just dimly exists.

A narrator can refer to a Babel of tongues in the mythic past, without actually putting them into dialogue. We can thus 'know' the strangeness without feeling excluded. It enables us to take in the *whole* past (by which I mean, of course, the whole of its representation), and to accept its conflict of varieties. Representations of the present, in the form of social realism they were beginning to take in the early nineteenth century, tended to put more of speech into dialogue, which immediately split up the reader's empathy. Kingsley and Scott used both strategies—their 'pasts' are strange but unthreatening, and the dialogue engages our interest while implying temporal direction, or progress. In 'The Doom of the Griffiths', however, the dialogue is scant no matter what the place in time. The 'translation' into a narrative voice seems just as necessary in the present as ever before.

Translations in the story occur with ease. Gryfydd becomes Griffiths; Owain's Welsh, Shakespeare's English. When Owain utters his curse, we do not 'hear' Welsh but rather the English of the Authorized Version of the Bible: 'Thy race shall be accursed'. The plant *Sorbus aucuparia* becomes 'a liquor called "diod griafol" '. Owen does not look for a key to his doom through his father's Welsh manuscripts; he turns instead 'to the old Greek dramas which treat of a family foredoomed by an avenging Fate'. But the easy movement between languages (the Welsh and English of several ages, Latin, Greek) does not guarantee enlightenment. The narrator has two methods. A translation may be given: "Tri pheth tebyg y naill i'r llall, ysgnbwr heb yd, mail deg heb ddiawd, a merch deg heb ei geirda' (Three things are alike: a fine barn without corn, a fine cup without drink, a fine woman without her reputation)'. Or it may not: 'Nest, your husband is dripping, drookit wet'. It seems that the dialect word 'drookit' is left to our imaginations (helped by the accompaniment of 'dripping'), while the Welsh is made clear. But *meaning* is not simply a synonym, or replacement; the Welsh saying does not illuminate the character of Nest, as it was meant to do. Nor does it relate convincingly to the couple's outcome. Obscurity does not live in the past, but moves along with time.

Time seldom relents. In the bloom of his marriage, Owen is happy. Moments occur when he forgets 'all besides the present; all the cares and griefs he had known in the past, and all that might await him of woe and death in the future'. It is an illusion. Soon he adopts the fatalism, or 'doom', of his ancestor: 'Neither words nor deeds but what are decreed can come to pass,' he says to the more pragmatic Ellis Pritchard. It could be something out of Carlyle's *Past and Present*—only it is darker. Owen's present recapitulates the murkiness of the past (we never understand the motives of treachery, or how the doom works); the past does not elucidate the present.

The Griffiths do not get strength from their past. They leave Wales altogether. The story ends not unlike an account of pre-Norman invasions: 'The house of Bodowen has sunk into damp, dark ruins; and a Saxon stranger holds the lands of the Griffiths.' It is as if the insularity of the Welsh family (held by the few words spoken to an ancestor) made decay inevitable. The Saxons may have been a blessing in disguise—in the way that Kingsley conceded the value of the Norman Conquest.

Only, Gaskell's resolution is not so simple. The narrator recalls the Welsh celebrating the announcement that 'Owain Glendwr' was to be 'the subject of the Welsh prize poem at Oxford'. It seems that Oxford has relented from a previous disparagement of the Welsh, and has finally chosen a Welsh hero for the subject of a Welsh prize. A happy blend of Saxon and Celtic culture. Or at least a concession. When we learn, however, that this Welsh hero has set the terms of the decay of a Welsh family (whose last son is, ironically, called Owen), making room for the encroachment of the Saxons, the neutrality of scholarship comes under question. The narrator claims to 'fully enter into the feeling which makes the Welsh peasant still look upon him [Owain] as the hero of his country'.[71] But the psychology of the 'peasant' in the story—the fatalism and the superstition—remain across a gulf from the narrator's cheerful interest. The story as a whole does not let 'Oxford' historicism escape mockery.

A SUMMARY

The three novelists shared with the linguists an attempt to cut through the fog of the past. At the same time, their historical fiction perpetuated the sense of mystery—the epic distance that resisted the realism they brought to the present. The 'other' languages of alien times came through in the smallest of fragments—'bits of granite'—seldom taken up by the characters, but rather handled by the author-as-editor. The concept of language as history is held apart from the narrator's ability to select and footnote and explain *with* language. As long as dialects keep their strangeness, they are objects of study—and language (in the voice of the narrator's present) retains its ability

---

[71] 'The Doom of the Griffiths', 229, 230, 247, 241, 245, 264, 250, 263, 269, 229.

to talk about itself, to comment. The trick is central to the authors' motifs of archaeology and natural history. The natural historian may be part of nature, but can see it whole none the less—in theory. Trench said that all languages must die, like people: 'Seeing then that they thus die, they must have had the germs of death, the possibilities of decay, in them from the very first . . .'. The linguist does not invent the rules, but charts the stages of a common life-span. Just as no person escapes death, however unique the events of his or her life, no dialect lives for ever in the same form. Not even standard English. But within the inexorable there is room for some movement, some agency, in the voice of each speaker: 'for while there is a law of necessity in the evolution of languages, while they pursue certain courses and in certain directions, from which they can be no more turned aside by the will of men than one of the heavenly bodies could be pushed from its orbit by any engines of ours, there is a law of liberty no less'.[72]

The desire to see liberty in the laws of nature finds a scheme in the author's manipulations of time. The historical fiction puts obscure moments of change into dialogue with a voice that keeps steady from past to present. Time is lengthened or abbreviated, depending on whether it is needed for revitalization or a tenable starting-point. The use of epic techniques (contraction and expansion of time, vagueness of origin, a voice more uniform than we hear in the present) achieves a past that is acceptable and, in fact, inevitable—without imposing such limits on the present. As I suggest with Gaskell's tale in particular, the awareness of this legerdemain comes more or less inscribed in the forms of translation.

All three authors put into their fiction a questioning of the very idea (and desirability) of a universal language—perhaps aware, as novelists, of how much they had gained from inaccessible sites of meaning. The epic tone ushers in the boundaries of nation. Kingsley's novel, in particular, suggests that optimism for the future of the nation requires an intermingling (rather than a resolution) of universal laws (or fate) and single, unrepeatable moments of glory. The novels do not take either

---

[72] Trench, *English: Past and Present*, 76, 95.

character or nation from acorn to oak. Nor does the genre 'apologize' (as many of the linguists did) for not doing so.

In other ways, too, the novels add to ideas about dialect and its place in language development. The bifocal view of language as both science and artefact is easier on the eye in the novels than in other kinds of prose. A single stratum of experience—the character's present—holds fragments of speech that may come from many points of origin, in time and space. One day in a life can expose many strata; in fact, the image of layers breaks down, when the narrator is not insisting upon it. The most 'developed' are those who use the tools at hand, if a bit awkward in shape. Dialect, as we saw in Gaskell's story, does not necessarily fill in the gaps of our knowledge; we may still be as clouded to meaning as before. But the exposure of the points of obscurity is both a science and a sign of a heightened sensitivity to the ways in which language alters perception. The novelists escape the question of how the single life fits into the evolution of the species by blurring (from the vantage-point of a literary heritage, of starting *in medias res*) both the past and the future. The only generative periods are what we see. By capturing a moment in the middle age, the fiction implies both 'made' and 'making', with characters who choose among the words they are given—often crossing period lines. The display of choice rubs away the gloss of fixed stages (often imposed by the narrator) and suggests instead a ground where fossils can start to breathe again. In the novels, at least, injections of the past may not only invigorate weary speech; they may also imply that language is not a describable history; that nothing vital is truly lost.

2

Rocks and Living Tongues:
Inductive Science and the Novels
of the Present

THE analogy between the two kinds of writer—of geology and of fiction—is not out of the blue. The people mixed in social groups. They documented exchanges. They traded forms of expression. Geology was 'in vogue'; it was not limited to academia, but was cheap to pursue, accessible, and of practical use. Prince Albert's interest gave it cachet.[1] John Herschel (a bright and well-known star among Victorian scientists) wrote to Charles Lyell on the topic, implying an easy link between three fields of research:

Words are to the Anthropologist what rolled pebbles are to the Geologist—Battered relics of past ages often containing within them indelible records capable of intelligible interpretation—and when we see what amount of change 2000 years has been able to produce in the languages of Greece & Italy or 1000 in those of Germany France & Spain we naturally begin to ask how long a period must have lapsed since the Chinese, the Hebrew, the Delaware & the Malesass [from Madagascar] had a point in common with the German & Italian & each other.—Time! Time! Time![2]

On a palette of geology, anthropology, and comparative philology, Herschel blended modes of inquiry and the problems that arose: How elastic was the concept of time? Could science get to the point of origin (assuming a single point)? Was much lost in the battering, or did the scars *increase* intelligibility? Did the changes work at a steady (and therefore usable) rate? If the novelists did not cling to images of layered stone, the impact of

[1] Janet M. Douglas, *The Life and Selections from the Correspondence of William Whewell* (London, 1881), 304.
[2] Adrian Desmond and James Moore, *Darwin* (London, 1992), 215.

their mental environment—ideas of time and organization—none the less affected their work. Against geological models, the structure of the fictional use of language can be set in relief, and curious patterns emerge.

Geologists in the eighteenth century had already developed a 'rude system of stratigraphic nomenclature', involving primary, secondary, and tertiary (oldest to youngest) deposits on the earth. Fossils and strata became 'classical data of historical geology'.[3] The method was adopted by students of mankind; the model of time in layers (the top layers being the most recent) could be applied to prehistoric human sites.[4] Kingsley in 1871 declared that 'When I consider the likenesses, and unlikenesses of the floras of India and of South America, my dreams carry me back to (dare I say) "secondary" rather than "tertiary" eras, and to slow mutations of land and water, causing slow migrations of forms.'[5] The use of fossils to date both organic and inorganic matter argued a temporal beginning and end to each species.

The image became linguistic. Thomas Arnold, in a lecture delivered at Oxford in 1842, spoke of the bearing of language upon history. He asserted the value of the writings of people who lived at the time under study, calling it a 'double lesson'. He believed that 'an impression of the style and peculiarities of any man's language is an important help towards realizing our notion of him altogether'. He pointed to Scott's *Fortunes of Nigel*, whose 'broad Scotch dialect' gave flesh and blood to James the First. The speech of the past, even while it narrated events, became at once part of them; likewise, the present historian must be aware of himself as both a recorder and a participant.[6]

Arnold's ideal historian immersed himself in two worlds, two languages, in order to understand true causes. His 'double lesson' image may be compared to the polarity that Carlyle set up between the writing and the events of history: 'Narrative is

---

[3] Stephen Jay Gould, *Time's Arrow, Time's Cycle* (London, 1991), 86.

[4] Peter J. Bowler, *The Invention of Progress* (Oxford, 1989), 82.

[5] Kingsley's letter to Charles Bunbury, in *Charles Kingsley: Letters and Memories of His Life* (London, 1877), ii. 389–9.

[6] Thomas Arnold, *Introductory Lectures on Modern History* (Oxford, 1842), 86–7.

linear, Action is *solid*.'[7] Arnold saw narrative as a kind of action—entering the present as itself; Carlyle envisaged history as a many-layered text, a palimpsest. The images are not the same, but they shared the idea that some languages, or forms of language, stopped at a certain point in time. William Gaskell regretted the decay of 'things of living power' in words that 'now seem to us so dead and strange'.[8] Lyell held that the 'extinction . . . of languages in general is not abrupt, any more than that of species', but added, 'a language which has once died out can never be revived'.[9] It augured more than simply fear of loss; it meant that words—and their parts—disclose identity and time, as fossils do. Bunsen, like Arnold, saw language as its own historical document. It exceeded the value of all others.[10]

Canon Farrar, in his account of Müller, described their excursion to the Malvern Hills in 1855, when Müller 'had only lately taken up the subject of Geology'. Farrar recalled, forty-six years later, the linguist's deep fascination with the 'odd fragments' in the field: 'I cannot but suspect that there was in his mind the perception of the close analogy offered by his own favourite study of the history of language. Those fragments of early strata were parallel to the presence of roots or old forms of words embedded in later linguistic strata.'[11] Hensleigh Wedgwood, introducing his *Dictionary of English Etymology* in 1859, argued that roots could never have existed prior to words. He used observation of a child's first speech to refute the idea that roots 'were implanted by Nature in the mind of man, as some people have supposed that the bones of mammoths were created, at the same stroke with the other materials of the *strata* in which they are buried'.[12] Wedgwood and Müller were often

---

[7] Thomas Carlyle, 'On History', in *English and Other Critical Essays* (London, 1967), 85.

[8] William Gaskell, 'Two Lectures on the Lancashire Dialect', in *Mary Barton* (1854; Halifax, 1993), 361.

[9] Charles Lyell, *The Geological Evidences of the Antiquity of Man* (London, 1863), 467.

[10] Christian Charles Josias Bunsen, *Outlines of the Philosophy of Universal History* (London, 1854), ii. 129.

[11] *The Life and Letters of the Right Honourable Friedrich Max Müller* (London, 1902), i. 168.

[12] Hensleigh Wedgwood, *A Dictionary of English Etymology* (London, 1859), vol. i, p. iii.

at odds in their analyses, but they shared a geological image of history. Schuyler, in his review of Wedgwood's book, suggested that 'all the related words should be grouped, and arranged historically; going "upward through the ages," that we may clearly see its development, and know just when and how it came into the language'.[13]

The three novelists, here, do not point to geology as a direct influence; yet they took up, in fiction, the same questions of origin, God, and plot. They shared an interest in how the teller of the tale altered the vision of time. It must be said, of course, that Scott did not trek across the Borders with a pickaxe and sack. He was interested more in stories than in rocks. Geological references in his novels are fleeting: for example, the letter of introduction to Hutton that Mannering takes to Edinburgh. We do not 'meet' the great geologist himself.[14] James Hutton, a late eighteenth-century earth scientist, is generally thought to be father of the concept of 'uniformitarianism', which, to quote Stephen Jay Gould, is 'loosely translated in textbook catechism as "the present is the key to the past" '. Hutton's *Theory of the Earth*, written in a difficult prose, did not find ready access to the public. It resurfaced in 1802, more persuasively, in the elegant and shorter adaptation by another Scot, John Playfair[15]— one of Scott's eclectic group of friends.[16]

Playfair appears, in quotation, on the title-page of Charles Lyell's *Principles of Geology*: 'The rivers and the rocks, the seas and the continents, have been changed in all their parts; but the laws which direct those changes, and the rules to which they are subject, have remained invariably the same.' The Victorians bought and read *Principles* 'as if it were a novel'.[17] Gould argues that much of its success was rooted in style: Lyell 'was a lawyer by profession—a barrister no less, skilled in the finest points of

---

[13] Eugene Schuyler, *Review of Wedgwood's English Etymology* (Andover, 1862), 2.

[14] Walter Scott, *Guy Mannering* (1815; London, 1905), 383.

[15] Gould, *Time's Arrow, Time's Cycle*, 67, 61.

[16] Edgar Johnson, *Sir Walter Scott* (London, 1970), i. 614.

[17] David R. Dean, 'Through Science to Despair', in James Paradis and Thomas Postlewait (eds.), *Victorian Science and Victorian Values* (New Brunswick, NJ, 1985), 114. Desmond and Moore also note the popularity of Lyell's book, in *Darwin*, 208.

verbal persuasion'.[18] Desmond and Moore add, 'He had a barrister's way with words and a beautiful command of foreign languages . . .'.[19] Lyell had been a student of William Buckland (1784–1856), whom one critic describes as the 'first British geologist of central importance to the Victorians', having taught the science also to Thomas Arnold, John Ruskin, and John Henry Newman, to name a few. Dean suggests that it was the 'Buckland controversy' that in 1839 threw Kingsley (who studied geology under the guidance of Adam Sedgwick) into a 'spiritual crisis'; he 'was rescued from despair by the optimistic fervour of Thomas Carlyle, with geological aid from Buckland and Hugh Miller'.[20] He was not the only one to struggle for a reconciliation between geological evidence and the Bible. That he finally won, at least in his own mind, is highlighted in a letter he wrote to Darwin after the publication (1859) of the *Origin of Species*: 'He found it "just as noble a conception of Deity, to believe that He created primal forms capable of self development . . . as to believe that He required a fresh act of intervention to supply the *lacunas* which He Himself had made".' Darwin was 'ecstatic', and cited Kingsley (along with Asa Gray) as proof that man can be 'an ardent Theist & an evolutionist'. The scientists—Darwin and Lyell among them—felt uneasy about the impact of their discoveries upon religious faith; Kingsley—who was to become chaplain to the Queen—symbolized the 'comically elliptical orbit' of a world that ached for consistency.[21]

Kingsley met Lyell in 1860.[22] In 'Town Geology' he lauds the 'venerable Sir Charles Lyell' as 'almost the first of Englishmen who taught us to see—what common sense tells us—that the laws which we see at work around us have been most probably at work since the creation of the world'. It is significant that Kingsley's edition of the *Principles of Geology*, the eleventh, included Lyell's new (if qualified) acceptance, after a long personal struggle, of Darwin's model of evolution. Kingsley

---

[18] Gould, *Time's Arrow, Time's Cycle*, 104.
[19] Desmond and Moore, *Darwin*, 202.
[20] Dean, 'Through Science to Despair', 112, 122.
[21] Desmond and Moore, *Darwin*, 477, 636, 548.
[22] *Charles Kingsley: Letters*, ii. 119.

gladly adopts Lyell's method: in particular, the idea that 'whatever changes may seem to have taken place in past ages, and in ancient rocks, should be explained, if possible, by the changes which are taking place now in the most recent deposits—in the soil of the field'. Kingsley presents geology as the ideal science, with transferable skills, because its 'most important theories are not, or need not be, wrapped up in obscure Latin and Greek terms. They may be expressed in the simplest English, because they are discovered by simple common sense.'[23]

Geology was popular, among Victorians, and no doubt the simplicity of prose was a factor, as well as the scattering of rocks in cities. Yet the very accessibility of the science made it all the more open to criticism from many angles. One huge category of dispute was religion. Kingsley, quick to embrace evolution, was perhaps atypical of Anglican clergy. Lyell's hesitation was closer to the norm—an unexpected twist, in the context of Lyell's Unitarian background. The Unitarians (with whom Darwin was connected) tended to challenge, without too much grief, the creationist science taught in Anglican schools at the time.[24] William Gaskell, for instance, was one Unitarian minister who followed modern science closely and who, like others of his sect, felt unthreatened by the works of Lyell and Robert Chambers (who popularized geology). God had set the laws in motion; science, uncovering their 'endless progression', looked towards God. Manchester, the home of William and Elizabeth Gaskell, and a hub of dissent, was gaining repute for an openness to scientific inquiry. A geological society began there in 1838. The city hosted the British Association meeting in 1842, attracting (among others) Herschel, Buckland, Whewell, and Roget.[25]

The acceptance of Chambers by the Gaskells is a rough but symbolic line between the Unitarians and Anglicans of their day. Chambers 'published his *Vestiges of the Natural History of Creation* (1844, anonymously) which went through four editions in just half a year'. It was quickly attacked by Buckland, Miller,

[23] Charles Kingsley, 'Town Geology', in *Scientific Lectures and Essays* (London, 1885), 33, 30.
[24] Desmond and Moore, *Darwin*, 413, 32.
[25] Jenny Uglow, *Elizabeth Gaskell* (London, 1994), 134–6.

and Sedgwick—whose collective influence on Kingsley was mentioned earlier. In an 1845 review of *Vestiges*, Sedgwick accuses Chambers of seducing maidens and matrons—of telling them that 'the Bible is a fable' and 'that he [Chambers] has *annulled all distinction between physical and moral*, and that all the phenomena of the universe, dead and living, are to be put before the mind in a new jargon, and as the progression and development of a rank, unbending, and degrading material-ism'.[26] Opposite Sedgwick stood Francis Newman—brother of John Henry (ironically enough), and a Latin professor at University College (a place, like Manchester, of dissenting ideas): 'Among Unitarians and freethinkers he was the man of the hour: an evolutionist—following *Vestiges*—calling for a new post-Christian synthesis.'[27] Elizabeth Gaskell's admiration and love for Newman is obvious in her letters. She applauded his wide influence. She was a fan, too, of Chambers, and sent him praise after reading his *Domestic Annals of Scotland*.[28] Chambers, whose love of history had years before won him the encouragement of Scott, wrote from an interest in the home life and dialects of the Scottish people, in addition to his geological work.

More acceptable to both ends of the religious spectrum was the mathematician and geologist William Whewell, Master of Trinity College, Cambridge. When Kingsley became Regius Professor of Modern History there, in 1860, Whewell took him under his wing, in spite of a distaste for *Alton Locke*. After Whewell's death, Kingsley wrote gratefully of his kindness.[29] Much earlier, Whewell had helped Lyell make a nomenclature for his geological research. In 1837 he became president of the Geological Society (in London), when Lyell's term had ended (Kingsley joined in 1863).[30] The year 1837 also marked Darwin's debut at the Society, where he gave a paper in the presence of Lyell and Hensleigh Wedgwood. Darwin, though a friend to many 'Cambridge clerics', balked at warming to the

---

[26] Nicolaas A. Rupke, *The Great Chain of History* (Oxford, 1983), 177–9.
[27] Desmond and Moore, *Darwin*, 376.
[28] Uglow, *Elizabeth Gaskell*, 456.
[29] *Charles Kingsley: Letters*, ii. 101, 227.
[30] *Dictionary of National Biography* (London, 1973), xx. 1367.

new president: he 'scorned anyone who found Whewell
"profound, because he says length of days adapted to duration
of sleep of man.!!! whole universe so adapted!!! & not man to
Planets.—instance of arrogance!!" '[31] Whewell may very well
have objected to Darwin's 'branch' metaphor, and its implication of a decentred man; yet he embraced scientific methodology,
and had a statue of Bacon put next to the one of Newton at
Cambridge.[32]

Whewell met Gaskell on a few occasions. He knew her at first
by chance. One of Gaskell's best friends, Susanna Winkworth,
translated from German the writings of Niebuhr, the historian.[33]
Whewell's English hexameters were included in the 1852 *Life
and Letters of Niebuhr*.[34] (Lyell refers to Niebuhr as summing
up the joy of geology: 'a bliss like that of creating'.[35]) When they
finally met in person, in 1855, Gaskell (unlike Darwin) did not
at all seem offended by Whewell's tendency to put man at the
centre of things. Whewell writes of having met her in Glasgow:
he 'took her over Glasgow Cathedral by way of getting for a
time out of the atmosphere of science'. Gaskell in turn gave him
a small book, an 'Okeawnt o the Greyt Eggshibishun be a Fella
fro' Rachde'. Whewell, in a letter home, describes it as 'a
specimen of the Lancashire dialect which I shall try to read to
Corrie and Janet; though being barbarians from Yorkshire, I
fear they are not well acquainted with our Lancashire Doric'.[36]
Gaskell later records enjoying a chat with him in London.[37]
Their religious differences shrank before a common pleasure in
language.

The 'Okeawnt' she gave him is rich in symbolic value. It turns
the tables—however briefly—on our picture of the times. It is
dialect writing about science—notable, because we tend to read
about the scientists who made an object of dialect, pulling it into
both methodology and general principles. Darwin, for example,

[31] Desmond and Moore, *Darwin*, 207, 199, 236.
[32] Douglas, *The Life and Correspondence of William Whewell*, 314.
[33] Letter dated 17 Nov. 1851, in Elizabeth Gaskell, *Letters* (Manchester, 1966),
172.
[34] *DNB* xx. 1373.
[35] Charles Lyell, *Principles of Geology* (1830–3; London, 1872), i. 87.
[36] Douglas, *The Life and Correspondence of William Whewell*, 442–3.
[37] Uglow, *Elizabeth Gaskell*, 225.

took pains to spell out his gardener's Shropshire accent.[38] Kingsley writes of his own father, a geologist and linguist, who echoed Bacon's 'magna est veritas, et prœvalebit' (truth is great and will prevail).[39] Wedgwood, Gaskell's cousin, in an important way shadowed Darwin:

[Hensleigh was] himself a philologist, looking for the 'laws' by which alphabets slowly change. He praised the Germans for understanding the 'organic' development of language and for tracing 'every descendant' of their own Gothic tongue. Languages had to be anatomized, their underlying unity exposed, ancestral sounds teased out. The analogy with Charles's zoology was overt. Just as he uncovered fossil sloths, Hensleigh was listening for 'fossil remains' in speech.

Desmond and Moore claim that 'Through Hensleigh and Herschel, Charles [Darwin] grasped the historical analogy.' Darwin had met Scott in Edinburgh in 1825, and was no doubt aware of the novelist's art of linking history, topography, and language. The Wedgwoods, Darwins, and Lyell made up a circle wherein 'language, genealogy and development were the hot topics'—though not all (including Hensleigh) accepted in detail the theory of a transmutation (natural evolution) of species.[40] Gaskell visited Lyell in 1859. In a letter of May 1864 she compares Roger, in *Wives and Daughters*, to Darwin: Roger's voyage across the seas, to find specimens for the English warehouse of biological knowledge, makes the source unmistakable. Gaskell writes of a number of social events wherein Darwin took part. There was a slight but mutual correspondence. In a letter to C. E. Norton—a close friend, who visited the Darwins at their home in Downe[41]—she reports that Meta (her second-eldest daughter) accompanied Darwin's sister on a voyage.[42]

By the mid-nineteenth century the contact between geology and the novel had, in a modest way, taken form. Dean observes that 'Emily Brontë's *Wuthering Heights* (1847) is the first major

[38] Desmond and Moore, *Darwin*, 290.
[39] Letter dated 1860, in *Charles Kingsley: Letters*, ii. 109.
[40] Desmond and Moore, *Darwin*, 216, 24, 218, 283.
[41] Ibid. 526.
[42] Elizabeth Gaskell, *Letters*, 581 (Oct. 1859), 732 (May 1864), 158 (July 1851), 630 (Aug. 1860).

British novel to be named for a geological process (erosion)'. He shows us Kingsley's attempt to dramatize in fiction his own, earlier struggle to fit principles of geology into the Anglican code: 'By 1848 Kingsley felt ready to speak out on behalf of his generation and did so in a provocative first novel, *Yeast*. It is the story of Lancelot Smith, geologist, who, like Kingsley himself, searches to find something beyond materialism, despite the inadequacy of traditional creeds'.[43]

The contact of genres did not stop at the insertion of characters who spoke, or thought about, earth processes. Their very speech was at times implicated. The novelists were aware of a general trend of comparison between language and geology.[44] One saw it emerge in the eighteenth century. J. G. Herder, for example, in his 'Essay on the Origin of Language', stated that 'In all aboriginal languages, vestiges of these sounds of nature are still to be heard . . .'.[45] Chambers later used the word 'vestiges' in the title of his geological treatise mentioned above. John Stuart Mill, looking back to the 'doctrine' of the Coleridge school, mentioned its treatment of language as a 'sacred deposit'— counteracting the synchronic approach of logicians.[46] History acted, through words, in the present; words, in turn, could be chipped from the bedrock to date an otherwise timeless (or readable) dialogue. Bishop Percy, whose *Reliques* deeply affected Scott, chose and ordered 'specimens of ancient poetry' in part to 'shew the gradation of our language'.[47] Tulloch draws attention to Scott's use of oaths for a contingent purpose: to date his stories without troubling the reader with inscrutable meanings.[48] The concept of 'dating' linked history, geology, and language. De Quincey, in 1839, called for a history of slang.[49] In

[43] Dean, 'From Science to Despair', 121–2.

[44] Tony Crowley, *The Politics of Discourse* (Basingstoke, 1989), 58.

[45] Johann Gottfried Herder, 'Essay on the Origin of Language', trans. A. Gode, in *On the Origin of Language* (New York, 1966), 91.

[46] John Stuart Mill, *A System of Logic* (1843; Toronto, 1974), books IV–VI, p. 685.

[47] Thomas Percy, *Reliques of Ancient English Poetry* (1764; London, 1794), vol. i, p. xiv.

[48] Graham Tulloch, *The Language of Walter Scott* (London, 1980), 92.

[49] Thomas De Quincey, 'The English Language', in W. F. Bolton (ed.), *The English Language* (1839; London, 1973), 205.

1851 Trench, borrowing a key geological image, extended it to all words:

'a popular author of our own day has somewhere characterized language as 'fossil poetry'—evidently meaning that just as in some fossil, curious and beautiful shapes of vegetable or animal life, the graceful fern or the finely vertebrated lizard, such as now, it may be, have been extinct for thousands of years, are permanently bound up in the stone, and rescued from that perishing which would have otherwise been theirs,—so in words are beautiful thoughts and images, the imagination and the feeling of past ages, of men long since in their graves, of men whose very names have perished, these, which would so easily have perished too, preserved and made safe forever.[50]

The images (of the present as quarry, as literature, as storehouse) are found in Lyell's *Principles of Geology*. In the preface to the tenth edition he justifies his work as an inquiry into 'permanent effects of causes now in action' (history in the present); he refers to such effects as 'a symbolical language, in which the earth's autobiography is written'. In the main text (eleventh edition) he describes geology as a focus upon the 'surface and external structure of our planet'. It is a sort of photographic realism: the outer form, in all of its vast but law-abiding detail, is the ideal object for inductive science. The observable gives us axioms for the obscure. By obscurity is meant time.

Lyell included language among the 'inorganic and organic': the very terms of geology could be used to date the history and geographical extent of the science. Werner, the eighteenth-century geologist from Saxony, for example, put his nation's stamp on such as 'greywacke' and 'gneiss'. Smith, an English geologist, 'adopted for the most part English provincial terms, often of barbarous sound, such as gault, cornbrash, clunch clay; and affixed them to subdivisions of the British series'. Locations of individual origin, then, got woven into the fabric of classification, and thus found a place in a system of identity that could be used outside historical consideration. Lyell's use of the

---

[50] Richard Chenevix Trench, *On the Study of Words* (London, 1851), 4–5. Linda Dowling identifies the 'popular author' who coined 'fossil poetry' as Emerson. Dowling, *Language and Decadence in the Victorian* Fin de Siècle (Princeton, 1986), 63.

word 'barbarous' shows the insertion of historic (socially inscribed) identities into scientific (socially neutral) means of differentiation—but it also suggests an eventual loss from view of the former. Science, as Kingsley kept insisting, was a level field. At least in potential.

Lyell attributed to his generation a 'growing importance ... of the natural history of organic remains'. In effect, it became a new way of classifying matter (living and dead), and of visualizing change over time: 'The adoption of the same generic, and, in some cases, even of the same specific, names for the exuviæ of fossil animals and their living analogues, was an important step towards familiarising the mind with the idea of the identity and unity of the system in distant eras. It was an acknowledgement, as it were, that part at least of the ancient memorials of nature were written in a living language.'[51] What Lyell suggests, here, is that a vocabulary has been made (in the present) to echo the fact that species and genera 'speak', or have identity, over time. The identity overtakes and passes the individual. Yet the artifice of the language—the fact that it has recently been adopted—becomes subsumed in the image of 'ancient memorials'; as if even the names had been written in stone by each embodiment. Lyell's metaphor turns the 'object' of science into both intention and fact. His ability to conflate 'methodological principles with substantive claims' has been well illustrated by Gould.[52] The point to be made, here, is that Lyell, in his own lifetime, saw language change to accommodate science; he used this phenomenon, even so, to argue that organisms held onto an identity ·far beyond the life of the individual. Darwin, too, had written that fossilized bones 'tell their story of former times with almost a living tongue'.[53] The 'speaker', in such a view, is composed of many lifetimes now gone, while giving the impression of a single, undying voice. The continuity of words over time is invoked to support a concept— of individuals connected by genealogy to wider categories— fundamental to the belief in evolution. It parallels an irony in the novels, where dialects are shown to be both continuous (from

[51] Lyell, *Principles of Geology*, vol. i, pp. x–xi, 1, 83, 86.
[52] Gould, *Time's Arrow, Time's Cycle*, 118.
[53] Desmond and Moore, *Darwin*, 144.

the origins of the national language) and in a process of change. It is not so much a contradiction as a flexibility of emphasis. Analysis of each new twist can suggest directions of meaning.

Max Müller in the 1860s compared the science of language to geology. He saw language as a product of nature, not of history. It grew.[54] His metaphors, however, are not exclusively organic. In 1868 he depicted our progress in other terms: 'we can see deeper and deeper into the shaft from which the ore of human speech is brought, and discover level after level that must have been left behind before the pure metal'.[55] Lyell read and respected Müller's work.[56] In the mid-nineteenth century, however, the analogy between the two areas of science was becoming more specific to fossils. Nicolaas Rupke describes the change in geology: 'The early *Transactions of the Geological Society* show a gradual shift from Wernerian stratigraphy (focused on Primary rocks and on mineralogy) to Cuvierian historical geology (focused on fossiliferous rocks and on paleontology)'.[57] Kingsley, in 'Town Geology', explains that the student can 'soon learn to distinguish the relative age of rocks by the fossils found in them, which he can now, happily, study in many local museums'.[58]

Fossils were becoming not only objects of study but central to a methodology. The idea of organic relics being used, in isolation, to judge the time-scale of the whole base of matter was of importance to the study of language in general, and of dialects in particular. According to Gould, the eighteenth century had already witnessed the idea that, while the 'material substrate' may not change, the *forms* of it do, and 'often in a definite direction so that each repetition passes with distinctive and identifiable differences'.[59] The word 'form', in both geology and the science of language, often meant a structure that allowed for identification in the process of development.

[54] Max Müller, *Lectures on the Science of Language* (1861; London, 1871), i. 2, 40, 80–1.
[55] *The Life and Letters of the Right Honourable Friedrich Max Müller* (London, 1902), i. 348.
[56] Lyell, *The Geological Evidences of the Antiquity of Man*, 454.
[57] Rupke, *The Great Chain of History*, 115.
[58] Kingsley, 'Town Geology', 3–4.
[59] Gould, *Time's Arrow, Time's Cycle*, 49.

Chevalier Bunsen (said to be the model for the Dean in *Alton Locke*[60]) wrote of languages containing, among other elements, 'deposits' from the primary formations of other languages. He argued that the original language must have consisted of 'inorganic' words—each being a whole 'sentence', or an independent unit of meaning. The aim of 'organic' formation was a greater use of the logic of parts of words, or inflexion. A language either remained inorganic or developed to organic perfection, before its necessary stasis and decay. The object of science was to chart the steps from one kind to the other.[61] Dialect, for many people, became a method of charting the stages of a language towards greater degrees of participation in a system of meaning that depended more on logic than on concrete images. The 'organic' nature of the more advanced languages, presumably, lay in their dependence, not on a static identity, but on a system that involved time (etymology and tense). Gaskell wrote a letter to George Smith thanking him for a copy of Bunsen's *Signs of the Times*—a title that admits him into the Victorian past-in-present club.[62]

William Gaskell had earlier compared the Lancashire dialect to 'bits of the old granite'.[63] Elizabeth Gaskell was writing *North and South* around the time of the publication of her husband's lectures in the back of the fifth edition (1854) of *Mary Barton*. Her main *North and South* character, Margaret Hale, grows more and more alert to the worth of the labourers in Milton (a northern industrial town: or, Manchester). She says to her father, 'There's granite in all these northern people, papa, is there not?' He answers, 'There was none in poor Boucher, I am afraid; none in his wife either.' She offers an explanation: 'I should guess from their tones that they had Irish blood in them.'[64] National slurs aside, it is interesting to see how she puts tone of voice (orthographically present in Boucher's speech) and a geological phenomenon into a gradient of value. Granite becomes an icon of lasting metamorphosis. Evidently, some

[60] J. W. Burrow, 'The Uses of Philology in Victorian England', in Robert Robson (ed.), *Ideas and Institutions of Victorian Britain* (London, 1967), 194.
[61] Bunsen, *Outlines of the Philosophy of Universal History*, ii. 93–5.
[62] Letter dated May 1856, in Elizabeth Gaskell, *Letters*, 389.
[63] William Gaskell, 'Two Lectures on the Lancashire Dialect', 371.
[64] Elizabeth Gaskell, *North and South* (1854–5; Oxford, 1982), 308.

forms of dialect are closer to the original language than others, though all have gone through change. Boucher's speech is weaker than, say, Bessy's. The Bouchers represent a race in decay. Boucher commits suicide rather than live out his degradation. He is a different sort of rock. Gould, writing of the eighteenth century, says that 'By recognizing the igneous character of many rocks previously viewed as sediments (products of decay), Hutton incorporated a concept of repair into geological history.'[65] Gould's thesis was that geologists were trying to reconcile images of cycle and progress. The Gaskells' use of granite, as a metaphor, draws into the dialect field the conflation of change and solidity: granite, now hard, becomes a malleable ingredient for the next stage in time, with its implication of the potential for progress rather than decay. The borrowing of geological time—with its extended scale— reduces the tragic impact of the idea that progress and decay are linked.

The huge time-scale, which replaced (for most) the biblical by mid-century, was in fact reflected by its reverse. Models of time, found in writings on geology, history, and language in the nineteenth century, suggest a briefer focus than that of their predecessors, encapsulating laws of process; the rest of time could be inferred. The novelists adopted the idea smoothly. Even 'epic' novels draw attention to their historical edges. In the background there may be taken for granted a pattern of cycles— history repeating itself—but the emphasis is almost always upon the details that make the chosen period unique. In *Principles of Geology* Lyell states the need to separate geology from cosmogony; history, likewise, ought not to be mistaken for speculations of origin.[66] Hutton's 'most famous' depiction of the earth's relics of change had been, in 1788, 'no vestige of a beginning,—no prospect of an end'. Lyell, too, 'eschewed speculation' about both limits of time. Gould saw both men as part of a move to narrow the scope of scientific research.[67]

Scott's contemporary and biographer, Lockhart, wrote of

---

[65] Gould, *Time's Arrow, Time's Cycle*, 65.
[66] Lyell, *Principles of Geology*, i. 5.
[67] Gould, *Time's Arrow, Time's Cycle*, 63, 123.

Scott's work as a 'Homeric mirror', implying both epic and realism in the context of a folk tradition. He insisted that Scott kept the 'unbroken energy of half-civilized ages'.[68] How far back does the energy go unbroken? Thomas Arnold traced the English language, and other characteristics, back to the coming of the Saxons, and no further. He argued that modern Englishmen were no more related to Romans and Britons, nationally, than to forest animals. Modern history, he claimed, must look only at the national life still in existence; since the coming of the Saxons there have been no new elements, but rather a variety of combinations, including race, language, institutions, and religion.[69] Scott, too, had attributed the origin of English to the Saxon invasion.[70]

Arnold was Lockhart's contemporary; Scott had learnt rather from Adam Ferguson, the father of a fellow student at Edinburgh.[71] In his *Essay on the History of Civil Society* (1767) Ferguson points to different modes of observation: 'What the savage projects, or observes, in the forest, are the steps which led nations, more advanced, from the architecture of the cottage to that of the palace, and conducted the human mind from perceptions of sense, to the general conclusions of science.'[72] He implies that the *method* of observation is a mark of historic time; that there is a deep structure, or process, of observation that gives identity, and breaks the line of continuity into types. Avrom Fleishman puts Scott into the context of the 'speculative school'—along with William Robertson, Adam Smith, John Millar, and Adam Ferguson—with its interest in discerning the universal laws that give history a shape of progress. It was the shape or form rather than the details that got the main focus.[73] This may seem an unusual setting for Scott, whose novels, after all, give highly specialized insight into bits of clothing, drinks, speech, and other forms of behaviour. But it offers a clue to why

---

[68] Johnson, *Sir Walter Scott*, i. 206.
[69] Arnold, *Introductory Lectures on Modern History*, 29–31.
[70] Walter Scott, *The Minstrelsy of the Scottish Border* (1802–3; Edinburgh, 1850), i. 29.
[71] Johnson, *Sir Walter Scott*, i. 76.
[72] Adam Ferguson, *An Essay on the History of Civil Society* (Edinburgh, 1767), 13.
[73] Avrom Fleishman, *The English Historical Novel* (Baltimore, 1971), 42, 50.

Scott stopped his dig for relics at a certain place in time; to why he was sometimes a bit careless in his 'transcriptions' of past speech.

Science was widely held to be unique to the modern period—defining it by a method of observation. Lyell used geology to discredit the idea that earlier races (as far as we know from the relics of their languages) were superior to the present. To those who pointed to the 'evidence' of artifical construction and abstract terms in Sanskrit, for instance, he gave as a counter-argument the geologist's vision: Paleolithic man existed long before the people who spoke any of the extant languages; the 'progenitors of mankind had a scantier vocabulary than the humblest savage known to us'; they had no abstract terms at all. The history of language, therefore, had a limited scope of proof, and should keep its aims between the lines. It was not, in any case, essential to push back any further. Lyell, defending *natural* history, insists that Darwin's ideas were none the weaker for the 'obliqueness' of a first cause.[74] Kingsley, in a letter to Max Müller, says that he believes man 'to be of any antiquity which he may be proved to be of', asserting both courage in the face of geology and expanding time, and the contingency of his belief upon facts, not speculation.[75] Lack of certain knowledge, about origin, was not to undermine the factual basis of modern science.

Uncertainty of material creeps into the novels. The footnotes and narrative insertions that explain unknown words do not go back earlier than the Anglo-Saxon period, and in many cases leave out etymology altogether—the obvious exception being *Mary Barton*. William Gaskell painted an image of old words as fruits that grow less 'racy and full-flavoured' over time; the etymology in *Mary Barton* illustrates the fear of decay. The question remains, though, of what can be done, given the incompleteness of our hold on the past. William Gaskell lamented the paucity of extant Anglo-Saxon material; the gaps between manuscripts made it hard to trace the 'colouring streamlets to their parent source'. He noted with relief the

---

[74] Lyell, *Principles of Geology*, ii. 485–6, 499–500.
[75] Letter dated 1871, in *Charles Kingsley: Letters*, ii. 349.

efforts to restore as much of the old dialects as possible. The Manchester Literary and Philosophical Society, for example, had begun to create a glossary, with the help of the Gaskells' friend Samuel Bamford. A sense pervaded that time was running out.[76]

Bishop Percy in the previous century had displayed history's silence on the matter of the Saxon 'oral itinerant Poet'; our notions of the minstrel had to be garnered from accounts found in Danish histories. Even when old texts were available, they were often marred by the several hands through which they had passed.[77] Carlyle, in *Past and Present*, later underscored the need for scrupulous editing, in an attempt to preserve the original, while recognizing that even the earliest *text* was an imperfect transcription of speech.[78] Tulloch, in his research on the historical novels, found that Scott borrowed 'period' words from historians; few came from oral literature. Others, like Chatterton, simply trawled through dictionaries.[79] The novelists took their samples from paper strata.

August Schleicher, in Germany, wrote a book that in 1869 was translated into *Darwinism Tested by the Science of Language*. He uses terms that couple natural history and the science of language, issuing as his premiss that 'What Darwin lays down of the animal creation in general, can equally be said of the organisms of speech . . .'. The 'history of the formation and progress of speech' may be considered 'the main aspect of the development of mankind'. He attests to the somewhat arbitrary nature of science and its deductions based upon a scattering of evidence, and highlights the primacy of written sources in the study of language: 'What we know now of those languages which, owing to an accident, we have been able to watch for so long a period of time, because the people who spoke them have been obliging enough to leave written records behind from a comparatively early time, may be otherwise supposed in respect of other families of languages, which do not

[76] William Gaskell, 'Two Lectures on the Lancashire Dialect', 361, 386.
[77] Percy, *Reliques*, vol. i, pp. xxiii, xvi–ii.
[78] Thomas Carlyle, *Past and Present* (1843; Oxford, 1918), 38.
[79] Tulloch, *The Language of Walter Scott*, 58, 63, 61.

possess those exponents of their earlier forms.'[80] As in biology, one must often take from the evidence at hand.

German historicism put emphasis upon the use of written sources as a basis for the 'reconstruction' of the spirit that underlay 'episodes in development'—Niebuhr's history of Rome being an example known to Kingsley and Gaskell.[81] Scott, well-read in German scholarship, was keen to discover the effects of Old German upon Scots. He, too, felt conscious that his own study of language was determined by extant written sources, and that these were limited. Introducing the ballad 'Auld Maitland', he claims that many of its words 'preserve traces of its antiquity'; according to his friend James Hogg (who also wrote intermittently in Scots), it takes a practised ear to date a poem by its diction. Even so, poems gradually lose 'their original sense or diction'; like old coins no longer in circulation, old words should be kept in a museum.[82] The vision faded a little at the sight of half-empty display boxes. Macauley, in his essay on Francis Bacon (1837), downplayed the idea that sixteenth-century women were exceptionally well educated. If they knew Greek and Latin, it was only by necessity, there being few other sources of knowledge: 'All the valuable books then extant in all the vernacular dialects of Europe would hardly have filled a single shelf.'[83]

It was a problem that haunted Lyell, and he wrote of the need to take into account 'the laws [in geology] which govern the recording as well as the obliterating processes'. He saw the analogue in language: old words were either supplanted or pared down; they might stay meekly in 'circulation' or be flung from it altogether. He insisted, however, that the lack of a complete set of documents did not erase the proofs that did exist. In terms that could be applied to geology and language, equally, he expressed a need to focus instead upon 'those monuments of the past in which the relics of the animate

---

[80] August Schleicher, *Darwinism Tested by the Science of Language*, trans. Alex V. W. Bikkers (London, 1869), 15, 18, 42–3.

[81] Bowler, *The Invention of Progress*, 52.

[82] Scott, *Minstrelsy*, i. 306–7, 315, 21, 20, 24, 22.

[83] Thomas Babbington Macaulay, 'Lord Bacon', in *Critical and Historical Essays* (London, 1903), ii. 132.

creation of former ages are best preserved and least mutilated by the hand of time'.[84] Gould shows the book metaphor passing from Lyell to Darwin. Lyell used it to argue that 'slow and continuous change will degrade to apparent abruptness as fewer and fewer stages are preserved'—as if only a few letters on a few pages remained of the original text. Gould then quotes from Darwin's *Origin of Species*: 'For my part, following out Lyell's metaphor, I look at the natural geological record, as a history of the world imperfectly kept, and written in a changing dialect; of this history we possess the last volume alone, relating only to two or three countries. Of this volume, only here and there a short chapter has been preserved; and of each page, only here and there a few lines.'[85] The analogy between dialects and fossils took a role, if seldom so explicitly, in the argument for the evolution of species. History was a form of nature; relics, a sign of hidden life.

THE FICTION

The metaphor of language as a germ, growing in complexity to fit the more abstract (yet more finely represented) needs of civilization, is central to the historic fiction, as we saw in the previous chapter. *Guy Mannering*, *Mary Barton*, and *Alton Locke* take place in the present of the nineteenth century. In them, the motif of etymology—of locating the meaning of a word through time—gives way (in very different measures) to that of the scientific method. The emphasis falls upon living memory to illuminate causes; facts in the observable moment are used to invoke both general laws and human motivations. This conflation, while mimicking the grander scale of time in the historical fiction, creates a subtle but important difference. The shadow of determinism moves slightly from a temporal to a spiritual zone: it is the Logos of God, more than the primary root, that counterpoints (while often supporting) the association of complexity and progress.

84 Lyell, *The Geological Evidences*, 462–3, 461, 470.
85 Gould, *Time's Arrow, Time's Cycle*, 135.

One scientist emerged in the nineteenth century as an icon of a glorious compromise. When caught between the urge to display the universe in all its infinite detail, and the fear of losing hold of organization (or meaning), Victorians could raise up Sir Francis Bacon from his sixteenth-century tomb. When Müller promised that we may become 'lords' of language if only we know how to use its laws, thus fitting together mastery and servitude, it was no soliloquy. He echoed what many were saying and attributing (often) to Bacon. Macaulay provides a clue to the rising fame of the Elizabethan sage: 'Two words form the key to the Baconian doctrine, Utility and Progress.'[86] Bacon became a sort of 'people's scientist' because he encouraged them to look at the world at hand; he could be cited as part of an erosion of class barriers, allegedly caused by science, with the demotion of obscure, expensive, and often foreign materials. Even Manchester labourers, such as we find in *Mary Barton*, got drawn into a march towards the command of nature's laws.

Guy Mannering offers a more equivocal view of Bacon—if not of the 'inductive method' itself. Scott had imbibed the method in part through Adam Ferguson, who wrote: 'Among the various qualities which mankind possess, we select one or a few particulars on which to establish a theory, and in framing our account of what man was in some imaginary state of nature, we overlook what he has always appeared within the reach of our own observation, and in the records of history.'[87] He puts 'our own observation' first. In *Guy Mannering*, though, the problem of *what* to observe is central to the plot, entwined around the figure of Bacon, in the 'voices' of Mannering, the narrator, and the Author. The latter admits to changing the original text of his story, whose plot once depended heavily on a faith in astrology, because it occurs to him 'on mature consideration' that people are less gullible than they used to be: 'In changing his plan, however, which was done in the course of printing, the early sheets retained the vestiges of the original tenour of the story, although they now hang upon it as an unnecessary and unnatural encumbrance.' He cannot erase the influence; nor can he testify to the exile of superstition. If

---

[86] Macaulay, 'Lord Bacon', 196.
[87] Ferguson, *An Essay on the History of Civil Society*, 3.

astrology is now less potent, in the imaginative eye, it has merely been replaced by other beliefs 'of a more gross and far less beautiful character'. Astrology, at least, 'was once received and admitted by Bacon himself'. The Author's choice of words implies that Bacon's mind could not be taken lightly; he is discountenanced by the fact that Bacon found any merit at all in the pseudo-science. In his 'Notes', at the back of the novel, the Author paraphrases Bacon (from *De Augmentis Scientiarum*) as saying that astrology 'is rather to be purified than utterly rejected'.

The novel does not clearly mark out the boundaries of acceptability. The precision of Mannering's astrological reading plays against his own reluctance to take it seriously. At one extreme is the laird, the old Mr Bertram, whose wandering mind is the bed of a total faith in starry predictions. Surely we are not to emulate. On the other hand, there is Meg Merrilies, who offers to read the stars for Bertram's son. Although it is the sceptical Mannering (from Oxford) who performs the task, it is hard to brush off Meg's superstitious mind. She plays a key role in the recovery of the lost boy—a role that is forwarded by her trust in the same 'science' that weakened Mr Bertram's reasoning. The old laird is a sort of parody of the inductive method taken to extremes: he 'never embraced a general or abstract idea, and his notion of the revenue was personified in the commissioners, surveyors, comptrollers, and riding officers, whom he happened to know'.

Astrology, teetering on the edge of science, presents the narrator with a conundrum. Observation, according to the inductive method, is key; astrology (in the time of the novel) depended upon a direct reading of the stars. The heading to chapter 4 cites Coleridge (from Schiller):

> Come and see; trust thine own eyes.
> A fearful sign stands in the house of life,—
> An enemy; a fiend lurks close behind
> The radiance of thy planet. Oh, be warned!

The narrator, on the other hand, compares astrology to the 'art of legerdemain' because of the 'thousand ways in which human eyes could be deceived'. Observation of stars and planets filtered through the method of reading them—the many 'abstruse calculations'; observation was not a method so much as the provider of raw materials. Guy Mannering ('or, The Astrologer') wavers a little, struck by the accuracy of his reading, and wonders if its success validates the means. He ponders the compromise, established by Bacon and Thomas Browne, wherein the 'influence of the stars' is taken for granted, while the 'application' by 'the knaves who pretend to practise the art' opens it to scepticism. Mannering ends by dismissing it altogether—though he cannot shake the qualms it raised—and so, 'like Prospero, he mentally relinquished his art'.

The comparison is apt. Prospero gave way to a new generation, and it is possible to read *Guy Mannering* as a record of steps away from magic towards realism. Mannering's tutor fully believed in the art that his student finally dismissed; Mannering's daughter is ignorant of the method, in spite of her birth 'in the land of talisman and spell', and she views it as a sign, merely, of romance, capable of throwing 'a mysterious grandeur about its possessor'. Miss Mannering thus brings astrology into a Jane Austen sort of world, where a heroine's flights of fancy cannot be sustained under the pressure of actual events. Lucy Bertram, taking it further, betrays not even a trace of her father's superstition. She bends her mind, not insignificantly, to the study of languages.

The differences, among characters, in their access to varieties of language offers perhaps the most interesting comment on the problem of method—of the degree to which we can trust what we see, and of how we turn our observations into laws. The following passage, taken from the moment of Harry's birth, gives a clue:

Mr. Bertram hastened to the lady's apartment, Meg Merrilies descended to the kitchen to secure her share of the 'groaning malt,' and the 'ken-no,' and Mannering, after looking at his watch, and noting, with great exactness, the hour and minute of the birth, requested, with becoming gravity, that the Dominie would conduct him to some place where he might have a view of the heavenly bodies.

A handful of linguistic associations can be found in the one sentence. The two flagged expressions of dialect place Meg in a long tradition of birthing rituals. Her linguistic 'belonging' in the Scottish household is later demonstrated by her loyalty to

Harry—in opposition, even, to the men who speak her own gypsy tongue. She is momentarily close (in a feudal sense) to the elder Bertrams, who trust absolutely in astrological prediction. Lady Bertram, who uses Scots dialect, puts Mannering's chart around Harry's neck, symbolically burdening him with his fate. The two sceptics in the passage are Mannering and the Dominie, and the gradient of disbelief between them reflects a linguistic curve.

At first it seems that, of the two, Mannering is the more scientific. Even in play he notes the time on his watch 'with great exactness'. The Dominie, on the other hand, is primarily a linguist. In spite of a difficult childhood 'he obtained a competent knowledge of Greek and Latin, and some acquaintance with the sciences'. Language took syntactic priority. His absent-minded behaviour—his failure to notice, even, the replacement of a whole suit of clothes—makes him a mockery of the inductive method. And yet he swears that 'the (pretended) science of astrology is altogether vain, frivolous, and unsatisfactory'. His incredulity reaches beyond Mannering's on a field of language. When Mannering tries (in jest) to persuade the Dominie of the credibility of his 'science', he throws at him a string of antique names to drown out the sound of Dominie's one 'vernacular' and 'modern' point of reference, Sir Isaac Newton (whose name, during that period, often came next to Bacon's). The two men exchange Latin tags—as if to tussle on that common ground. At first it seems that Meg is the only one affected by Mannering's rhetoric: 'As for Meg, she fixed her bewildered eyes upon the astrologer, overpowered by a jargon more mysterious than her own.' Mannering deliberately 'pressed his advantage, and ran over all the hard terms of art which a tenacious memory supplied'. The narrator's use of 'memory' implies that Mannering is at present a non-believer. He throws at the Dominie 'a thousand terms, of equal sound and significance'. Here the narrator claims his own distance from the jargon, suggesting by 'equal' an absence of meaning. The Dominie, likewise, remains 'unshrinking' in the teeth of 'this pitiless storm'. Mannering, however, does not. His own distance from such terms is later questioned by the narrator, who wonders at the extraordinary coincidence of a 'fate' shared by Harry Bertram and Sophia Wellwood. He asks whether it 'was really one of those singular chances . . . or whether Mannering, bewildered amid the arithmetical labyrinth and technical jargon of astrology, had insensibly twice followed the same clew to guide him out of the maze'; or he might have been 'seduced by some point of apparent resemblance'. Mannering's detachment remains uncertain until the end of the book, where he gets the last word: 'here ends THE ASTROLOGER'.[88]

Scott's ambiguous use of Bacon's name suggests that, for him at least, Bacon stood not so much for inductive science as for the need to find a compromise between trust in destiny and active morality. The Dominie, though a figure of fun in many ways, knows almost every language (ancient and modern); his knowledge of the library's system is both scientific and a mystery to others; neither one of these skills (of both system and detail) distracts him from trying vigorously and against the odds to find his young charge. And yet his vagueness towards much of the world around him—including the jokes at his expense—cannot be taken as the best model. His goodness, and his scholarship, prevent him from imagining the motives of others unlike himself. He embodies a mixture of accumulated knowledge and original goodness that may win him a place in the hearts of his friends, but that hardly furthers the plot. There is too much of caricature and not enough realism for us to accept him as a viable, modern role model. He is rather like a *good* monster of Frankenstein's creation—linguistically adept, a slap in the face of ancient science, and a hint that natural benignity does not thrive in the world unaided. He needs the worldliness of one such as Bacon, or Mannering, to give destiny a realistic shape, while the others gain hope from his axiomatic certainty that good must prevail.

For Gaskell and Kingsley, induction figures more positively as a method intertwining realism and faith, while the dynamic of voices in their fiction gives a clearer view of how the rhetoric of geology (and related natural sciences) fits into their (differing) perspectives on language, and of how linguistic variations in the present determined readings of the past.

[88] *Guy Mannering*, pp. xxxvi–ii, 622, 43, 29, xxxvii, 31–2, 153, 25, 15, 23–5, 31, 604.

Figures of the scientist in *Mary Barton* and *Alton Locke* reveal different uses of the inductive method: Kingsley's approach is more diachronic; that is, he records many dialects and arranges them thematically to accord with his model of evolution and progress. Gaskell, on the other hand, takes a more synchronic approach. She puts less emphasis upon the progress of time, but highlights the boundaries of space, showing how different *forms* of knowledge, within one region, can actually— at any given point in time—help to strengthen community bonds. The shifting emphases, in both writers, invite a query into the value-laden relationship between linear time and improvement.

Mary Barton is complicated by a feature that may have been an afterthought, or a fifth-edition patchwork: the inclusion of William Gaskell's lectures. Far from dovetailing with the main body of the novel, the lectures often read against the grain. William Gaskell valued ties between past and present; he buttressed the union with allusions to Carlyle, who told poets to put away Cant and to know their Facts in a gesture that blurs the line between science and art.[89] The Gaskells put *Mary Barton* into an equivocal position regarding science: Lyell wrote of the need to observe present changes to interpret the past; William's lectures , by contrast, declare that 'Language thus ever runs backward, and very often, in order clearly to understand what it *is*, we must know what it *was*.'[90] Yet *Mary Barton*, the lectures aside, depicts a preoccupation with fact-gathering and processes of the moment, far outweighing—both in sheer bulk and in imaginary force—the impact of the 1854 addendum.

Mary Barton's narrator lauds the typical Manchester worker for his enthusiastic pursuit of facts, citing Newton as the inspiration. The Oldham weavers read Newton's *Principia* at the loom. Their ability to think in the abstract is held up to any prejudice against their speech: 'Mathematical problems are received with interest, and studied with absorbing attention by many a broad-spoken, common-looking, factory-hand.' The narrator admits, however, some ground for incredulity, by adding that it 'is perhaps less astonishing that the more

[89] Carlyle, *Past and Present*, 78.
[90] William Gaskell, 'Two Lectures on the Lancashire Dialect', 361.

popularly interesting branches of natural history have their warm and devoted followers among this class'. As a class, the workers provide (for themselves and the more genteel) a reliable bank of regional data, while hungering to expand their own sense of region. Their close involvement in science draws validity not from similar work done in the past, but rather from a very present skill. Their use of language, too, appears to derive as much from use as from inheritance: the workers insert 'Ephemeridae' and 'Phyrganidae' into their speech, but leave aside elements of standard English that would simply replace (without adding to) the Manchester dialect. Job Legh, surrounded by jars and specimens, is the fullest-drawn example. Jem may look to Canada as an escape from the taint of a murder charge, but Job sees it as a hunting-ground for new insects. For Jem and Mary, Canada is free of certain burdens of history— though not completely, because of human memory. Job also views it geographically—as a guarantee of different species, because of its location in space. Will Wilson, who travels far and wide by sea, collects strange creatures without caring how they fit into the Linnaean world. His frame is thus more *local* than Job's—though Job inhabits only a basement room in Manchester. Will finds no need for a universal language, and hassles Job for using Latin: 'You're one o' them folks as never knows beasts unless they've called out o' their names. Put 'em in Sunday clothes and you know 'em, but in their work-a-day English you never know nought about 'em.' For Will, the language of science is a register of both class and national identity; he uses dialect in a more consciously political way, defending his birthplace. For Job, language aspires to atemporal precision; to locating things in a value-free, unbounded system.

Precision, however, undermines his conceptual flexibility: 'Writing was to him little more than an auxiliary to natural history; a way of ticketing specimens, not of expressing thoughts.' To a degree the narrator colludes. A malediction on the workers' attempt to seize the power of 'combination' likens it to the 'agency of steam; capable of almost unlimited good or evil'. Because of the relative nature of its outcome, the narrator calls for some 'high and intelligent will', and decries the lack of calm wisdom among the 'operatives'. But then, to counter such abstractions, the narrator opens a new paragraph with a terse

'So much for generalities. Let us now return to individuals.' The
narrator, like Job in that instance, feels uneasy beyond the reach
of palpable facts. Unlike Job, however, the narrator can slip into
alternative modes of thought, making Job's adherence to
observable data look rigid, forbidding him access to any hazy
belief (for instance) in mermaids.

What Job loses, in his quest for categorization, is fluidity
among ideas that depend on metaphor. He cannot believe in the
mermaid as a species, so he cannot use it to look more closely at
the motif of seduction and attraction—a motif central to the
murder plot. The legal system hangs on precise terminology—
and Job relishes both its jargon and logical method. He can
relate to the barrister, hired to defend Jem, who sees new
evidence not primarily in the light of its ability to free Jem,
whose innocence he doubts, but as 'opportunities for the display
of forensic eloquence which were presented by the facts'. Job's
own fondness for Jem gets clouded not only by the evidence
against him, but also by a delight in the language of law. Mary,
on the other hand, experiences the input of new modes of speech
as a hindrance at best, and at worst as a frightening environment: for example, in Liverpool, 'The cries of the sailors, the
variety of languages used by the passers-by, and the entire
novelty of the sight compared with any thing which Mary had
ever seen, made her feel most helpless and forlorn . . .'. The
jargon of the subpoena and the slang of Liverpool crowd around
her, and hobble her attempt to collect the proofs of Jem's
innocence. The novel may not exalt her slowness to adapt, but it
does invoke our sympathy and respect for Mary in the trial. Her
single voice rings against the more precise, but ill-informed,
legal framework. Truth does not seem to require a full score of
dialects. The narrator, though 'omniscient', limits the record of
voices to those experienced first-hand: we are *told* that Charley
spoke to the old sailor 'in slang, which to Mary was almost
inaudible, and quite unintelligible, and which I am too much of
a land-lubber to repeat correctly'.[91] The tone lacks apology, or
sense of any real loss to the story, and puts the narrator on a
level with Mary—no superhuman observer, but a person who

[91] Elizabeth Gaskell, *Mary Barton* (1848; Harmondsworth, 1976), 75–6, 466,
201, 406, 223, 395, 351–2.

can be located (however broadly) on a map, like the working-class scientists. The novel underlines the limits of the recording voice, while upholding the belief in degrees of authenticity—a scale that rises or falls not according to the person's linguistic versatility (never absolute, in any case), but to motive.

Gaskell involves language variation in an attempt to mesh a neutral, inductive method into the teachings of the Bible; to find a dynamic of detached tolerance (expressed through standard and biblical English) and local involvement (standard, but more often Manchester dialect). The narrator's (standard) voice is at times a shaky bridge. William Gaskell's lectures belie the focus on immediate, or near present, details—central to the working-class vision in the novel—often looking to other writings or to abstract principles, and allowing mere speculation to stand. They bring to the fore a slim outline of past, racial characteristics, linking these to forms of speech; they assume a parity of historical dialect and racial type in order to 'explain' divisions of the present. The novel, in contrast, portrays manifold responses by drawing out events that took place in the living memory of its characters. In both texts moments of history are juxtaposed to indicate universal laws at work; in the novel proper most of the evidence for interpretation happens in Mary's lifetime. The reader is not sent back centuries to identify and place forms (of language and behaviour) into a hierarchy of value, or to predict developments; a lifetime is enough. The lectures take the opposite approach. Where they fit most neatly into the novel's scheme, perhaps, is by vindicating the amateur's role in science; not only praising the efforts of Samuel Bamford to collect dialect words, but also admitting the author's (William Gaskell's) own lack of expertise in the field—the 'little attention' he was able to give to the subject.

William Gaskell augmented his philological background with the essays of Carlyle, who appears in quotation on the title-page of *Mary Barton* in the first edition. Carlyle encouraged the retrospective, linguistic glance: 'As Mr. Carlyle has said, "The word I speak to you to-day is borrowed, not from Ulphilas, the Mœso-Goth only, but from all men since the first man began to speak".'[92] Carlyle figures even more prominently in the novels,

---

[92] William Gaskell, 'Two Lectures on the Lancashire Dialect', 361.

letters, and essays of Kingsley, who believed his writing to be 'instinct with the very spirit of science'.[93] In *Hypatia* Kingsley develops the Carlylean method found in Gaskell's lectures: 'The universal fusion of races, languages, and customs' are shown to produce 'a corresponding fusion of creeds, an universal ferment-ation of human thought and faith'.[94] Yet his own, non-fictional position on science would seem to reject any withdrawal into a contour map that had not first been thoroughly surveyed. In 'Science' he articulates a deep respect for the inductive method. He traced it from the Chaldeans onwards; he saw Hypatia herself as part of a futile attempt, among the Graeco-Romans, to reconcile the method with 'all the nature-dreading superstitions of the Roman world'. The Jews, he argued, 'taught that science was probable; the Greeks and Romans proved that it was possible. It remained for our race, under the teaching of both, to bring science into act and fact.' He beheld Spenser's *Faerie Queene* (with its partly synthetic construction of an older language) as a 'resuscitation' of Hypatia's motive; it was not until the eighteenth century that any substantial work was done to advance science 'by boldly observing and analysing facts'.[95]

Kingsley rejected the Comtean philosophy with its model of science as ineluctable heir to all religious visions. He insisted that they coexist. Without discarding the basic tenet of necessary cycles, he adapted it to his own purposes, asserting the claim that 'the whirligig of Time' would allow the sun to set on Comtism: 'and Realism, and we who own the Realist creeds, may have our turn'. He looked instead to the psychologist Alexander Bain, who offered 'an older, simpler, more human, and, as I hold, more philosophic explanation' of human emotions.[96] Bain, as I will show in Chapter 4, developed a model of language acquisition that closely related the mother tongue to needs of the body and heart, felt in childhood. Kingsley no doubt respected Bain for combining the physical

---

[93] Charles Kingsley, 'Science', in *Scientific Lectures and Essays*, 249.
[94] Charles Kingsley, *Hypatia* (1853; London, 1882), p. x.
[95] Kingsley, 'Science', 233–5, 238–9.
[96] Charles Kingsley, 'The Natural Theology of the Future', in *Scientific Lectures and Essays*, 336.

context with ideals of family structure; his realism included not a few axioms. He criticized Comte, not because the philosopher scorned facts, but because he neglected the all-encompassing truths that might give them integrity. In 1868 in a letter to F. D. Maurice, Kingsley announced a suspicion that Comte was 'not an inductive (the only truly positive) philosopher, but a mere systematizer and classifier'. He wanted, in tandem with fact-collection, the sort of organic model of civil growth that one finds in the writings of Maurice, Carlyle, and Bunsen.

Kingsley's remarks on realism, science, and language assume a nexus of racial etymology and close observation, with an assurance that the latter will flesh out generalizations. His anxieties about the waterproof nature of his own reconciliation between God and science appeared in a letter of 1857, wherein he refers to himself as 'the strangest jumble of superstition and of a reverence for scientific induction'. He saw Bacon as a fusion of those elements, and associated the rising status of the Baconian method with changes in literary technique—in particular, with realism. His treatment of speech in the novel bears witness: in a letter to George Brimley in 1857 he counsels the young writer to 'have people talk, as people do in real life, about all manner of irrelevant things, only taking care that each man's speech shall show more of his character, and that the general tone shall be such as never to make the reader forget the main purpose of the book'. Revelation entailed more than just idiomatic expression. He admired Lyell's chapter on the 'Analogy of Language and Natural History' (in the *Antiquity of Man*) because it was not a 'mere "illustration" ' but instead 'a real analogue, of the same inductive method applied to a set of facts homologous, though distinct'.[97]

Homology, as opposed to analogy, denotes a genealogical connection, rather than a structurally determined but otherwise unrelated response to needs in common. Kingsley saw induction as a key to the past: as both method and (in its presence or absence) measure of society's mental development. In his mind, the collection and description of present facts—words, accents, and body shapes among them—could not be isolated from evolutionary implications. He pointed to 'the remarkable

[97] *Charles Kingsley: Letters*, ii. 274, 18–19, 40, 168 (letter dated 1863).

absence of any etymological instinct in the ancients, in consequence of their weak grasp of that sound inductive method
which has created modern criticism'.[98] He promoted natural
history as the route to 'that inductive habit of mind, that power
of judging fairly of facts, without which no good or lasting work
will be done, whether in physical science, in social science, in
politics, in philosophy, in philology, or in history'. He cements a
bond between Christianity, earth processes, and the origin of
language by quoting the Psalmist, who said that the heavens
'declare the glory of God; and the firmament showeth His
handiwork. There is neither speech nor language where their
voices are not heard among them.'[99]

The Dean in *Alton Locke* puts philology on a level with
natural history and tries to help Alton get round the problem,
since he is unable to tackle it directly. He affirms that
Christianity does not collide with science, except in appearance;
the two must not go out of their way to accommodate each
other, 'and where they seem to differ, it is our duty to believe
that they are reconcilable by fuller knowledge, but not to clip
truth in order to make it match with doctrine'.[100] The novel's
title is no accident: we have already noted Kingsley's desire to
'work clear of Locke'.[101] He defended his love of geology by
claiming for it the ability to help townsmen see and hear around
them 'that great book of nature, which is, as Lord Bacon said of
old, the Word of God revealed in facts'.[102] Although Locke in
the previous century had encouraged close attention to one's
own environment, Kingsley rejected in essence his philosophy.
Bunsen spoke for Kingsley, too, in the *Outlines of the
Philosophy of Universal History*, where he referred to Locke's
view of human life as 'degrading and materialistic'; he, like
Kingsley, saw in the works of Maurice and Carlyle a progress
towards 'the course indicated rather than traced by Bacon', the
faultiness of whose speculations did not overshadow (for

---

[98] Charles Kingsley, 'Superstition', in *Scientific Lectures and Essays*, 203.
[99] Kingsley, 'Town Geology', 13, 23–4.
[100] Charles Kingsley, *Alton Locke* (1850; Oxford, 1987), 170.
[101] Letter dated 1854, in *Charles Kingsley: Letters*, i. 380.
[102] Kingsley, 'Town Geology', 151.

Bunsen) the 'spirit' of his system. Bunsen, like Kingsley, saw the workings of time within the present:

The phenomena of mind (e.g. in language) must first be treated as elements in themselves, considered as single facts: this would constitute the forms of what there *is*, or of evolved existence. But all historical phenomena are connected with each other by the law of cause and effect, subordinately or collaterally: they are the elements of a process of evolution, according to the special laws inherent in the nature of the phenomenon; therefore, in the case alluded to, of language.

Bunsen saw the first process—fact-collection—as philological; the second, historical. The combined method brings to the focus on detail a structure of laws inferred from previously recorded events.[103] It allows the presence of axioms to be acknowledged during the very process of induction.

Alton Locke uses a like strategy, in other terms. Sandy tells Alton that true poetry 'begins at hame': 'Gin ye want to learn the spirit o' the people's poet, down wi' your Bible and read thae auld Hebrew prophets; gin ye wad learn the style, read your Burns frae morning till night; and gin ye'd learn the matter, just gang after your nose, and keep your eyes open, and ye'll no miss it.'[104] Like Bunsen, with a racier dialect, Sandy equates the historical (organic) element with a language that pre-dates the English of the standard Bible; both style and facts are closer at hand, but not independent of the laws that informed earlier (cross-national) writings. Poetry may begin at home, as far as the poet's *method* is concerned, but only because hidden principles connect him to words far distant in time. Kingsley admired Burns for having 'welded' together 'the Norse Scotch and the Romanesque English'; Burns was close to his ideal poet, having risen from the masses still able to speak their tongue, for 'when he speaks to the wanderer and the drudge, he speaks to the elemental and primeval man, and in him speaks to all who have risen out of him'.[105] In recounting the dream that comes to him in illness, where he passes through evolutionary stages, Alton wonders how he can have feelings previously unknown.

[103] Bunsen, *Outlines of the Philosophy of Universal History*, i. 14, 25, 32.
[104] *Alton Lock*, 88.
[105] Charles Kingsley, 'Burns and his School', in *Literary and General Lectures and Essays* (London, 1890), 158, 183–4.

He asks, 'Has the mind power of creating sensations for itself? Surely it does so, in those delicious dreams about flying which haunt us poor wingless mortals, which would seem to give my namesake's philosophy the lie.' His life story may be read as a movement in method from the particular to the universal. As a child, he was forced by circumstance to restrict his observations to a very narrow sphere—the front garden, or Battersea-fields. And yet he turned the limitation to good account; it 'concentrated the faculty into greater strength'. He speaks of natural history as a sort of predecessor to the humanities, for 'the study of human beings only develops itself as the boy grows into the man'. As the Dean later points out, such fields as philology require a privileged background of wide-ranging study; whereas natural history—the poor man's science—involves the same method, with fewer materials.

Sandy gives Alton a boost towards wider knowledge; Farmer Porter embodies a dearth of book-learning, like others in the novel who speak the dialect of the Cambridgeshire fens. Yet Kingsley does an interesting thing with the equation of illiteracy and superstition. Porter's broad dialect (non-standard vocabulary, accent, *and* grammar) seem at first to connote a great distance from the scientific method. He comes to Sandy for help in finding his lost son, 'by any ways o' conjuring like', amazed by the pile of books in the shop. Sandy and Alton pull his leg—Alton by plucking the word 'efreets' (evil spirits) from the *Arabian Nights*, Sandy by offering 'a meeracle or twa'. Their words reduce the bulky farmer to 'an awed and helpless voice'. Education has power. Kingsley does not let it go at a simple polarity, however; he makes Porter an emblem of the latent scientist in every man. As Ferguson argued in *An Essay on the History of Civil Society*, as Scott implied in his comments on Bacon in *Guy Mannering*, and as Kingsley stated in his essay on 'Superstition', the mentality of the occult does not detract from but may in fact lead to the inductive method. Sandy therefore concedes (after not a little mockery), 'Aweel—I'm no that disinclined to believe in the occult sciences.' In reference to magic lanterns, mesmerism, and hallucinogens, he says: 'Doot- less they were an unco' barbaric an' empiric method o' expressing the gran' truth o' man's mastery ower matter. But the interpenetration o' the spiritual an' physical worlds is a gran' truth too; an' aiblins the Deity might ha' allowed witchcraft, just to teach that to puir barbarous folk—signs and wonders, laddie, to mak' them believe in somewhat mair than the beasts that perish . . .' In other words, 'witchcraft' is a step towards an insight into the laws that govern particulars; the laws that both govern man, and allow him (if he knows them well enough) to master the earth in turn.

Nor is science the final destination. Alton chafes from the very beginning against the role of pure scientist. He is a poet. Unlike Sandy, who practises phrenology, he finds himself unable to 'dissect and map out my own being, or my neighbour's, as you analysts do'. Take away 'a single faculty' from the whole, and you 'destroy the harmony, the meaning, the life of all the rest'. Even as a child, when he collected flowers and insects, he 'pored over them, not in the spirit of a naturalist, but of a poet'. He was not another Job Legh. The Dean tells him that in order to become a poet, he must 'become a scientific man', like Goethe, whom he pronounces 'the great poet of the day; just because he is the only one who has taken the trouble to go into the details of practical science'. But Alton had already discovered greatness in Tennyson, for confirming his intuition of the sublime in the dykes of Battersea-fields, and 'in the long gravelly sweeps of that lone tidal shore'. The advice of the Dean, who does not in the end give Alton much lasting aid, is superseded by Eleanor's. She repeats the Dean's assurance that miracles are in fact revelations of natural laws, not yet known; she reminds Alton of 'Bacon's golden rule—"Nature is conquered by obeying her" '; yet she goes further by shifting the emphasis from the 'outward nature' to 'as Bacon meant, the inner ideas, the spirit of Nature, which is the will of God'. Much is revealed in her notion of the way the mind works: 'The unconscious logic of association is often deeper and truer than any syllogism.' She therein discriminates between axioms, erected for the problem, and eternal truths— 'the finger-mark of God'.[106]

Alton does not grasp Eleanor's strategy until near the end, when she voices a change in emphasis: from a secular interest in nature, felt most strongly in childhood, to a passion for abstract

[106] *Alton Locke*, 338, 9, 197, 424 (ed's note), 9, 168, 98, 370, 385.

or spiritual laws. There is no deep contradiction; in her eyes the burden of empirical knowledge rests on the hypothesis, with an axiomatic pull. Finding no proofs to the contrary, she avows the presence of God in even the minutest phenomena.

Her method bears a likeness to the *rapprochement* that Lyell set up in the *Principles of Geology*. Gould shows how Lyell used rhetoric to create (rather than mirror) a dichotomy between speculation and empiricism. As in each of the novels, one finds a distrust of claims ungrounded in the senses—without the rejection of abstract principles that one might expect. Lyell turns the empirical approach into an argument for universal (and timeless) laws.[107] We only speculate upon that which we do not observe (in his book, temporally measured changes of process); empiricism, on the other hand, *obliges* us to extract timeless laws from the processes at hand. Wedgwood took the same view in 1866 when he criticized Müller for his 'supposition of a primitive man with a constitution of mind essentially differing from our own, whereas what we require is an indication of the process by which language might have come to a being in all respects like ourselves'.[108]

Ironically, Eugene Schuyler had attacked Wedgwood in 1862 by insisting (contrary to what he saw in Wedgwood's *English Etymology*) that 'The object is now to obtain all the facts; when we have these, we may endeavor to see in what manner they can be explained. The theory must grow from the facts.'[109] The relevance of induction to the study of language had gained wide acknowledgement by the 1860s. In 1869 Schleicher affirmed that 'Languages are organisms of nature'; that 'they rose, and developed themselves according to definite laws'; that the methodology of the science of language 'is generally altogether the same as that of any other natural science'.[110]

Kingsley's fake autobiography explores the duality of the scientist's role as both organism and shaper of language. It enables Alton to display his first, untutored impressions along with the conclusions drawn by experience; to tell us he is a Cockney, in standard English. The genre makes him both

---

[107] Gould, *Time's Arrow, Time's Cycle*, 111.
[108] Hensleigh Wedgwood, *On the Origin of Language* (London, 1866), 7.
[109] Schuyler, *Review of Wedgwood's English Etymology*, 3.
[110] Schleicher, *Darwinism Tested by the Science of Language*, 20–1.

'scientist' and experiment. As poet, his duty is to observe and record and distil the essence of what he sees. He is the perfect note-taker because his own lack of experience opens him to unfiltered, sensual input—or so we are told. The irony is that he cannot write about what he does not know, first-hand: most of the world is to him a 'fairy-land', unseen, and he implies from the start that he will limit his observations not only to London, but to a class within the city. Yet his standard English, markedly unlike the dialect of the other tailors, and his ability to slip into a biblical idiom suggest that books are a form of experience beyond location; similarly, his dreams authorize him to describe evolution. Again, it reinforces the idea that people are not the products, entirely, of geography. In *Alton Locke* the alternative modes of knowledge (books, dreams, the inspiration of God) are a source of the precepts that even the most 'innocent' observer brings to bear upon his material. Eleanor and the Dean tell Alton roughly the same things: that he is suited for the task (of science or art) by lack of experience; that miracles are simply undiscovered laws of nature. The 'unknown' becomes a way of attuning the qualities of precognition and ignorance that give Alton the art of artlessness—making him a true poet of the people, able to speak of and for them, without their limitations of voice.

Eleanor echoes the Dean's words, but alters the conclusion: Alton's destiny lies not in science but in philanthropic art, with an emphasis—upon universal laws—that precedes the evidence. She orders him (her knight) to go into primitive societies to bring home a fresh aesthetic and 'fresh spiritual and physical laws' of human existence, 'that you may realise them here at home—(how, I see as yet but dimly; but He who teaches the facts will surely teach their application)—in the cottages, in the play-grounds, the reading-rooms, the churches of working men'. Questions, for her, take the Socratic form, implying that answers need to be drawn out, aided by one (or One) who already knows. Speculation, unaccompanied by some guiding force, wastes precious time—as does the random collection of facts. The Dean, we may infer, is not entirely wrong; but he lacks Eleanor's focus on the belief (in God's order) that instructs their choices of material. Eleanor wants Alton to prove the integrity of mankind, over time, by living in 'older' (present but uncivilized) societies. The Dean took for his own mission a much narrower topic, and instructs Alton to do the same:

your plan is to take up some one section of the subject, and thoroughly exhaust that. Universal laws manifest themselves only by particular instances. They say, man is the microcosm, Mr. Locke; but the man of science finds every worm and beetle a microcosm in its way. It exemplifies, directly or indirectly, every physical law in the universe, though it may not be two lines long. It is not only a part, but a mirror, of the great whole.[111]

Eleanor's late reign over Alton displaces the Dean, but it does not refute the image of the world in a grain of sand; it suggests rather a change in method—finding laws not in a single creature, but in the differences between societies that imply large sweeps of time. Her notion, of temporal changes existing (among men) in the present, becomes a variant of the 'scientific' model, containing both the natural 'organism'—free yet of willed change—and the already present outcome.

The backward-glancing narrator puts on display the details that feed into his conclusion, giving the impression that theory and facts emerge in tandem; an impression not unlike Kingsley's advice to Brimley, to let the author's purpose govern the extent to which he represents true speech, without losing all trust that the facts (the variants) will speak for themselves. The concluding pages to *Alton Locke* use a mixture of standard and biblical English (the Standard Version), with none of the varieties that appeared earlier. The novel ends with Alton's poem, written in 'standard' words that derive mostly from Anglo-Saxon, considered by Kingsley to be the most scientific.[112] It implies, in concert with the more explicit theme, that a language for all can be found in the present and the past—meshing the personal voice with a national, Christian heritage.

Elizabeth Gaskell's portrayal of the inductive method puts the accent on a different sort of relationship between object and observer. She indicates a different ground for her quarrel with idle speculation. One jarring effect of the lectures attached to *Mary Barton* arises from William Gaskell's breezy use of deduction: he finds himself 'disposed' or 'inclined' to draw

---

[111] *Alton Locke*, 5, 384, 368, 166–7.
[112] Brenda Colloms, *Charles Kingsley* (London, 1975), 60.

various etymological conclusions; it seems to him 'reasonable to conclude', based on the history of the Danes, that the Saxon invaders married Britons, thus blending the languages.[113] His approach is not unscientific, for he uses what he knows to explore the unknown, but it lacks the novel's wariness. *Mary Barton* shows how even the most likely deductions can go astray, to the point of hanging the wrong man. The novel exhibits a strong need to verify through the senses—most elaborately in the murder case, where the facts put Jem in so bad a light that even his closest friends doubt his innocence. Speech gets drawn into the problem in brief passages, as when Mary detects the accent of family in Esther's appeal; she thinks it the ghost of her mother speaking, until Esther presses into the room. In *Alton Locke*, extra-sensory knowledge comes from books, dreams, and God's will; in *Mary Barton*, there is a knowing that is peculiar to the bonds of kinship. It does not contradict the physical world; the facts give it validation, or a greater degree of accuracy. When Will Wilson returns after a long voyage at sea, he calls at his aunt's house. Alice, alone, recognizes the voice, and 'with the instinct of love (for in all usual and common instances, sight and hearing failed to convey impressions to her until long after other people had received them), arose, and tottered to the door'. Blinded by tears, she touches his face with her 'sodden, shrivelled hands', not to discover, but to make sure of what she already knows.

One exception deserves notice. When Esther finds the scrap of paper (once a valentine) that Barton had used in his gun, the writing on it convinces her of Jem's guilt. In this instance, their old friendship—the hours Jem spent writing her letters for her, because she was 'ashamed of sending her own misspelt scrawl', and the admiration she felt for the 'extraordinary graces and twirls' of his script—works against both of them in Esther's attempt to uncover the truth. Mary, who had not learnt her writing from Jem, does not know for certain that he sent it; she only suspects. On half of the valentine Mary had written down the poem that Job had recited to her father, 'a bit on a poem as is written by a weaver like oursel'. Like Alton, however, the poet (Samuel Bamford) used standard English—ironic in light of the

---

[113] William Gaskell, 'Two Lectures on the Lancashire Dialect', 362.

salute given him by the lectures for trying to preserve the Lancashire dialect. The valentine, then, represents Jem's love—unrecognized by Mary, but obvious to Esther when it is too late for her to retract the warning that she now believes turned Jem to violence. It also marks the working-class irony: the likelihood that their own pleas for a healthier life will go unheard unless spoken in the voice of the governing classes. Everyone hears a gun. As an attempt both to speak from the heart, and to adopt a speech that will be recognized, the valentine is a linguistically charged piece of evidence that obscures more than it illuminates. Its unique position in the novel does not so much contradict the model of the senses confirming a previous awareness, as point to the chance of deception in areas that we may feel to be sacrosanct. The novel reveals some basis for Esther's mistake: her mind suffers from 'her violent and unregulated nature, rendered morbid by the course of life she led, and her consciousness of her degradation'. As town pariah, and barely literate, she hardly embodies an ideal of calm induction; yet the wider involvement of language in the material of her mistake complicates the hope for all of us that by listening we understand.[114]

Speculation, in *Guy Mannering*, occurs similarly among folk who would not normally be rated among the scientists; yet in Scott's novel the crux of the matter lies not in sympathy among kin, as in *Mary Barton*, or in the need to assume God's order, as in *Alton Locke*. It lies, more generally, in the inadequacy of names, illustrating the need for a subtler level of classification. At Otterscope Scaurs, where men of the farming community take Brown (or Bertram) to fish, an accident happens. One man drops his torch in the water just as another is hauling in a salmon. No one saw it clearly, but some assume he did it on purpose. Unaware of his true motive, the fear of being detected by Brown, they reason that he did it from sheer spite and a sense of his own inferiority. When Brown asks for the man's name, all they can tell him is 'Gabriel':

'Ye see, sir,' said an old shepherd, rising, and speaking very slow, 'the folks hereabout are a' Armstrongs and Elliots, and sic like,—twa or three given names; and so, for distinction's sake, the lairds and farmers

---

[114] *Mary Barton*, 194, 290, 154, 290.

have the names of their places that they live at,—as, for example, Tam o'Todshaw, Will o' the Flat, Hobbie o' Sorbietrees, and our good master here, o' the Charlies-hope. Aweel, sir, and then the inferior sort o' people, ye'll observe, are kend by sorts o' by-names, some o' them, as Glaiket Christie, and the Deuke's Davie, or may be, like this lad Gabriel, by his employment; as, for example, Tod Gabbie, or Hunter Gabbie. He's no been lang here, sir, and I dinna think onybody kens him by ony other name.'

The 'inferior sort o' people' are a lesser-known quantity— unlocated by place—and Gabriel attracts suspicion because he is doubly strange. His one advocate, the shepherd, approves of him because he lives up to his limited name: 'he's a fell fox-hunter'. Otherwise, he is a prime target for unflattering speculation in the small community.

As in Esther's case, however, their guesses are not totally wrong; they hit upon a measure of truth. Scott's novel differs from *Mary Barton* rather in the greater faith it puts in the legal profession for sorting out the facts. Mannering tells his lawyer, Mr Pleydell, that he is finished with astrology: 'you are the only Ptolemy I intend to resort to upon the present occasion. A second Prospero, I have broken my staff and drowned my book far beyond plummet-depth.' Pleydell's analysis of Meg's scroll depends not on personal knowledge, as in Esther's recognition of Jem's writing, but upon a wider application of principles: 'the letters are uncial or semi-uncial, as somebody calls your large-text hand, and in size and perpendicularity resemble the ribs of a roasted pig'. He, like Colonel Mannering, can read it none the less.[115] Kingsley, half a century later, might well have had the Colonel in mind when he concluded that 'the finest type of civilized man which we are likely to see for some generations to come, will be produced by a combination of the truly military with the truly scientific man'.[116] Scott inherited a fear, spelt out in the *Edinburgh Review*, that scientific progress faced 'the difficulty of a proper expression in a country where there is no standard language, or at least one very remote'.[117] The

[115] *Guy Mannering*, 232–3, 502–3.
[116] Charles Kingsley, 'The Study of Natural History', in *Scientific Lectures and Essays*, 198.
[117] Quoted in J. C. Bryce's introduction to Adam Smith, *Lectures on Rhetoric and Belles Lettres* (Oxford, 1983), 7.

Colonel's 'modern' approach to the mystery of Ellangowan runs parallel to, without totally subverting, the occult methods of 'our Egyptian sibyl', Meg Merrilies. Her kind of knowing depends less upon any conspicuous weighing of facts than it does upon her identity with the motives of her people, tangled by her maternal passion—absent in the Mannering household. On the surface, however, it would appear that most of the clarity comes from Mannering's ease among kinds of science— all of which combine, in their focus on precise terminology, to outwit Glossin, whose very name suggests the need for translation into a readable text.

A SUMMARY

Geologists at the end of the eighteenth century began to shift their focus to organic (from inorganic) proofs of change. A parallel trend, in language, was the growing interest in the sound of words: in the invisible Hebrew vowels, Grimm's law, the attempt to write the accent of Cockney workers. The elusiveness of sound, like corners of the earth worn down over time, gave new form to the anxiety of loss—of time slipping through our fingers at each tick of the clock. Speech was an act of the moment. As in geology, the organic nature of language implied both life and decay.

Not too distant from anxiety, however, lay a new ability to reconcile each particular act with a belief in universal laws. The word 'spirit' could be derived from the motion (physical and punctuated) of breath. Geology was invoked, at times, to prove that life was not random, or without direction: the huge scale of time could be unfolded to argue that language was not in a state of decay. If it seemed that Sanskrit, for example, was more abstract and (therefore) sophisticated than some present dialects, it was an optical illusion, deriving from our myopic view of time. If we were able to hear the first utterances of savages—to hear all of the history of speech—we would know that language has advanced. The loss of ancient languages, then, was both regretted and inconsequential. More emphasis was put on adaptability.

The novels bring language (especially dialect) into conflicting models of time—in particular, the question of how the method of realism (induction: the objective recording of facts on a local scale) accords with a priori assumptions of process and (to be treated in the next chapter) progress. Narratives of change on the earth's surface—the texts of geology—were spilling through the presses at a time when narrative, in fiction, was becoming more explicitly a medium for noting (and commenting upon) changes in speech and writing. There was a shared invocation of Bacon's approach. The value of empirical research—the collection of facts in the discovery of laws—was a potential threat to the faith in a theological line of development. What if the facts overran the axiom? Geological narratives (histories of the earth) were no watertight protection against heretic leaks, against the possibility that natural growth and history were completely at odds. In the novels, attitudes towards non-standard language (stated and implied) show a tendency to pit the 'history of language' against the possibility that it lacks any necessary direction at all. What if language (the object of scientific observation) evolves totally outside any system of morality? What happens to individual agency, in such a model? *Guy Mannering*, *Mary Barton*, and *Alton Locke* present us with a scientific model that cuts across time (in theory) to illuminate the unknown through the known. The entry of language—as an object of study bound up with a character's identity—gives to the raw material of science the appearance of a dynamic of elements (characters) whose interaction effects change on a path that can be charted.

The focus on organic remains and living signs accompanied the taste for induction. The metaphor of language as an organism made it easier for such as Kingsley to invoke the pattern of genealogy, rather than let the multiplicity of facts suggest other, non-inherited kinds of order—or total chaos. Magic was set up as a precursor to induction: each of the novels (and their references to astrology, mermaids, and the occult) hint that magic and metaphor are needed to remind us of the God in the works. Magic, like Victorian induction, allows an openness to phenomena; both, along with the trope of metaphor, imply that general laws operate amid the vastness of detail.

3

Decadent Strength:
Models of Progress

> The formation of different languages and of distinct
> species, and the proofs that both have developed through a
> gradual process, are distinctly parallel.[1]
>
> (Darwin)

LYELL noted a lack of unity among philologists as to the strict
meaning of 'language'. They drew wavy lines between language
and dialect.[2] Most agreed, however, that while people spoke
differently, they belonged to one species. Kingsley posited that if
in nature you find 'a regular series of gradations' between two
different objects, you might 'suppose them to be only varieties of
the same species'. He acknowledged the vast gulf between
Norwegian and Negro, but invoked gradations to prove a
common origin.[3] Lyell reported that 'some naturalists' held the
Negro to be distinct, but argued that the blending of races over
time made all humans capable of 'intermarrying and producing
fertile offspring'—a characteristic that roughly determines our
notion of a species. He compared the difficulty of picturing the
formation of a species, in nature, to that of 'the growth and
establishment of a new language'.[4] It was a useful analogy, but
Lyell did not take it further. He instead remarked that 'No
language seems ever to last for a thousand years, whereas many
a species seems to have endured for hundreds of thousands.'
Modern Germans, for instance, cannot understand their

---

[1] Charles Darwin, *The Descent of Man* (1871; New York, 1874), 106.
[2] Charles Lyell, *The Geological Evidences of the Antiquity of Man* (London,
1863), 458.
[3] Charles Kingsley, 'Town Geology', in *Scientific Lectures and Essays* (London,
1885), 91–2.
[4] Charles Lyell, *Principles of Geology* (1830–3; London, 1872), ii. 481, 475–6.

Teutonic ancestors of the ninth century; the two languages are therefore distinct. It did not mean that the languages marked out different species, or even races; it pointed, rather, to the difficulty of proving an invisible process.

Lyell imagines trying to explain to an illiterate audience why it is that languages *sound* different, if the theory of 'transmutation' be true: 'how comes it that the tongues now spoken do not pass by insensible gradations the one into the other, and into the dead languages of dates immediately antecedent?' He compares the philologist's problem—of drawing lines between languages or dialects—with that of the biologist who must somehow prove why an organism belongs to one species and not another.[5] Lyell thus applies biological terms to language whilst arguing that a single species (human) can use many different 'species' of tongue, in a manœuvre that both makes language a product of nature, and gives it (and humanity) a unique place in the scheme. Darwin's phrase '*distinctly* parallel' (my italics) is apt. Müller also saw language as a field of physical research, *and* warned against mixing the sciences of language and ethnology; he firmly held that the classification of races and languages should be independent of one another.[6]

Lyell set language apart from evolution by denying literary critics the right to argue about the validity of transmutation, or evolution. They had not undergone initiation. They had not been faced with the uncertain mark of a species. The geologist, on the other hand, had to know when to set an organism apart from all the shades, or varieties, that make up a related species. Geologists, too, held a 'fragmentary record' in their hands. Geology stood, in this respect, closer to the study of past languages than to the criticism of extant texts. Lyell looked at trends among languages and concluded that, as science showed in other realms, the stronger (more civilized) nations would replace the weaker, resulting in one race and one language (likely Anglo-Saxon in nature)—with multiple dialects. He did not predict total hegemony. He argued, however, that the tendency for one type to compete with another made it certain

---

[5] Lyell, *The Geological Evidences*, 457–9.
[6] Max Müller, *Lectures on the Science of Language* (1861; London, 1871), i. 40, 373.

that all races, from the Negro to the Caucasian, belonged to one species; two rational species could not possibly coexist.[7] The sign of rationality is language.

Lyell investigates the process of selection among words. He notes the continuous introduction of new 'words, idioms, and phrases', most of them ephemeral. He wonders about the laws of invention and selection, the number of terms being limited by the capacity of the human memory. In such a finite 'universe', an old word will either be replaced or cut back in meaning. The process only appears haphazard: 'there are nevertheless fixed laws in action, by which, in the general struggle for existence, some terms and dialects gain the victory over others'. Factors at play in their selection include brevity, euphony, aristocratic fashion, popular writers, orators, preachers, and centralized government.[8]

Lyell's terms allude to a joint process of intrinsic and social causes. Few nineteenth-century writers gave deeper analyses of why one language, dialect, or word supplants another. Schleicher's offering was typical: 'In the present period of the life of man the descendants of the Indo-Germanic family are the conquerors in the struggle for existence; they are engaged in continual extension, and have already supplanted or dethroned numerous other idioms.'[9] As in geology, the linguist watches the visible process repeat a heritage, characterized by the image of a physical take-over. The fact of domination is axiomatic, while the nature of it (degrees of biological, divine, or social input) gets little expression; outcomes, on so slim a line of cause and effect, seem inevitable from the start. In a like vein, William Gaskell 'explains' the mixture of languages in England as a tendency for Saxons to take Briton wives and to adopt some of their vocabulary while promoting more extensively their own forms of speech. He derives this process of selection (with its linguistic outcome) from a later, documented case in the history of the Danes, leaving us with a vision of unchanging structures

[7] Lyell, *Principles of Geology*, ii. 490, 486.

[8] Lyell, *The Geological Evidences*, 463.

[9] August Schleicher, *Darwinism Tested by the Science of Language*, trans. Alex V. W. Bikkers (London, 1869), 64.

of process, unsupported by a chronicle of *why* one form of speech endures beyond another.[10]

In 1861 Schleicher published the 'family tree' theory of linguistic evolution.[11] The 'family' metaphor loaded the inquiry into the nature of language—whether a form of language, like the colour of skin or hair, might be inherited rather than learned; whether languages developed from a single point or many. Lyell attested that the general question of biological inheritance among the 'intellectual faculties' had not, by mid-century, been settled. He also looked into the model of inheritance itself, to see if there might not be some other way of accounting for the form of any given species. He refers to geologists 'speculating on the co-existence of vertebrates, insects, and cephalopods in the Silurian strata', and to the difficulty that many found in accepting 'so early a co-existence of the three types'. He admits 'that the highest parts of their organization, which discharge the same functional duties in all three, have been independently super-induced by the action of outward conditions, and that we need not derive them by inheritance from some common starting-point'.[12]

When anatomists talk about the form of a species, they make a distinction between analogy and homology, especially when making comparisons. If two (or more) species have a feature in common, the question of origin arises. Did the one species evolve from the other, thus inheriting the feature, or did the two species develop it of their own accord, having in common not an origin but a circumstance of environment? Homology denotes a common origin; analogy, a like solution to a shared problem. Stephen Jay Gould in the 1980s gave us a simpler way of looking at it, using an arrow and circle to illustrate geologists' efforts to solve questions of similarity and difference in form: 'These two kinds of similarity—by genealogical connection, or time's arrow, and by separate reflection of the same immanent

---

[10] William Gaskell, 'Two Lectures on the Lancashire Dialect', in *Mary Barton* (1854; Halifax, 1993), 362.
[11] Martyn Wakelin, *The Archaeology of English* (London, 1988), 175.
[12] Lyell, *Principles of Geology*, ii. 493, 498–9.

laws, or time's cycle—join forces when we try to reveal nature's complexity.'[13]

The 'cyclic view of history' gained momentum from Gibbon's *Decline and Fall of the Roman Empire*; Adam Ferguson took from it the idea, for instance, 'that a civilized society could be corrupted by luxury'. The image of a cycle appeared in the writings of Carlyle and the two Arnolds, father and son; Matthew Arnold strove to reconcile it with optimism in the dawning of a better age. Bowler links it to organic metaphors, also found in their works, by arguing that 'the analogy of growth can be exploited in two ways: one can concentrate solely on the phase leading through to maturity, or one can include the complete life cycle and accept that it ends with an inevitable decline'. The despair in the reactions of some to this ineluctable end could be avoided by imagining a torch being passed along from one dying person, or civilization, to the nascent.[14]

Yet in the nineteenth century a different way of thinking about progress took on more shape and clarity. The model of 'a branching tree rather than a ladder', animating some works on philology and natural science, had implications. Bowler claims that it threatened, potentially, 'the teleology inherent in the progressionist assumption that all social development tends toward a single goal'. He attests (as do Desmond and Moore) to Darwin's recognition of 'a close parallel between his theory and the process of change revealed by philology'.[15] There could be many goals, arising from unseen variables in the environment, as well as in the organism itself. Success for one might mean disaster for another, even within a species. It may be more meaningful to talk of progress in each event, rather than making it a chart of the whole, if what we now call 'progress' wears a different aspect to the species in the future.

Philology, none the less, did not give up the notion of inherited form. Lyell put grammar into the 'analogy versus homology' model, using it to favour the belief that languages derive common structural features by inheritance, rather than by

---

[13] Stephen Jay Gould, *Time's Arrow, Time's Cycle* (London, 1991), 197.
[14] Peter J. Bowler, *The Invention of Progress* (Oxford, 1989), 59, 51, 58, 50–1.
[15] Ibid. 68.

similar responses to an external circumstance. He wrote, for example, of eight varieties that 'have all such an amount of mutual resemblance, as to point to a more ancient language, the Aryan'. Grammatical forms were the most trustworthy, as evidence of origin, because they (unlike vocabulary or pronunciation) were the least readily adopted.[16]

Earlier, in the *Principles of Geology*, he had written of biological 'Variation and Selection'. When intermarriage occurs in a 'limited geographical area', a sameness of 'bodily and mental structure' begins to emerge among the children. Inheritance outruns environment; the structure endures long after the area (physical and social) has changed. From his reference to the mind as well as the body, we may infer that Lyell included language among the inherited traits. More direct evidence appears, soon after, when he equates the opacity of variation and selection, in biological terms, with the unclear idea we have of 'the growth and establishment' of language, even in the recent past. The mixing of 'heterogeneous materials' results in a 'unity and permanency of character'. When a language (he points to English) is 'transplanted' into a new region it shows a 'want of pliancy'. He seems to be arguing in favour of an almost exclusively homologous (inherited) approach. At some point, however, pressures of the region begin to be felt:

The modifiability of the language and its tendency to vary never cease, so that it would readily run into new dialects and modes of pronunciation if there were no communication with the mother country direct or indirect. In this respect its mutability will resemble that of species, and it can no more spring up independently in separate districts than species can, assuming that these last are all of derivative origin.[17]

The tenacity of the basic structure of a language comes through in Lyell's emphasis on the total isolation from the country of origin that is needed for change to occur. Nor will the change be of a radical kind; he limits it to 'new dialects and modes of pronunciation', rather than predicting new languages. The inability of 'species' to grow from the pressures of a region

---

[16] Lyell, *The Geological Evidences*, 455.
[17] Lyell, *Principles of Geology*, ii. 475–6.

alone implies that the character of each derives more from the original language than from the environment.

A new time-scale was opening, and with it a sense that we needed to rethink our models of chronology. Trench in 1855 gave a lecture on time and language: 'The great innovator Time manages his innovations so dexterously, spreads them over such vast periods, and therefore brings them about so gradually, that often, while effecting the mightiest changes, he seems to us to be effecting none at all.'[18]

Not all languages change at the same rate. Max Müller used the polarity of gradualism and interruption to distinguish between 'savage' and 'civilized' groups of people. Nor was he isolated in doing so. He quotes from Dr Rae in *The Polynesian* (no. 23, 1862): 'where writing is unknown, if the community be broken up into small tribes, the language very rapidly changes, and for the worse'. Missionaries became sources of linguistic detail. Müller drew evidence of the flux of 'barbarous jargons' from such works as Gabriel Sagard's *Grands Voyages du pays des Hurons* (1631); he cited the Jesuit report of a multiplicity of tongues in North America, deeming it proof not of a 'high state of civilisation' but rather the lack of any concentrated, central power, and the consequent lack of 'great national empires'. The reference to missionaries is of particular value to a study of Kingsley's fiction: divine order meets a babble of savage (but still human) tongues.

Müller believed that, while the earlier impulse of language was towards 'unbounded variety', it was brought into check by a feeling of nationalism. Higher civilization demands a more 'stationary' language—just as it tends away from nomadic societies; Müller derived the word 'Arjan' from the meaning 'cultivator of the land'. His etymology invokes an image of movement on a stable field. His racial suppositions did not allow for any neat exclusion of continuity or rupture; both had to be at work. He compares the stationary language of a nation's classic literature to 'the frozen surface of a river'. The ice does not break of its own accord; 'political commotions' rise up from below, caused by a foreign threat, or class struggle, or

---

[18] Richard Chenevix Trench, *English: Past and Present* (London, 1855), 44–5.

religious controversy. Language responds to the circumstances of the nation. When the centres of civilization are destroyed, 'it is then that the popular, or, as they are called, the vulgar dialects, which had formed a kind of undercurrent, rise beneath the crystal surface of the literary language, and sweep away, like the waters in spring, the cumbrous formations of a bygone age'.[19]

Müller's image is almost anarchic. Gould draws a parallel between science (in the nineteenth century) and the Whiggish outlook of history, dubbing the science of that period the 'ultimate tale of progress'.[20] Debate tended to fly around the nature of that progress, rather than questioning it at a more fundamental level. Yet by 1838 Darwin was writing, 'there is no absolute tendency to progression'. He challenged Lyell's (and most philologists') conviction that organisms and language grew from simple to complex forms: 'Some animals—parasites, for example—had even simplified, and if these died out, others would "degenerate" to fill their niche.' He wrote, 'It is absurd to talk of one animal being higher than another,' arguing that our own criterion of success—the 'intellectual faculties'—would be of little use to a bee.[21] Lyell in the 1850s tried to qualify Darwin's position: 'When Mr. Darwin says that he does not believe in a law of necessary development, he means that simple and unimproved structures may sometimes be best fitted for simple conditions of life, and that even a degradation instead of an advance in structure may occasionally be advantageous.' Lyell then goes on to insist that 'in the long run' the higher (more complex) organisms will 'prevail', and that their 'final predominance' is by no means 'left to chance'. Lyell qualifies his own earlier belief in steady progress, without giving it up entirely: the 'final success' of higher organisms is 'certain, though many adverse circumstances may retard the rate of progress'.[22] Years later he would claim that 'Progressive improvement in language is a necessary consequence of the progress of the human mind from one generation to another.'[23]

[19] Müller, *Lectures*, i. 38, 58–9, 62–3, 276, 66.
[20] Gould, *Time's Arrow, Time's Cycle*, 5.
[21] Quoted in Adrian Desmond and James Moore, *Darwin* (London, 1992), 275, 232. [22] Lyell, *Principles of Geology*, ii. 494.
[23] Lyell, *The Geological Evidences*, 467.

He tried to keep out the element in Darwin's writing that Banton calls the 'bogey of chance'.[24] As Gould reminds us, 'No logical necessity can extract an implication of progress from the fact of evolution.'[25] Evolution can simply mean change.

Bunsen argued that 'Nature always tends towards perfection, and the image of God, hidden under deviations from the perfect type, returns, *jure postliminii*, as soon as outward impediments are removed.'[26] He implies that God, nature, and history coexist. Gould tells the story of how Lyell tried to find a record of gradualism among all the 'bits and pieces of apparent abruptness'. Darwin looked for history in the 'quirks' (e.g. our tail-bone) of present organisms. Only a 'perfect' structure 'covers the tracks of its own formation'. Perfection in all organisms would argue for a single moment of origin; Darwin cited the 'oddities and imperfections' as proof of evolution. Gould sees the principle as 'a general argument for history'; linguists, too, must detect history 'when current usage does not match etymology'.[27]

In the novels, the 'oddities' of speech and writing are shown to function in both the present and the (implied) past. The failure of a non-standard form to 'work' in the novel's present— to do what the speaker or writer wanted—often coincides with a narrative voice that argues a model of progress. We can thus imagine that 'bad' English is not so much a value statement as a comment on history. Yet there are moments in each novel that open a door to another way of thinking about varieties. The narrator in *Guy Mannering* wonders if society might not lose too much by sloughing off the impediments. The only person to speak the truth in the court room in *Alton Locke* uses a dialect that otherwise implies (through narrative comment) a backward life. Yet it is Gaskell's work that most audibly suggests that 'imperfections'—rather than prove development—might instead be part of an atemporal need for people to draw upon private histories to survive the present.

[24] Michael Banton, *The Idea of Race* (London, 1977), 81.
[25] Gould, *Time's Arrow, Time's Cycle*, 170.
[26] Christian Charles Josias Bunsen, *Outlines of the Philosophy of Universal History* (London, 1854), ii. 101–2, 108.
[27] Gould, *Time's Arrow, Time's Cycle*, 134, 43, 84.

THE FICTION

The nexus of history, geology, and language is most visible, perhaps, in the novels of Thomas Hardy, whose 'literary language is a deliberately heterogeneous assortment of words from many layers of historical usage, and reflects one of the most interesting comparisons of the Victorian period: that of the strata of the mind to geological strata'.[28] You do not find, in the novels of Scott, Gaskell, or Kingsley, a man facing his own insignificance in the fossil of a trilobite. Often in their novels the comparison looks faint, or disappears, while the part that can be traced gives insight into how they tried to account for and organize the often great differences within a single, present species.

Edgar Johnson, likening Scott to Darwin, notes that Scott chose for his novels the 'great watershed moments in history, those great turning points, which are pregnant for human affairs'.[29] The Waverley novels, on the whole, do not present a gradual motion through time but rather one that is punctuated by events, represented in stages. Fleishman writes of the speculative historians of the eighteenth century: 'their picture of the past was a reconstruction of the major stages in the course of civilization, often without hard data, but deduced from generalizations about the forms of all social phenomena'. Scott drew upon the 'stages of human progress', believing them to be 'fairly uniform among various societies—e.g., the Highlanders are compared by Scott to American Indians—and their peculiar strengths and weaknesses are explainable by their place in an evolutionary sequence'. In other words, Scott differentiated forms of culture not only by location, but also by time.[30] In *Guy Mannering* we are told that 'the progress of time', while diminishing the gypsies in number, has not greatly altered them in kind. They cannot blend in; they are 'the Pariahs of Scotland, living like wild Indians among European settlers, and, like them,

---

[28] Dennis Taylor, *Hardy's Literary Language and Victorian Philology* (Oxford, 1993), 11.

[29] Edgar Johnson, *Sir Walter Scott* (London, 1970), ii. 1262.

[30] Avrom Fleishman, *The English Historical Novel* (Baltimore, 1971), 41.

judged of rather by their own customs, habits, and opinions, than as if they had been members of the civilized part of the community'.[31] It is not a region, so much as a truncated phase of growth, that accounts for the gypsies' isolation and gradual decay.

All three novelists hint at layers of change by locating 'relics' of older tribes among the civilized. Each refers to North America, whose native inhabitants were generally believed to represent an earlier stage of human development; dispute remained as to whether all races began at the same point (and place) in time, or were of different origins. In either case, the manifestations in the present, and the comparisons that arise, were seen to offer a key to the problem of differences that the living reader sees among classes. Some efforts towards justification are greater than others.

Guy Mannering presents the simplest model of stratification. Groups (races or families) come and go over the centuries, with few marks given for being the first. Scott plays with the usual mystery encircling old family names. He describes Godfrey Bertram, a typical laird: 'His list of forefathers ascended so high that they were lost in the barbarous ages of Galwegian independence; so that his genealogical tree, besides the Christian and crusading names of Godfreys and Gilberts and Dennises and Rolands without end, bore heathen fruit of yet darker ages,—Arths and Knarths and Donagilds and Hanlons.' The names, while marking status and role in a particular time and place, convey little about the present man; yet the narrator links the weight of genealogical information to Godfrey's weak nature. His body cannot support the roll-call: 'In fact, his physiognomy indicated the inanity of character which pervaded his life.' There is a hint of poor breeding in the observation that he 'was one of those second-rate sort of persons that are to be found frequently in rural situations'. He, like the gypsy Meg, represents the tail end of a dying tribe. Their difference in strength may be connected to the fact that his tribe once had political clout in the land, while hers never did; the remnants of Ellangowan are thus supported by lucrative gains of the past,

---

[31] Walter Scott, *Guy Mannering* (1815; London, 1905), 59–60.

while the present gypsies, lacking the attention that history gives to success, depend upon physical prowess for survival. Even among the upper classes, however, it becomes clear that a string of old names does not alone secure good fortune. The parents of Charles Hazlewood, for instance, would rather he marry the rich Miss Mannering than the pretty, well-born, but penniless Lucy Bertram. Scott is not contrasting the present with the past. The Hazlewoods, while seeming in their preference to ignore the value of inheritance, in fact replay the ambitions that once brought the laird's old family to power.

Lucy's most devoted attendant is the Dominie—an ugly, 'ungainly figure'. His physical endurance comes out when the people he loves are in danger; otherwise, his body does him little credit. Scott caricatures him as the 'poor scholar, from Juvenal's time downward'. A college education fails to spread over him the patina of the upper classes; rather, 'the harsh and dissonant voice, and the screech-owl notes to which it was exalted when he was exhorted to pronounce more distinctly,—all added fresh subject for mirth to the torn cloak and shattered shoe'. His low birth and unexamined name give him the timelessness of genre; it suits his role as a (relatively) impartial access to the history of language—a comical Jacob Grimm, perhaps, with whom Scott held correspondence. Mannering finds him invaluable, for 'this sort of living catalogue and animated automaton had all the advantages of a literary dumb-waiter'.[32] The Dominie thus embodies a truce, in his ease *and* in his awkwardness with language, between the need to move freely through the strata of development, and an alertness to the values of the present.

The image of a 'literary dumb-waiter' is germane to the three novels treated in the previous chapter, and here. Alton, in *Alton Locke*, devotes a whole chapter ('Dream Land') to his delirious trek through the stages of evolution. Eleanor drops his soul into a cavern, 'and I fell and fell for ages'. He reaches 'the lowest point of created life', where he becomes 'a crowd of innumerable polypi', unable to speak, or think, or even experience his individuality. The paragraphs are visibly divided, giving a layered effect—though, because we do not have the original

---

[32] Ibid. 9, 8, 14, 15, 622 (ed.'s note), 339.

manuscript, we can only assume that Kingsley had some input into the first edition, on which the present World's Classics edition is based. Even at his lowest point, he is able to hear Eleanor predicting that he will move up the ladder to reach manhood again; and he refers to speech and to thought as latent capabilities that are struggling to emerge over the ages. The process is punctuated rather than fluid; he is one species, then another, with sleep in between. The idea that all races go through the same stages of evolution appears when Alton awakes in the form of a 'baby-ape'—able only to howl—with a face that 'might have been a negro child's'. Articulation wars against the flesh: 'Long melancholy mopings, fruitless strug-glings to think, were periodically succeeded by wild frenzies, agonies of lust and aimless ferocity.' He first begins to understand human speech, 'not of the words, but of the facts'. When he finally becomes a human child, he lies on the breast of Eleanor, whom he suspects may be 'some ideal of the great Arian tribe'. He at last can pray in direct speech.

His earliest words precede the Tower of Babel, implying a time of a universal language that has since become fractured and politicized by human greed. At some point in time historical development began to mirror biology—both exhibiting laws in the present that had been active throughout. Crossthwaite accuses their own government of keeping wages at a starvation level, and swears it will some day 'be known, the whole abomination, and future generations will class it with the tyrannies of the Roman emperors and the Norman barons'. When Alton complains that refinement has become 'an everlast-ing gulf between man and man', and wonders why the upper classes do not help men like himself overcome the barrier, Sandy warns him of the 'monopoly' of manners. Thus, while speech represents a pinnacle of evolution, and a uniform latency throughout its stages, it also appears in the novel as a demarcation among classes—a mode of personal advancement that gives power to those who do not deserve it, threatening the upper classes with the decay that must follow a state of perfection out of step with the laws of nature. Even the Dean sees that the upper-class youth are 'painted over by the artificial state of society'. Alton had earlier been surprised at the 'fluency and eloquence', the 'excellent English', spoken by 'men of my own class—and lower still, perhaps, some of them'.[33] The novel suggests that men universally contain the potential, at least, of 'perfect' speech; yet, by representing that potential with standard English, the novel undermines its own vision of humanity returning to a pre-Babel, classless state. Its political and biological model, of languages that go extinct when their speakers do, contests its own 'back to the garden' imagery.

Mary Barton uses language more directly to gauge time; but, like *Alton Locke*, it involves class in an ambiguous way. The footnotes, with their etymological detail, seem on the one hand to draw speakers of the Manchester dialect back into the fold of inherited English. William Gaskell illustrated his lectures to prove (more or less) that the Celtic words in the dialect were not late introductions, but help date it to the time of 'original' Celtic presence in the area; he then derives the force of Lancashire industry from its racial inheritance. He takes the cobbler's word 'camming' (wearing out of shape) and traces it back through his own childhood experience to Tim Bobbin, Shakespeare, and Skelton—as if each represented a layer of time and place: 'This word "cam," then, is a genuine Celtic word, and I see no reason why we should not receive it as one that has kept its ground in this locality from the time of the true Britons.'[34]

Yet working-class characters in the novel, John Barton in particular, are declared unable to use similar powers of reasoning; unable to fit the details of their life into a historical pattern. The narrator excuses their 'use of opium'—their taste for a timeless oblivion—by putting to readers (of a higher class, presumably) the question 'Have you taught them the science of consequences?' The comparison between Frankenstein (by whom Gaskell meant the scientist's monster) and the 'actions of the uneducated' implies a lack of historical sense, and a latency (as in *Alton Locke*) that could prove dangerous. The monster, after all, learned to read more swiftly than the rich young foreigner. He simply lacked the 'right' background. Barton, too, gets so torn apart by his environment that his very powers of

---

[33] Charles Kingsley, *Alton Locke* (1850; Oxford, 1987), pp. 336, xxi (ed.'s note), 341, 343, 106, 78, 108.
[34] William Gaskell, 'Two Lectures on the Lancashire Dialect', 369, 363, 364.

reasoning fail him, and he grows incapable of any thought but the most synchronic: the distinction, in a slice of the present, between rich and poor.[35]

Gaskell's fusion of working class and ahistorical thought does not simply contradict her husband's stratification of language; instead it creates, at the very least, a juxtaposition of one layer and many. Winifrid Gérin understands the theme of *Mary Barton* to be the breakdown of communication.[36] William Gaskell's notes and lectures, with their endorsement of dialect speech, may be seen as part of the narrator's urge to 'give some utterance to the agony which, from time to time, convulses this dumb people'.[37] They may also be put in the context of linguistic segregation. Herder, in the eighteenth century, had compared the number of 'tonal modes' in human nature to the number of 'modes of sensitivity', concluding that the greater the difference in nervous structure, between species, the more impaired the communication. The further we are from a species of beast, the less we comprehend its 'natural language'.[38] Ferguson considered man's 'use of language and articulate sounds', along with his body, reason, and relationships, to be 'so many attributes of his nature: they are to be retained in his description, as the wing and the paw are in that of the eagle and the lion'.[39] Müller, over half a century later, felt that comparative philology and the history of language had paved the way for evidence of natural evolution.[40] Such equations of language and evolution became part of inquiries into what makes a language, what a dialect, what merely an individual's speech pattern. The specification of language, in other words, implied time in a structure that Elizabeth Gaskell modified, but did not entirely break.

---

[35] Elizabeth Gaskell, *Mary Barton* (1848; Harmondsworth, 1976), 219.
[36] Winifred Gérin, *Elizabeth Gaskell* (London, 1976), 85, 88.
[37] *Mary Barton*, 37–8.
[38] Johann Gottfried Herder, 'Essay on the Origin of Language', trans. Alexander Gode, in *On the Origin of Language* (New York, 1966), 89.
[39] Adam Ferguson, *An Essay on the History of Civil Society* (Edinburgh, 1767), 4–5.
[40] *Life and Letters of the Right Honourable Friedrich Max Müller* (London, 1902), i. 122.

In Scott's novel, differences can take the linguistic form of imprecise terminology. When Mannering gets lost in the Scottish bog, far from Oxford, the silence is broken by 'the deep cry of the bog-blitter, or bull-of-the-bog (a large species of bittern)'. The gypsies who inhabit the region 'were at an early period acknowledged as a separate and independent race by one of the Scottish monarchs', and given a legal status akin to the common thief. Over the years they were joined by famished 'men of the North', and 'lost, in a great measure, by this intermixture the national character of Egyptians, and became a mingled race'. The ambiguity of their blood line comes out in mingled speech, and in what they are called: 'gypsies, jockies, or cairds—for by all these denominations such banditti were known'. Guy Mannering, the 'new man' of the novel, changes the pattern by rebuking his daughter for the suggestion that speech matters to the speaker's identity. When Julia asks if her new companion has much of the Scottish accent, he replies, 'do you think I care about *a*'s and *aa*'s, and *i*'s and *ee*'s?' Yet notably his lack of prejudice acts in favour not of a gypsy, but of a lady of noble descent. Glossin, on the other hand, may be seen as an alternative 'new man': a 'shrewd, worldly, bustling man of business', who cares less about racial inheritance than about manipulating to his own advantage disputes over the inheritance of land and wealth. He dreams of settling among the country gentlemen and becoming 'in Burns's language,—

The tongue of the trump to them a'.'

The author's note informs us that 'The "tongue of the trump" is the wire of the Jew's harp,—that which gives sound to the whole instrument'. *Guy Mannering* may warn against too crude a use of speech to classify the speaker, but it still holds on to the idea that vocal sounds can guard us against making false identifications. Ambiguity of name often represents a harmful, inherited split in society.[41]

Mary Barton, with its stronger focus on a living present, shows less concern for the historical authenticity of names than for the rooting of a system of nomenclature in the place and time of the observers. She draws out the 'class of men in Manchester'

---

[41] *Guy Mannering*, 4, 57–9, 166, 288.

(indeed, in all of Lancashire) who exist unknown, 'who may yet claim kindred with all the noble names that science recognizes'. The men belong to a type; among them are the botanists 'equally familiar with either the Linnaean or the Natural System, who know the name and habitat of every plant within a day's walk from their dwellings'. Their enthusiasm brings intimacy to the sort of knowledge that the system tries to make universal. To intimacy it brings a tone of impartiality: they are ready to catch 'any winged insect', to 'pore over every new specimen with real scientific delight'. The partiality of their observations is rather circumstantial than deliberate: 'beautiful families of Ephemeridae and Phyrganidae' get special notice because they emerge at the time of 'the great annual town-holiday of Whitsun-week so often falling in May and June'. Gaskell's social observation grounds the urge to classify in real time and space.

The novel attempts a contradictory manœuvre: to invoke science as an escape from the political struggle, and to highlight the inadequacy of the Linnaean system to meet local problems. Yet it is not so much a contradiction as an uncertainty, on the reader's part, as to the weight of the balance. The weaver forgets the monotony of the loom under the spell of Newton; the narrator offers no hint of awareness of the political message behind such a displacement. On the other hand, the representation of Job Legh, who of all the characters feels most ardent about the collection and identification of species, is most unable to bring his skill to bear upon the human facts around him. His knowledge, far from merging with the common set of skills, looks esoteric: his eyes are 'wizard-like'; his 'whole room looked not unlike a wizard's dwelling'; 'rude wooden frames of impaled insects' hang on the walls, the table is strewn 'with cabalistic books' and 'a case of mysterious instruments'.[42] The description bears no little resemblance to Farmer Porter's impression of Mackaye's book shop (in *Alton Locke*), an assumption of working-class awe in the face of science that jars against the earlier impression given of the worker's innate tendency to observe and classify. Job's attentiveness to the natural world makes him oblivious to Margaret's suffering; she, at any rate,

[42] *Mary Barton*, 75–6.

feels the need to support his activities, and fine needlework—the only acceptable option before she becomes a paid singer—hastens her blindness. She develops a different mode of precision, to the point of being able to identify Jem by his cough in a strange city; but she, like Job, cannot see clearly into Mary's position. The novel gives the working class the problem (and merit) of identifying their own environment, statically, but leaves in question their ability to adapt the skill to meet living, changing concerns.

Alton Locke shows a similar mindfulness of the potential for stasis in systems of classification. There is, as well, a sense of their artificial nature; they do not label minutely enough the changes that create each species. The Dean occupies 'a room lined with cabinets of curiosities, and hung all over with strange horns, bones, and slabs of fossils'. When he enlists Alton's help to arrange 'this lot of shells, just come from Australia', he does not foresee the result of his own aim to teach a working man the fundamentals of science in a very short time; he does not imagine that Alton will then put himself on the same plane, intellectually, as any man of property. Equipped with 'Cuvier's "Animal Kingdom", and a dictionary of scientific terms' the tailor quickly sees how to make sense of what he finds. The only difference between the two men, in the past, was an access to the right vocabulary.[43]

Alton Locke supports *Mary Barton* in the judgement that classification, and its attendant jargon, can obscure the fluid reality and bar people unjustifiably from voicing an opinion. Yet Kingsley's novel adds a twist. It projects into the future the potential for all men to use language equally; in the meantime, fragments of the narrative could be invoked to prove that conditions of the past give legitimacy to the belief that language mirrors biology. Four years later William Gaskell made the analogy between the study of language and the analysis of old coins and clothes; by these we know the man, he suggests, even centuries down the road.[44] Alton had reached the same conclusion: 'Class costumes, relics though they are of feudalism, carry a charm with them. They are symbolic, definitive; they

---

[43] *Alton Locke*, 164, 167–8.
[44] William Gaskell, 'Two Lectures on the Lancashire Dialect', 361.

bestow a personality on the wearer; which satisfies the mind, by enabling it instantly to classify him, to connect him with a thousand stories and associations . . .'.

Language, too, gives an immediate message. Alton becomes acquainted with his cousin, just down from Cambridge. As they walk together, Alton feels the difference in their speech: 'there were stories of boat-races and gay noblemen, breakfast parties, and lectures on Greek plays, flavoured with a spice of Cambridge slang, all equally new to me—glimpses into the world of wonders, which made me feel, as I shambled along at his side, trying to keep step with his strides, more weakly and awkward and ignorant than ever'. At Cambridge, watching the boat race, Alton feels overwhelmed at first by the clamour: 'Oh, the Babel of horse and foot . . .'. Soon, however, the vision of young men straining at the oars produces in him a sense of national pride: he grows conscious of 'that grim, earnest, stubborn energy, which, since the days of the old Romans, the English possess alone of all the nations of the earth'. It makes him feel included: 'My blood boiled over, and fierce tears swelled into my eyes; for I, too, was a man, and an Englishman . . .'. For a while he runs at the head of the cheering crowd, until physical reality catches up with him, and he falters in a weakness both inherited and exaggerated by his poverty. At that very moment, rich onlookers break into upper-class speech, pushing Alton once more from the swell of voices, and onto the ground.

On the one hand, by relating Alton to a Cambridge gent, and emphasizing the bond by labelling him throughout as 'my cousin', Kingsley suggests that Alton's disadvantages are social, or political. It seems to contradict the link he makes between physical form and exclusion from types of speech. But we are never asked to see Alton as the lowest form of humanity, except in his own delirious episode. The fact of his connection, by birth, to a member of the university goes hand in hand with the otherwise discrepant feature of his own speech, which remains closer to the standard than his cousin's; George's speech, interlarded with Cambridge slang, may symbolize a higher class, but it also locates him in a city—while the ideal of the standard involved a non-localized set of values. Aristocrats were in any case not the sole arbiters of correct language: 'Are ye gaun to be like they puir artistocrat bodies', challenges Sandy, 'that wad suner hear an Italian dog howl, than an English nightengale sing . . .?' Poetry must come from one's own geographic roots. Sandy voices one of the novel's deepest contradictions when he tells Alton that a poet must find his own form of writing:

wha wants mongrels atween Burns and Tennyson? A gude stock baith, but gin ye'd cross the breed ye maun unite the spirits, and no the manners, o' the men. Why maun ilk a one the noo steal his neebor's barnacles before he glints out o' windows? Mak a style for yoursel, laddie; ye're na mair Scots' hind than ye are Lincolnshire laird; sae gang yer ain gate and leave them to gang theirs; and just mak a gran, brode, simple Saxon style for yoursel.

Sandy at once makes each dialect equal—deeming Tennyson and Burns great poets in spite of their different uses of language—and gives historical authenticity to Alton's 'native' style, without explaining why Cockney should be any closer to Saxon than the Lincolnshire dialect. He undercuts his own claim that each man's 'barnacles' (spectacles) are best adapted to his own use; a man may be a man for all that, but some voices are closer than others to the nation's 'original' speech. He mixes the concept of biological inheritance ('stock') with the imperative to 'mak' a style. He speaks of poetry as Alton's 'doom': 'Some's folks booels are that made o' catgut, that they canna stir without chirrupping and screeking.' Later, Alton would muse, 'There are men whose class no dirt or rags could hide, any more than they could Ulysses. I have seen such men in plenty among workmen, too; but, on the whole, the gentlemen—by whom I do not mean just now the rich—have the superiority in that point.' Alton turns the contradiction into the sort of play on words that enabled Shakespeare to reconcile nature and art in *The Winter's Tale*. When Alton encounters a garden, on his break from London, it transports him from the misery of his class:

as I wondered at the innumerable variety of beauties which man's art had developed from a few poor and wild species, it seemed to me the most delightful life on earth, to follow in such a place the primæval trade of gardener Adam; to study the secrets of the flower world, the laws of soil and climate; to create new species, and gloat over the living fruit of one's own science and perseverance.[45]

[45] *Alton Locke*, 144, 69, 131–2, 86, 99, 117, 116.

He, like the Dean, feels natural history to be a more primitive form of science than the arts; unlike the Dean, he connects his poetry to political action, and feels chagrined by his gardening fantasy. Fortified by Sandy, then Eleanor, he makes poetry into both a product of nature—the instrument of the natural leader—and a force he can shape.

Lyell imagined people asking why God should not have created new, entire languages rather than setting in motion gradual change. 'Where', he asks, 'are the memorials of all the intermediate dialects which must have existed, if this doctrine of perpetual fluctuation be true?' He knew, however, that time erases evidence, and concluded that the extinction 'of languages in general is not abrupt, any more than that of species'.[46] The novel, as a genre, participated in models of succession—its structure shifting amid techniques of authorial intrusion, gradual plot development, crises, and the focus on main characters.

Scott's depiction of the causes of change fused ideas of uniformity and interruption. Concerning the former, his novels show the influence of such men as Ferguson and Percy. Ferguson believed that 'Natural productions are generally formed by degrees.' If children were stranded on an island, their social development would mirror the rise of all races towards civilization.[47] Percy, too, made available to Scott the notion of steady improvement, announcing that the poems in his collection had been put in 'order of time' to show 'the gradation of language and idiom'.[48] Yet Scott, in his own edition of ballads, drew attention to the dependence of progress upon the gifted individual who changes a nation and its language.[49] Both Percy and Scott threw their comments deliberately into a controversy about the origin of ballads; both believed extant ballads to be remnants of 'the single creation of bards or minstrels in the employ of a king or chief' rather than the collective products of

---

[46] Lyell, *The Geological Evidences*, 457–8, 467.

[47] Ferguson, *An Essay on the History of Civil Society*, 1, 6.

[48] Thomas Percy, *Reliques of Ancient English Poetry* (1764; London, 1794), vol. i, pp. xiv, 2.

[49] Walter Scott, *The Minstrelsy of the Scottish Border* (1802–3; Edinburgh, 1850), i. 12.

whole communities. For both, 'The *Volk* was a receptacle not an author.'[50] By highlighting the moment of unique production, Scott puts into question the logic of Percy's attendant model of gradation. In *The Life of John Dryden* (1808) Scott exposed his ambivalent view of the ballad—both as an art form and as a step towards higher culture. He wrote of Pope's genius, arguing that while others might 'by dint of a good ear, and a fluent expression' learn to imitate, the result of their efforts 'like a favourite tune, when descended to hawkers and ballad-singers, became disgusting as it became common'. Dryden won his approval by admiring 'old ballads, and popular tales'; by reviving (like Pope) the ancient poets; by using old words and idioms in a style that was none the less current. Yet the thread running throughout Scott's biography of the poet is the uniqueness of Dryden in the history of English literature—akin to the roles of Bacon and Newton in the acceleration of philosophy and natural science. Dryden was the first to prove the English language 'capable of uniting smoothness and strength'.[51]

Fleishman refers to Scott's ability to 'weld' the uniform and the unique 'into a coherent view of the world', attributing it to his exposure to the speculative school of history: 'there is progress, or at least novelty, as between past and present, but it proceeds along rationally predictable lines and is similar where conditions are similar'.[52] Scott's commentary on the poets, however, suggests that his view was not so neatly linear; that language could degrade with use; that it took the genius of the individual to ensure overall (if not smooth) progress. In *Guy Mannering* we are asked to trust in God's order, and not to be swayed by the disorderliness of human perception. The quotation from Hudibras—referring to 'strange turns in the world's affairs'—is countered by reminders of divine power and the need for the individual to invoke God's aid 'in sincerity and truth'.

The cacophony of tongues in the novel—the misconstructions

[50] John Sutherland, *The Life of Walter Scott* (Oxford, 1995), p. 75.
[51] Walter Scott, 'The Life of Dryden', in *The Works of John Dryden* (London, 1808), i. 478–9, 460, 510, 523, 481, 485.
[52] Fleishman, *The English Historical Novel*, 42.

below the surface of apparent communication—find an antidote in the figure of Bertram, who is singular not in his ability but in his readiness to adapt: 'He had learned the language and feelings of the country even during the short time of his residence . . .'.[53] The brevity of his change, against the obstinacy of language in others, shows that what appears to be a single, short event can actually be the better mirror of the larger scale of God's intent. The novel manages thus to give little ground for argument between gradual and rapid change, by making time contract or expand with the individual's response.[54] The progress of language, in Scott, may reflect slow racial movements, but the leaders of progressive change tend to exhibit the greatest linguistic facility, bringing about the 'watersheds' that in turn affect everyone's tongue. Scott thus uses language to show a coexistence of stagnancy, decay, and progress—while placing his chips on the latter as the ultimate pattern.

The model of the 'strong' language overriding the 'weak' bows under pressure of doubts about the very criteria of survival. Dialect, the so-called relic of past strength, may in the novels be spoken by characters with the toughest bodies; it may affect the choice of a mate in either direction; it may be heard at either end of a line of moral development. Scott allowed the uncertainty to remain. Gaskell put dialect in the realm of haphazard selection, pointing to more than one conclusion. Kingsley got tangled up, thematically, in an effort to join standard English to freedom of choice and an ideal of leadership.

In *Guy Mannering* the belief in a best language, and the bid for social as well as biological cultivation, vies with a caution that we have no real way of calculating the worth of the parts of society that get sloughed off in the name of progress. In a footnote the 'Author' discusses the breeding of foxhounds, extolling the Pepper and Mustard race for their intelligence and fidelity as well as for their adroit bodies: 'Those who, like the Author, possess a brace of them, consider them as very desirable

---

[53] *Guy Mannering*, pp. 18, xxix, 235.

[54] Stephen Jay Gould argues that a 'new' theory may simply be a change of temporal view: for instance, in his own thoughts on evolution he arrived at 'punctuated equilibrium'—the realization that where a species may be 'glacially slow' (to us), geologically it appears 'sudden' (*Time's Arrow, Time's Cycle*, 2–3).

companions.' Yet verbal and physical fitness, honed by a breeder's choice, do not always meet in a human character. After the skirmish between Dinmont, Brown (later known as Bertram), and the rogues, Dinmont shrugs away the handkerchief held out to him to protect his wound from the cold air. He tells Brown that 'The best way's to let the blood barken upon the cut,—that saves plasters, hinney.' Brown's response, over-lapped by the narrator's voice, reveals that 'he had never known such severe strokes received with so much apparent indifference'. Dinmont replies, in direct speech, 'Hout tout, man! I would never be making a hum-dudgeon about a scart on the pow . . .'. The contrast in voices, at the moment of Dinmont's immunity to attack, links his dialect with an inherent likelihood of survival (he surpasses even the trained soldiers of Brown's experience), suggesting a split between social and biological aims.

Elsewhere, the narrator tells us that the farmers in the south of Scotland 'are a much more refined race than their fathers', and that the manners of such as Dinmont 'have either altogether disappeared, or are greatly modified'. Dinmont's successors 'now cultivate arts unknown to the former generation', aided by the fact that 'the best of luxuries, the luxury of knowledge, has gained much ground in their hills during the last thirty years'. Just after the narrator stresses the gap between Dinmont's habits and the reader's, Dinmont and his wife break into the text with strong dialect. The timing insinuates that their language, too, disappeared under the new regime of cultivation. If all of the other changes are for the good, socially, is the change in language any different? The narrator offers no comment. By offsetting Dinmont's strength with an approval of changes that make him obsolescent, Scott hints at the danger of unexpected loss in the wake of goals based on imperfect understanding.

The narrator speaks of the rejects—the 'long-remembered beggar' and the 'decrepit dame' who end up in a workhouse, the 'daft Jock' who dies in jail, and the 'old sailor' whom the county banishes 'for no better reason than that he was supposed to speak with a strong Irish accent'. The removal of such people from our lives may do more damage than we know at the time: 'We are not made of wood or stone, and the things which connect themselves with our hearts and habits cannot, like bark or lichen, be rent away without our missing them.' When the beggar goes to the workhouse, the farmer's wife loses 'her usual share of intelligence, perhaps also the self-applause which she had felt while distributing the "awmous" (alms), in shape of a "gowpen" (handful) of oatmeal, to the mendicant who brought the news'. Many people censure the laird for ridding Ellangowan of its 'nuisances'; the sudden change makes them aware, in an instant, of values on the fringe. In a collective voice they bemoan the laird's habit of 'helping' the poor by 'just dinging down a saxpence in the brod on the Sabbath, and kilting and scourging and drumming them a' the sax days o' the week besides'. Scott creates a relativity of fringes: the dialect speakers (themselves on the wrong side of the verbal track) learn the value of those even lower in status. The narrator's translations and quotation marks draw attention to the distance between the reader and the outcast, while the tree and stone analogy insists upon the interconnectedness of all human life.

Hierarchy and symbiosis do not always contradict each other; in fact, they shape the feudal society that Scott tried to evoke. His use of both models parallels his arbitration between the concept of outworn social features (including language) and the belief in their potential (rather than played-out) value. Bertram is a Scot, but feels that the English 'would hardly acknowledge me a countryman'. Again, there are degrees of living beyond the pale. Because he is an outsider, he must prove his mettle by the sword, echoing the aspect of feudalism that appealed to Scott— the testing of a man by his strength and judgement, instead of title. The modern army, in order to survive, must select its men according to ability. A mysterious birth gives Bertram the status of one whose inherent fitness won him a role in life; on the other hand, his impeccable control of standard English (in writing and in speech) makes him a man of the future—a new Scot. He observes that the English find it advantageous to reconcile the values of 'good birth' and trained skill. It is as if the wisdom of selection operates below the surface, and the choice that looks precarious at the time is in fact the best in the long run: 'The English are a wise people. While they praise themselves, and affect to undervalue all other nations, they leave us, luckily, trap-doors and back-doors open by which we strangers, less

favoured by nature, may arrive at a share of their advantages.'[55]
The strangers, in turn, contribute their skill, having had (unlike
those privileged by birth regardless of merit) to prove it each
step of the way. In effect, biologically inherited strengths check a
system that *assumes* a concord between biology and social
forms of cultivation.

Elizabeth Gaskell creates a similar dynamic, with less confidence in the underlying wisdom of the selection process. In *Mary
Barton* the dialect speakers live closest to the line marking out
the unfit on the simplest level: they breathe the reality of
'clemming' (starving to death). Some shake off the fever; others
do not. Some endure hunger; others cannot. Speech plays no
part in handing out fortitude on the streets of Gaskell's
Manchester. Esther, dressing gaily to attract male customers,
becomes known as 'the Butterfly'. It is her bid for survival, to be
singled out among prostitutes. Her nickname places her among
objects of science, whose adaptation may be studied, and it gives
ironic edge to the impression that the dialect-speaking workers
undergo a kind of evolution that is closer to nature than to
society. Esther's costume fails her: Mary and Jem find her lying
'crushed' in 'what appeared simply a heap of white or light-
coloured clothes'. The novel compares her to 'a wounded deer'
dragging its limbs.

Within the working class, language plays an unpredictable
part in determining who survives. Mary gets no bonus from her
employer for speech that is closer to the standard than Sally
Leadbitter's. Success or failure depends more upon stamina—
the ability to sew until dawn breaks, if necessary. Margaret,
whose blindness threatens to ruin her, uses her voice to escape a
world she cannot physically manage. Her escape, however,
illustrates a need to reach beyond her class; a need that others
share, and one that often finds its outlet in language. The
Chartists chose their delegates, not according to bodily form:
'Had they been larger boned men, you would have called them
gaunt; as it was, they were little of stature, and their fustian
clothes hung loosely upon their shrunk limbs. In choosing their
delegates, too, the operatives had had more regard to their
brains, and power of speech, than to their wardrobes.' The

[55] *Guy Mannering*, 213, 210, 214, 53–5, 186.

workers turn to language to evade biological determinism. They
see their survival in the honing of *mental* characteristics. It is a
reversal of Scott's check against the excesses of social cultivation: the workers use the cultivation of language to balance the
heavy impact of nature on their lives. They want to take part,
deliberately, in the process of selection, and must use language
to break up the hierarchy that has made their existence a lottery.
To strengthen their position, however, they draw upon a verbal
skill they deem 'natural'. Job, for instance, refers to 'the gift of
language', which makes it easier for some to negotiate legal
terms. The narrator suggests that orators are born leaders:
'Masses of people when left to their own free choice, seem to
have discretion in distinguishing men of natural talent . . .'.
Irony appears on two counts: nature is being used to outwit
nature, and one sort of hierarchy replaces another. Both
phenomena, however, echo Bacon's idea that nature can be
beaten with her own laws.

The individual, in other words, may be cast aside by nature's
selection; but *Mary Barton* focuses on the ability to choose,
where the choices people make become part of the order that
decides their fate. The interplay of pawn and decision-maker
can be observed in a dialogue between Mary and her rich lover
Mr Carson, towards the end of chapter 11. We immediately
note a difference in appellation: it is not 'Miss Barton'. The class
barrier between them, raised by Carson as a reason to avoid
marriage, appears even on so simple a level as a comparison of
their names. Mary's will cannot change it. Yet the one dialect
word interpreted for us, in a chapter that contains her rejection
of both Mr Carson and Jem, is 'liefer'. Mary tells Carson that
she 'would far liefer that you should say you will never think of
me again, than that you should speak of me in this way. For
indeed, sir, I never was more in earnest than I am, when I say to-
night is the last night I will ever speak to you.' The author's
footnote gives 'rather' in translation for 'liefer', and quotes
(aptly) from Chaucer's *Troilus and Criseyde*: 'Yet had I *levre*
unwist for sorrow die.' The editorial apparatus holds Mary in a
history of language and romantic stereotypes that determine her
place in relation to Carson, at a time when her dialect signifies
both the past (with its own political barriers) and a strength (the
Celtic fire) that fed, according to William Gaskell, the economic

furnace that raised the Carsons above Mary in class. After admitting that his mother was a 'factory girl', the young Carson yet refers to the 'disparity' between himself and Mary, greater than what had lain between his parents. A lot can happen from one generation to the next. Even so, the use of the word 'liefer' to indicate the gap bespeaks—directly and symbolically—Mary's resolve to end all communication with Carson.

In *Guy Mannering* Mrs Bertram is limited to Scots, while her husband wavers from Scots to standard English, and a sprinkling of Latin. They are, however, of the older generation; the younger people choose mates of a similar language, without expressing concern over the issue. In *Mary Barton* the greater use of dialogue at moments of selection brings language closer to the foreground. When Mary denies that she can ever love Jem, as a wife, she speaks in a form that is closer to the standard than his. It is closer, in fact, to Carson's, in the same chapter. Carson initially put marriage out of the question because of the difference in class—not language, explicitly—but he overcomes the barrier, at least on the surface, when Mary steps back. Her new stand against him takes form in her own translation of his words: 'if I had loved you before, I don't think I should have loved you now you have told me you meant to ruin me; for that's the plain English of not meaning to marry me till just this minute'. Morally, she and the narrator become one, just as their languages merge into each other. Many of her thoughts come to us indirectly, through the narrator's voice; furthermore, her direct speech sounds more like the narrator's standard than in other parts of the book. The effect is complicated. On the one hand, it suggests that the speaker of standard English has more control over the events in her life; in her dialect 'self' Mary might not have exerted her determination to love the man she marries. On the other hand, the erasure of most language gaps in the chapter (except for Jem's speech), and the greater linguistic affinity between Mary and the narrator, give Mary a more easily perceived access to the universal language of 'plain English': the kind of judgement that depends on moral autonomy, rather than variety of speech. The narrator, indeed, doubts the wisdom of choices made on the basis of language alone, as we can see in comments about the London orator. He may be gifted with language, and chosen for his gift, but the

choice involved 'little regard [for] temper and principles'.
Furthermore, the delegates speak a 'more homely and natural
language' amongst themselves than in his presence. The narrator,
unable to merge with their cause, does not join them in their
language; but they are held to be truer to nature than the orator,
whose use of language as a tool is not unlike the rhetoric with
which Carson plies Mary, and which stands apart from the
narrator's own form. Perhaps it is easier for the narrator to
blend voices with Mary at a crisis of love, rather than of politics.
In any case, 'plain English' is the language of moral choice,
taking the form of sexual selection.[56] Mary struggles to free Jem
from a tangle of jargon and verbiage. Not all moments of
triumph come across in her usual dialect, though; one feels as if
the author did not trust her readers to locate in dialect a choice
unbounded by nature and circumstance. Love, as the prime
factor in Mary's decision, pushes both biology and social
cultivation to the side, while her access to the language of both
Jem and the narrator creates a triangle of shared values.

The idea of 'plain English' appears in *Alton Locke* as well. Alton
bewails the fact that clergymen use 'the strange, far-fetched,
technical meanings' instead of a simpler language. He urges that
a teacher go down to the level of his pupil, and not the other
way around, insinuating a hierarchy of knowledge that reaches
its potential through the medium of plain speech. At first the
American preacher Mr Windrush impresses Alton with a
'brilliant declamation' and 'forcible epigrammatic antithesis'.
He invokes science to prove that nothing bad exists; that
everything reflects an order; that the best way to honour God is
to submit to circumstance, on the premiss that whatever is, God
intended. The laws of nature are irrevocable. Crossthwaite
becomes so enamoured of the preacher that he mimics his very
language, to Sandy's astonishment: 'But Johnnie, lad—guide us
and save us!—whaur got ye a' these gran' outlandish words the
nicht?' Sandy inserts pithy sarcasm, in Scots, among the much
longer declamations of Windrush, like a pin pricking a balloon.
   The novel as a whole does not unequivocally deny the
preacher's argument. Windrush echoes the insistence that 'a

---

[56] *Mary Barton*, 72, 463–4, 233, 314, 237, 182–4, 237.

man's a man for a' that'. He takes it too far, though, for
Mackaye's taste, when he concludes that problems must be left
to correct themselves; that the toad and the thief are as
legitimately a part of nature as any of us, and should therefore
be left undisturbed. In some ways, he is the American
counterpart of O'Flynn, preaching (rather than acting upon) a
sort of antinomianism. O'Flynn, the Irish editor, had got himself
into trouble with the law on account of his unorthodox beliefs,
'and showed himself as practised in every law-quibble and
practical cheat as if he had been a regularly-ordained priest of
the blue-bag; and each time, when hunted at last into a corner,
had turned valiantly to bay, with wild witty Irish eloquence'.
Alton cites O'Flynn as an example of his belief that few men, if
any, are all good or all bad. Windrush in a like vein argues that
the polarity of good and evil should be altered into a gradient of
goodness, or nature. Both characters support the thesis of *Guy
Mannering*'s narrator, that the people we cast aside often
contribute more to society than we observe, throwing a curve
into the notion of linear progress. The novel parts from
Windrush, however, by prescribing the *use*, and not just the
acceptance, of the grades of ability in nature. Alton admires the
'stately limbs' of the Cambridge scholar, but notes that upper-
class inbreeding can also lead to 'over-bred imbecility', requiring
an occasional dip into the working-class population for a
renewal of strength. It was a bid for hybridization, without
using the term.

It enters the linguistic domain when Alton and Crossthwaite
meet the dragoons. Alton exclaims that 'there is something
noble to the mind, as well as to the eye, in the great, strong man,
who can fight—a completeness, a self-restraint, a terrible
sleeping power in him'. Crossthwaite, on the other hand, sees
the Horse Guards simply as a body of men protecting those who
get fat while he and his family starve. One of the dragoons, four
times the size of the tailors, is a countryman of Crossthwaite's,
speaking the dialect that the tailor discarded: 'I'm gaun be
moorthered wi' a little booy that's gane mad, and toorned
Chartist', he mocks, when Crossthwaite accuses him of betray-
ing his people. Alton wonders why the two men, who share a
background (and language) cannot speak together: 'You and he
might have cracked many a joke together, if you did but

understand each other . . .'. His friend's automatic rebuff
centres on the belief that genius and brute strength never mix;
whereas Alton dreams that they might. In the 'Dream Land'
chapter, when the Aryan people move West to fulfil God's plan,
they encounter a barrier of rock. Only the dwarfs hold the
knowledge needed to bore the mountain, and the Aryans
negotiate: 'Then the dwarfs taught us smith-work; and we loved
them, for they were wise; and they married our sons and
daughters; and we went on boring the mountain.' The exchange
of skills creates a happy kingdom, until the strongest people
begin to dominate the resources, drawing upon themselves the
hatred and envy of the weak. Alton pictures himself as a poet
who leads the whole tribe back to an interdependence that
accommodates inequality. Selfishness is not the key to survival
of the tribe, he implies.

In the same dream he imagines watching his cousin, dressed
'like an American backwoodsman', digging for gold by a tree,
where Alton (in an earlier stage of evolution) was attempting
without success to grab for the beautiful girls that were nestled
among the branches. The tree cracks, and seems about to fall on
the cousin. Alton tries to warn him: 'but how could a poor
edentate like myself articulate a word?'[57] The tree rushes down,
'and, leaving my cousin untouched, struck me full across the
loins, broke my backbone, and pinned me to the ground in
mortal agony'. The dream associates lack of articulation with
selfish and 'sense-bound' destructive impulses. The insect
images recall the scene among the farm labourers, who 'were
swarming restlessly round a single large block of stone, some
relic of Druid times', where their leader stood, in what was 'the
earthwork, probably, of some old British town'. They appear to
be of a different time, if not race, from the workers in the city, just
as in *Mary Barton* the country folk show a bucolic air in contrast
with the sharp, clever faces of those in Manchester. Alton had
been 'struck with the wan, haggard look of all faces; their lack-
lustre eyes and drooping lips, stooping shoulders, heavy,
dragging steps, gave them a crushed, dogged air, which was
infinitely painful, and bespoke a grade of misery more habitual

[57] Elizabeth Cripps, in the Explanatory Notes to *Alton Locke*, defines 'edentate'
as 'An animal without incisor and canine teeth' (p. 447).

and degrading than that of the excitable and passionate artisan'.
The novel presents the language of their leader (as far as Alton
'can recollect') in a long abuse of the farmers who 'makes slaves
on us'. Before the speech, Alton prepares us for tedium: 'His
words, like all I heard that day, were utterly devoid of anything
like eloquence or imagination—a dull string of somewhat
incoherent complaints, which derived their force only from the
intense earnestness, which attested their truthfulness.' The
labourers have not chosen a London orator to represent them,
unlike the workers in *Mary Barton*; they only glare 'with sullen
curiosity' when Alton appears in his 'Londoner's clothes'. The
dialogue ends in 'pandemonium'—a word that synthesizes vocal
chaos and the fires of hell. The only word that Alton gets across
to the hungry workers is 'bread', inciting them to violence
against his will, and once again he merges incoherent babble
with sensual impulse and needless destruction.

Alton looks to a future synthesis (or hybridization) of physical
and mental prowess, and believes it requires people now and
then to select among those who on the surface seem little
qualified to effect social improvement. Mackaye offers an
alternative. He advocates a rule of selection whose criterion is
generosity:

Let a man prove himsel' better than me, my laddie—honester, humbler,
kinder, wi' mair sense o' the duty o' man, an' the weakness o' man—
and that man I'll acknowledge—that man's my king, my leader, though
he war as stupid as Eppe Dalgleish, that could na count five on her
fingers, and yet keepit her drucken father by her ain hands' labour, for
twenty-three yeers.[58]

As Scott's novel had done, *Alton Locke* points out the social
benefit of requiring proof of superiority, rather than letting
people choose a leader on the basis of social or biological
privileges alone. Scott often played the two modes against each
other, illustrating blind spots in each. *Mary Barton* introduces,
as an external gauge, the factor of love. For Mackaye the factor
is ethics, even when they oppose social and biological 'impera-
tives'; whereas for Alton, and the novel as a whole, the
development of moral agency intertwines itself with the cultivation of an alliance between genius and health, making irrelevant

[58] *Alton Locke*, 288, 209, 212, 191, 146, 44–6, 344, 340, 259, 271, 214.

(ultimately) for fear of greed. Associations made between survival and speech, moreover, suggest that in the triad he foresees—of morality, strength, and eloquence—the latter will not be Cockney in form.

For the three novelists, varieties of language enter the decisions their characters make; dialect and the standard are involved in a woman's choice of a husband, in a county's tolerance of its residents, and in a worker's bid for representation. Selection, as a narrative device, makes us focus on the character's agency, while at the same time drawing him or her, and the forms of language in question, into a vision of the past and future—into a model, and its problems, of evolution. When a worker, for example, chooses a delegate, he takes into account (consciously or not) past events that have made one form of speech more readily listened to than another, though he may be thinking only of the goals the delegate is meant to attain. Many of the characters show awareness of the potential in language to fit their needs, and in their ability to manipulate; many, too, feel strongly about inherited qualities that make a language unique. The images of language as a tool, and as a sign of genealogy, combine—as do the fields of linguistics and biology in the nineteenth century.

Adam Ferguson saw that people could approach an object (and language) as a static form, and *create* a language to describe it, when the truer course would be to grow with the object and the language. The inanimate approach, though fitting language to a need, could not be communicated to other people, while the latter process implies both a forming of language (to circumstance) and a merging of it with the development of the mind.[59] Scott puts into his novel a similar blend of analogy and homology. Mannering and a rural Scotswoman, speaking in different dialects, fill gaps of understanding easily enough to suggest that the particularity of the form comes next to circumstance, the latter enabling the characters to predict each other's speech. Both dialects point to the same issue, and become mutually intelligible when characters share a location

[59] Ferguson, *An Essay on the History of Civil Society*, 274.

(of place and event). Gaps of time may be overcome, too, by the use of footnote translations for the reader, where the gap is further elided by the omission (in most cases) of etymological detail. The author tends to give a modern equivalent, rather than explain the word's development, giving us little reason to feel that the meaning of the older word is trapped in its own time.

Translations of the gypsy dialect, however, do not entirely shake the possibility that some forms of language got frozen at an earlier stage, beyond the reach of any dictionary. Meg's occasional use of non-gypsy words appears to 'the old gypsy man' to contradict the fact that she is in other respects 'true-bred' and loyal to her tribe; his comment affirms a parallel of lineage and vocabulary. The narrator, too, hints in places at a connection between the gypsies' nomadic life and marriages, and the obscurity of their language. They have trouble communicating even amongst themselves: 'With more of this gibberish, they continued the conversation, rendering it thus, even to each other, a dark, obscure dialect, eked out by significant nods and signs, but never expressing distinctly, or in plain language, the subject on which it turned.' Coupled with the earlier statement about the obsolescence of their race, the muddle of their speech implies their inability to adapt to a new environment; their meaning dies out with the words, instead of finding a new form. Scott shows it dying, not dead, by including both a direct dialogue we can understand (more or less) and a description of its nonsensical, unrepeatable nature.[60] Thus, while some forms of speech perform a given task with equal ability, no matter what the chronology of their development, the waning of the gypsy dialect suggests that language may conform to biological variation, where the disappearance of an anatomical form (from the inheritance pool) means that it is most likely gone for ever, along with its niche. The surviving, exchangeable dialects (or languages) in Scott's novel belong to societies far outweighing the gypsies in population and economy.

Dennis Taylor points to the example of one of Scott's mentors, Dugald Stewart, who 'cited the error in Tooke of confounding

[60] *Guy Mannering*, 76, 5, 252.

"the analysis of a language, after it has assumed a regular and syntactical form" and "the gradual steps by which it proceeded to that state" '. Taylor adds that 'Much of Saussure is present in this statement.'[61] Stewart's distinction between two approaches was based on the theory that a language was in (historical) flux until it became consistent enough in itself to produce meaning independent of the past. If we put *Guy Mannering* into his model, we can see the gypsy dialect as a product of a society still in flux, undeveloped. It functions in the novel as a form, of society and language, too weak to withstand the pressures of historic change.

The idea that some dialects, only, are developed enough to exist on the merits of structure alone gives a clue to Scott's lack of perfect ease with the premiss of 'general laws'. Harry Shaw, writing about *The Heart of Midlothian*, claims that the text resists 'the promotion of any language to an ahistorical, universal, and natural status, even though the novel's larger rhetorical force depends upon just such merging and pro-motion'.[62] The contradiction, however, may be understood better if we apply to the novels a 'split' that Tony Crowley makes between two methods of studying language, both, in this case, historical. The split occurs in nineteenth-century philology, between internal and external emphases in the history of language. The 'internal' refers to a focus on syntax and grammar, outside any historical context, with the idea that a language moves organically from a synthetic to an analytic state. The 'external' refers to the features that are affected by 'historical pressure'. Crowley writes: 'Another way of putting it would be to say that according to this scheme the "essence" of the language and nation (the internal), remains always organi-cally ordered in terms of its development and only the "accidental" features of language and nation (the external or historical), are constantly open to change.'[63]

Guy Mannering, in several ways, tries to mesh the universal and the historical through the medium of language. It features the language of astrology as a string of jargon that acts like a

---

[61] Taylor, *Hardy's Literary Language and Victorian Philology*, 228.
[62] Harry E. Shaw, 'Scott's "Daemon" and the Voices of Historical Narration', *Journal of English and Germanic Philology*, 88/1 (Jan. 1989), 31.
[63] Tony Crowley, *The Politics of Discourse* (Basingstoke, 1989), 47.

smoke-screen from antiquity, bewildering rather than illumin-
ating the listener, with the sheer weight of its obscurity rather
than by virtue of any structural effect; and yet the accuracy of
Mannering's prediction, and the author's claim to a prototype in
real life, adds to the sense in the novel of eternal laws at work in
the universe. The 'accidental' nature of the jargon, and the
narrator's urging of coincidence, put in relief (rather than
contradict) the certain and repetitious quality of Bertram's fate.
The gypsies play an 'accidental' role in the novel, using
Crowley's definition. Their life-style and language are unsettled:
they affect but do not feel a part of the course of national (and
natural) inheritance. Meg comes closest of all her kin to being
'true-bred', as gypsy and Scot, by speaking both central and
marginal languages, and by helping the lost boy recover his
estate. Mannering, as a visiting Englishman, may also be seen as
a point of external pressure, using a non-essential jargon to
make his presence felt.

The novel, however, does not place the gypsies and the
English in the same circle on the margin of Scotland. Mannering
becomes part of the inner (legal) workings of the Scottish
society, reflected by his ability to understand (if not perfectly)
the Scots dialect. His method of restoring Bertram to the land,
and his use of several languages, puts him closer than Meg to the
changes—legal and linguistic—apparent in Scotland at the time.
Scott, a lawyer by training, saw in the uniqueness of the Scottish
legal system a way of differentiating his country from England,
without disrupting Britain as a whole. Meg's hold on the
'essence' of events is the repetition of an old (anglicized) ballad.
Her inactive role in the legal structure, and her relation to the
gypsies by nature and language, puts her closer than Mannering
to elements of Scottish society that were beginning to fade. She
is the more 'accidental' of the two, in that sense, however strong
her character. Scott was hardly reluctant to give fire and pathos
to even the most fleeting of traits.

Lyell had said that varieties of speech did not depend on barriers
of land alone; they were in fact more greatly influenced by
genealogy.[64] Yet our potential to see how different forms

---

[64] Lyell, *Principles of Geology*, ii. 475–6.

emerge depends as well upon a *spatial* awareness of development. We must keep in mind, here, the tension between place
and time. Scott, in *Guy Mannering*, tilts the emphasis to the
latter. In *Mary Barton*, on the other hand, we find most
vividly—and audibly—a sense of space. There occurs no sheer
break from the 'mother country': when Jem and Mary emigrate
to Canada, letters cross the Atlantic. In England itself, however,
large variations in dialect seem to issue from regions divided by
train travel. The sailors in Liverpool are a 'new race of men' to
Mary, who requires the aid of a local boy to 'interpret' their
speech. The confusion is a factor of both geography and
occupation: Mary 'had hitherto seen none but inland dwellers,
and those for the greater part factory people'. When Charley
speaks on her behalf to an 'old tar', the slang 'to Mary was
almost inaudible, and quite unintelligible', increasing her sense
of isolation and despair. The narrator begs off repeating the
language, being 'too much of a land-lubber to repeat correctly',
thus asserting her own location.[65] Gaskell herself had had a
much different experience: in 1831 (before her twenty-first
birthday) she spent a summer with the Holland family in
Birkenhead and Liverpool, and wrote to a friend with the news
that 'I do like Liverpool and the Mersey and the accent and the
people very much.'[66]

The narrator takes on a curious role in the novel, insisting
both upon the linguistic uniqueness of each region, and upon the
ties of emotion underneath. In the preface we are told that 'the
state of feeling' among the characters in the novel is confirmed
by events 'among a similar class on the Continent' in 1848—the
year of *Mary Barton*'s publication. When Mary takes the train
out of Manchester towards Liverpool, she finds it bewildering,
especially to her ear, and she looks back to her own city 'with a
feeling akin to "Heimweh" '. The use of the German word for
'homesickness', at a moment of strong regional attachment,
suggests that in Mary's feeling there is a universality of which
she is unaware. When she arrives in Liverpool, she follows the
directions of a policeman 'with the *savoir faire* of a town-bred

---

[65] *Mary Barton*, 352.
[66] Quoted in Jenny Uglow, *Elizabeth Gaskell* (1993; London, 1994), 66.

girl'. Again, the foreign phrase hints that Mary is not as bound
to her region as she imagines. It is one of a number of places in
which the novel implies, through a choice of language, that
social barriers are learned rather than fixed. Job's familiarity
with legal terms is presented as the 'air of a connoisseur'; the
French origin of the word augments the feeling that it is a
difference more cosmetic than inherited. He translates
'subpoena' for Mary, who comprehends at once its nature and
threat.

Throughout the novel, the act of translation diminishes the
otherwise strong sense of regional uniqueness, as if to urge that
dialects do not represent a trenchant isolation; at the same time,
the focus on the need for mediation adds to the force of
geographic identity. For instance, the narrator supposes that few
of us know 'The Oldham Weaver' (Alice calls it 'The Owdham
Weaver'): 'Not unless you are Lancashire born and bred, for it is
a complete Lancashire ditty'.[67] The song contains 203 dialect
'flags' and words, only two of which are translated (in William
Gaskell's footnotes). Sheila M. Smith believes that it was 'taken
down from a singer. The correct sound of Lancashire speech is
carefully reproduced in print.'[68] By writing out the song for us,
and describing how it is sung, the narrator bridges a difference
of birthplace; in contrast, the retention of dialect form indicates
not only where a bridge is unnecessary, but also where
translation might weaken the impact of expression. It is the core
tension of the novel: between an insistence upon the universal,
and validation of a local speech.

In *Mary Barton* spatial barriers of language may, in essence,
be overcome. It is hard to make a similar claim for traits of the
body—keeping in mind that Gaskell, like many of her contemporaries, drew a fuzzy line between mental and physical
characteristics. The ambiguity of the line can be seen when the
narrator accounts for differences between Mary's father and
mother. John Barton comes from Manchester, where a glance
into a crowd reveals 'an acuteness and intelligence of countenance, which has often been noticed in a manufacturing
population'. His wife, on the other hand, 'had the fresh beauty

---

[67] *Mary Barton*, 38, 343, 345, 314, 71.
[68] Sheila M. Smith, *The Other Nation* (New York, 1980), 200.

of the agricultural districts; and somewhat of the deficiency of sense in her countenance, which is likewise characteristic of the rural inhabitants in comparison with the natives of the manufacturing towns'. Gaskell later repeats the contrast, comparing farm labourers to the factory workers of Milton, in *North and South*. The Bartons are, to some degree, determined both physically and mentally by the place of their birth; the lack of any real distinction in manner of speech, however, diminishes (in the reader's mind) the impact of mental inheritance. We must be told, later, that the young Mary is more intelligent than her mother. It would be impossible to derive it from their dialogue alone. In another instance, Gaskell uses dialect (Scots, this time) to enable a character to overcome a disadvantage of inherited form. When Jem encounters the 'other man', Harry Carson, he at once feels himself thrown into a poor light by 'the gay, handsome young man approaching, with a light, buoyant step'. It is no wonder, then, that Mary should prefer the superior body: 'for [Carson] seemed to the poor smith, so elegant, so well-appointed, that he felt his superiority in externals, strangely and painfully, for an instant. Then something uprose within him, and told him, that "a man's a man for a' that, for a' that, and twice as much as a' that." And he no longer felt troubled by the outward appearance of his rival.' Thus, while characters in the novel inherit more than just a face and limbs from their ancestors, prettiness of form does not necessarily match clarity of mind; nor are features of speech felt to be as essential a demarcation. In other words, Gaskell juxtaposes language and biology; the former is the least bound by laws of inheritance, or homology.

In this, the two Gaskells vary. The footnotes, contributed by William, stress the inherited elements of language, connecting the Lancashire dialect (in fact there were several Lancashire dialects) with earlier forms. Wilson approaches John for some money, explaining 'I donnot* want it for mysel . . .'; a friend of theirs is 'down wi' the fever, and ne'er a stick o' fire, nor a cowd† potato in the house'. The event itself illustrates the resourcefulness of the two men, who bring not only their hearts but also their wits to bear upon an unexpected tragedy. Their speech, however, appears less impromptu. The footnotes show its ancestry:

* 'Don' is constantly used in Lancashire for 'do'; as it was by our older writers. 'And that may non Hors *don.*'—*Sir J. Mandeville.*
'But for th' entente to *don* this sinne.'—*Chaucer.*
† 'Cowd', cold. Teut., *kaud.* Dutch, *koud.*

A second example of charity offers the same tension. Job tells the story of Margaret's infancy—of when her parents, by death of fever, left her an orphan with their landlady in London. Her grandfathers set out to rescue her, little able to afford the journey. They decide to take much of the road by foot, and in doing so gain a sense of the gradual changes over the social landscape. They leave Brummagem (dialect for Birmingham) 'which is as black a place as Manchester, without looking so like home'. Their spirits lift, for 'th' day were fine, and folk began to have some knowledge o' th' proper way o' speaking, and we were more cheery at thoughts o' home (though mine, God knows, were lonesome enough)'. Job's narrative is peppered with dialect words and pronunciations, several of which are derived (the footnotes inform us) from the Anglo-Saxon. Once again, the footnotes counter the weight put by the main text on the locality, the unique form, of the men's approach to common suffering; on the spatial barriers that must be overcome. William not only conflates the Manchester dialect with all speech forms in Lancashire; he also puts direct translation (present definition for present word) into the same format as the illustrations of lineage—suggesting (by implication) that spatial and temporal differences are much the same, connected to each other by inheritance. The main body of the novel, by contrast, hints at the greater pressure of existing circumstances.[69]
It would be simplifying the case to say that the novel and lectures contradict each other outright. After all, land barriers and genealogy mesh together in Lyell's *Antiquity of Man,* where he argues that 'the geographical relations of living and dead languages favour the hypothesis of the living ones having been derived from the extinct'; no language, he adds, 'can have had two birthplaces'. Each generation tends 'to adopt without change the vocabulary of its predecessor', while able to adapt to new conditions by inventing new words; in both respects, language may be compared 'to the force of inheritance in the

[69] *Mary Barton*, 41–2, 226, 97, 150.

organic world'.[70] The uniqueness of place, in other words, creates variety; the variations are proof of unique characteristics. Genealogy need not rule out shared laws of adaptation, however idiosyncratic the expressions of them.

Critics often dicuss Gaskell's novel alongside *Alton Locke*; yet William's lectures, drawing more upon genealogy, are the more fitting link to Kingsley's novel. *Alton Locke* is the tale of a working man who slips through barriers by teaching himself to read and write. No one, we are told, need succumb entirely to circumstances of birth. Forms of intelligence (including a knowledge of languages) may be interchanged; no one is bound to a particular form. The Dean, for example, refers to the mental powers that are stimulated by the working man's science— natural history. It is akin (to a greater degree, even) to what the more privileged scholar experiences in the study of philology or mathematics. Eleanor extends the law of analogy across time: she bids Alton to go to the tropics, to observe the 'primeval' man, to 'bring home fresh conceptions of beauty, fresh spiritual and physical laws of his existence', and to apply these at home in London, 'in the cottages, in the play-grounds, the reading-rooms, the churches of working men'. Here, though, one can see how the use of analogy—of laws operating over time—supports the belief, not in the unity of a species, but in variety of inheritances. The working class in nineteenth-century London (in Eleanor's model) bears a closer kinship to tropical natives than to the nineteenth-century London middle class. The novel, in spite of its own insistence upon the need for social remedy, draws heavily upon a matrix of genealogy to argue that the remedy lies within. A different configuration is all the Londoners need; one that makes better use of their racial origins.

Kingsley's use of language points to a vaguely Aryan base, departing in detail, if not in structure, from William Gaskell's bias towards the Celtic element. In Alton's dream-vision, the 'sacred' notion of family (the nouns of relationship) issues from the knowledge of an 'All-Father'. The term denotes 'Odin, the chief Scandinavian god, in the Icelandic *Eddas*'. Alton envisions the spread of 'Titan babies, dumb angels of God, bearing with them in their unconscious pregnancy, the law, the freedom, the

[70] Lyell, *The Geological Evidences*, 461, 465, 467.

science, the poetry, the Christianity, of Europe and the world'. Their language (when they achieve it) diversifies, as we found out earlier in the novel; but the differences are not necessarily ill wrought. So we are given to understand by the '*** ambassador', who was based, by one claim at least, on the real figure of Bunsen—Prussian ambassador to London, patron of Müller, and historian of language. The ambassador, in the novel, refers to Alton's poetry as proof of 'the undercurrent of living and healthful thought which exists even in the less-known ranks of your great nation'. He then asks if Alton understands the German language. When Alton admits ignorance, the ambassador insists that he learn, arguing that 'We have much to teach you in the sphere of abstract thought, as you have much to teach us in those of the practical reason and the knowledge of mankind.' Each language, then, expresses the mental characteristics of a nation—an argument that William Gaskell had applied to a county in his glamorization of a past mix of Aryan and Celt. The ambassador explains: 'I am anxious to encourage a truly spiritual fraternization between the two great branches of the Teutonic stock, by welcoming all brave young English spirits to their ancient fatherland.' The Germans are 'true brothers'.

Alton has two reactions. The first is to exalt himself on the attention given him by a great man. He becomes 'utterly "*tête montée*", as I believe the French phrase is—beside myself with gratified vanity and love'. A fit of asthma cools him down to 'something like a rational pitch', and he composes a poem—the only one in this 'autobiography' of a poet—using a touch of dialect, in the style of a ballad. In a few paragraphs, then, the novel connects abstract thought with the German tongue, practical reason with the English, and vanity with the French. Alton's ultimate response to the ambassador's advice is to second it by writing in a style that draws from an older (and, with its 'simple' vocabulary, more Teutonic) form of English evoking a humble life. He thus steps into his own contradiction. Earlier, when he discovered the poetry of Alfred Tennyson, he asked himself why each generation selects its own poet. He decided that the 'latest poet' is most popular among his generation because 'he, living amid the same hopes, the same temptations, the same sphere of observation as they, gives utterance and outward form to the very questions which, vague and wordless, have been exercising their hearts'.[71] Yet both Alton and Tennyson use a ballad form and older themes, while trying to come to grips with present anxieties. Both limit their experimentation with dialect. Close parallels between biological and linguistic development involve Kingsley's fiction—to a more complicated degree than Gaskell's or Scott's—in controversies about the rate, direction, and nature of human evolution.

Alton's 'life' can be read as an attempt to harmonize two modes of writing: an impassioned voice that speaks to and of the moment, underscoring the abruptness of events; and a voice that negotiates between extremes, making the change from one phase to another look gradual. Alton identifies briefly with O'Flynn, but puts him in a slightly comical (and therefore alien) light as a ranting Irishman who grabs hold of the wrong end of the stick. It builds an association between 'paroxysmic' writing and self-centred ambition. On the other hand, the Dean's insistence upon ridding Alton's verse of topical anger seems an act of self-protection—not just a belief in slow evolution. The dilemma, of not knowing which mode to keep prominent, has some foundation in a confusion of metaphors that beset scientists of nature and of language in the mid-nineteenth century (and before). Müller may have warned against drawing too close an analogy between variations of language and of race, but biology had a way of sliding into the picture; conflicting images—depicting change as either progress or cycle—moved back and forth across disciplines. Social and biological histories merge.

It does not follow, necessarily, that the later novelists drew from the more scientific writings; or that influence is a one-way road from science to fiction. Scott, of the three novelists, had the least exposure to formal articulations of relative progress in either philology or natural history. He adopted a discourse of developmental *stages*. Like Ferguson, who compared the British at the time of the Roman invasion to North American natives of his present day,[72] Scott included the notion of cycles in his

---

[71] *Alton Locke*, 165, 384, 343, 447 (ed.'s note), 343, 241, 431 (ed.'s note), 241–2, 97.   [72] Ferguson, *An Essay on the History of Civil Society*, 114.

picture of improvement over the largest scale of time. He took up a well-worn marriage of values—of essence and change—and made it play a part in his fiction. In *Guy Mannering* a distinction is made between nature and human history. While riding past the stones of a ruin, Mannering thinks of the 'ancient chiefs' who built the fortress, and of how amazed they would have been if able to look ahead to the downfall of their mighty race. He wonders at the vanity of the individual, for 'Nature's bounties are unaltered. The sun will shine as fair on these ruins, whether the property of a stranger, or of a sordid and obscure trickster of the abused law, as when the banners of the founder first waved upon their battlements.' The human contains both elements, natural and social. Bertram (as Brown) tries to read in Meg's face 'something that promised those feelings of compassion which females, even in their most degraded state, can seldom altogether smother'.[73] Races of people tend to draw upon qualities already at work in their design, in order to reach higher levels of refinement. Human history tends (in Scott's novel) to argue a social progress that never quite escapes the input of nature; modifications carry a whiff of the past. It was an idea that Chambers (geologist and biographer of Scott) took into his own work, postulating that 'lower' races were less-developed versions of the more advanced.[74] Nature, in other words, imposes upon social history the figure of return, and the compromise is the image of a spiral, positing the necessity of ordered steps.

Yet the novel resists falling into so easy a formulation, as we can see from two parallel events. Bertram, like Mannering, journeys past an old ruin. He does so on purpose, choosing 'that unusual tract which leads through the eastern wilds of Cumberland into Scotland' in order to see the remains of the Roman wall. His thoughts run along a line similar to Mannering's, with an interesting difference. The vanity of human desire occurs to both men, but Bertram sees a gradation among outward forms. Artefacts of the more recent stages in the science of war will soon vanish, while those of antiquity remain. Bertram, looking at the wall, sees a facsimile of the Roman language: 'Their

[73] *Guy Mannering*, 123, 246.
[74] Bowler, *The Invention of Progress*, 91.

fortifications, their aqueducts, their theatres, their fountains, all their public works, bear the grave, solid, and majestic character of their language; while our modern labours, like our modern tongues, seem but constructed out of their fragments.' Ancient architecture, built of more lasting material, seems closer than the modern to the essence of nature, out of which people construct their social histories. Mannering portrays nature as a counterpoint to society; Bertram, as a degree of concord with human artefacts, be they physical or linguistic. The difference is subtle, because both characters use the idea of nature to evoke human folly; yet it offers a choice between two kinds of check to the belief in a steady grade of progress. Mannering's is a more unilinear view of societies advancing out of the ruins of their predecessors; Bertram's, though similar in its notion of building with fragments, may be taken to mean that progress depends not so much on a society's place in time, but on the materials at hand. The modern scientist is no less intelligent or well adapted, but his materials are less permanent. How can progress be measured without them?

Both characters admit the change that 'progress' derives much of its significance from the viewpoint of each assessor. Within Scott's picture of developmental stages lurk hints of a less sequential pattern. Sir Robert Hazlewood may have benefited from the 'decadence of the Ellangowan family'; his own family may be on the rise; but his language betrays him. He affects 'a species of florid elocution, which often became ridiculous from his misarranging the triads and quaternions with which he loaded his sentences'. The biological image, of one family growing out of another's decay, is turned into a mockery by a social (linguistic) 'accomplishment'. Sir Robert is waxing and waning at the same moment. He himself attests to ambiguity in the concept of progress when he calls Glossin a 'gentleman'. When Mannering gazed at the ruined fortress, he wondered at a world in which a 'sordid and obscure trickster' might take over a family seat. It was Glossin he meant. Later, though, Sir Robert names Glossin 'the gentleman who has purchased Ellangowan'. His son objects, and Sir Robert replies, 'Why, Charles, I did not mean "gentleman" in the precise sense and meaning, and restricted and proper use, to which, no doubt, the phrase ought legitimately to be confined; but I meant to use it relatively, as marking something of that state to which he has elevated and raised himself,—as designing, in short, a decent and wealthy and estimable sort of a person.'[75] Sir Robert implies that the 'proper' use is limited to a rung on the social ladder; he wants to extend its meaning to fit an individual's adaptation to the world around him. A similar debate occurs in Gaskell's *North and South*, providing a useful comparison. Margaret finds it hard to grant Mr Horsfall the status of gentleman; Thornton admits to preferring the term 'true man' as a gauge of character. Margaret presses him on the difference, and Thornton answers, 'A man is to me a higher and completer being than a gentleman.' The term 'gentleman' places a man only 'in his relation to others', whereas 'man' puts him also 'in relation to himself,—to life—to time—to eternity'. Thornton complains that the word 'gentlemanly' is 'often inappropriately used, and often, too, with such exaggerated distortion of meaning, while the full simplicity of the noun "man," and the adjective "manly" are unacknowledged—that I am induced to class it with the cant of the day'.[76]

In Thornton's mind, 'man' is closest to nature, embodied by Robinson Crusoe on his island, shorn of (most of) the accoutrements of society. It matters to the factory owner that the two words—man and gentleman—be kept apart to effect a mental distinction between two concepts of selfhood, natural and social. The social is but a part of the natural whole. Thornton wants to adapt the norm of language to fit his idea of man's place in the universe better; he derides the norm as 'the cant of the day', insisting upon the truer priority of his own usage. Sir Robert, by contrast, gets stuck between two values. He balks at giving up the notion of a 'proper' use of words—for precision keeps the distinctions (in this case social) that have served him well in the past. On the other hand, self-interest prompts him to loosen up a definition in a move that could, if he gave it much thought, shake apart his own order of things. He is an object of fun because he introduces the very element— relative status—that threatens his own, linguistically manoeuvred position. Thornton invokes no such laughter; his attempt to reform English usage is very much in accord with his own

[75] *Guy Mannering*, 194–5, 416, 417, 484, 485.
[76] Elizabeth Gaskell, *North and South* (1854–5; Oxford, 1985), 164.

ambitions, which demand that he be evaluated by performance rather than by an inherited position. We can laugh at the irony of his rhetoric, perhaps. He supports his case by deriding as cant a term that people have found useful; where, by his own logic, such usefulness ought to give it some authority. Yet he makes the inconsistency work for him, unlike Sir Robert, whose words say more than he would care to know.

Sir Robert, then, introduces the concept of relative progress in two ways. The most obvious is prompted by a desire to give Glossin a status that would enable his wealth and strategy to benefit Sir Robert; as a mode of self-interest, it discredits judgement by individual measures. In the larger scale of the novel, however, Sir Robert is himself a parody of a certain kind of order; of the idea that progress flows inevitably through the rise and fall of noble families, each benefiting from the decay of the one past. The idea is never discarded completely, for Bertram fleshes out both concepts, rising first on his own merit—adapting to the language and customs of each environment—then taking up a noble lineage. Genealogy clearly mattered to Scott, but he slipped a wedge into the idea, later articulated in the sciences, that progress takes a less linear form than hitherto supposed.

Bunsen in 1854 avows that 'every language contains within itself an element of progress, which upon some crisis may become the element of death to the old and of life to the new language'. The death of the old is ameliorated by an onset of growth. The organic metaphor, however, is not allowed to imply steady change—on a historical scale—for 'No language dies without a great crisis occurring in the tribe or nation which speaks it.' What appears to be a single fact—the 'phenomena of mind (e.g. in language)'—is in truth an element 'of a process of evolution'. A crisis, then, like human tragedy, has only the appearance of a unique event. Using Bacon's power of influence (as Scott had done) to argue the reality of the single fact—its weight in the search for truth—Bunsen nevertheless concludes that each point in time is the finite form of the infinite mind. The tragic figure who builds, destroys, and endures the destruction of a nation (affecting its speech) is but part of a larger scheme of progress. Language, for Bunsen, is the best proof that the contradiction (between individual and atemporal emphases) lies only on the surface.[77]

Scott, in *Guy Mannering*, invokes God in the attempt to reconcile different rates of progress; Gaskell, in *Mary Barton*, draws in the Bible to mediate between figures of progress and chance. Jenny Uglow points to the scientific element in Gaskell's later works, *Sylvia's Lovers* and *Cousin Phillis*: both re-create 'the contemporary debate between "development" and "catastrophe" theories of the geological formation of Earth itself', but in human terms. Her characters experience both 'the gradual accumulation of years' and 'the violent shock of the new', while she looks for unchanging values they can hold onto. Their conflicts 'are related specifically to language and form'. Uglow makes a distinction, however. Predominant in *Sylvia's Lovers* are elements of 'predatory competition and random accident', while Hope Farm, in *Cousin Phillis*, is pre-Lyell and pre-Darwin: 'a teeming confusion which appears chaotic, but is ultimately interlinked, harmonious and orderly: "From stage to stage, the vital scale ascends." '[78] In *Mary Barton* two primarily different experiences of change coexist in the same city: workers oppose the rich, 'the even tenor of whose seemingly happy lives appeared to increase the anguish caused by the lottery-like nature of their own'; the agony of the poor 'convulses' them, while they are unable to speak it. Gaskell's use of 'seemingly' and 'appeared', of course, undermines the polarity; what remains, none the less, is an association between unrecognized speech forms (that of the working people) and a sudden, unpredictable movement through time.

Gaskell was aware of the 'bogey of chance' even before it took shape in Darwin's *Origin of Species*. John Barton's features, for instance, tell of an earnestness that may work 'either for good or evil'. Of all the characters in the novel, he is singled out as a 'visionary'. The narrator tries to detach the word from its limited association with Chartism and communism, to give it a wider, more auspicious meaning: 'It shows a soul, a being not altogether sensual; a creature who looks forward for others, if

---

[77] Bunsen, *Outlines of the Philosophy of Universal History*, ii. 92; i. 32, 35–6.
[78] Uglow, *Elizabeth Gaskell*, 540–1. Uglow quotes from James Thomson, 'Autumn' (*The Seasons*).

not for himself.' Barton represents, among the workers, a shift away from their mute, animal nature. That is why Gaskell often lets him speak for himself, in spite of her claim that the workers are dumb. He possesses 'a ready kind of rough Lancashire eloquence'. The others may be less advanced in speech, but they lean towards the skill in Barton, suggesting a bent in nature for greater articulation. Barton, though, as a modern Frankenstein's monster, becomes the central figure in a great set-back, not only to Chartism, but to faith as a whole in the rough speech of the heart. Where Mary succeeds in quelling legal jargon with her native speech, her father dismally fails. The parallel stories make it hard for the reader to maintain trust in necessary progress; and the short time-scale of the novel gives little room for belief in what Lyell called the 'final predominance' of higher organisms. Another scene from *Mary Barton* illustrates the point. When Margaret relates to Mary the success of her 'musical début', they both picture a rise in the blind girl's fortunes. Margaret reassures her friend, 'I'll not forget to give thee a lift now an' then . . .', adding, 'may-happen I may make thee my lady's maid!' She sings, 'An' ye shall walk in silk attire, | An' siller hae to spare.' But Mary begs her to stifle the ballad and give her 'something a bit more new'. Margaret complies, and sings from verses written by a lecturer at the Mechanics' Institute (where William Gaskell frequently spoke), only this time in standard English. Mary is not the only one who welcomes it: 'As a factory worker, listening outside, observed, "She spun it reet* fine!" ' (William's footnote translates: '*"Reet", right; often used for "very" '). The ballad represents for Mary an old world of lost loves and lady's maids; yet the new song hardly guarantees a better world. It contains two parts, each exclaiming over 'What a single word can do!' In the first, a word can thrill 'all the heart-strings through'. In the second, it can blast away hope. The new song is a change from the old, but not necessarily in a good direction.

Mary, in her quest to prove Jem's innocence, also grasps the knowledge of accidence. Looking for Will in a strange (and strange-sounding) city, she knows that her plan could be baffled if 'some little accidental occurrence' had led him away from his intended route. The only weapon she carries is memory, as do the other main characters, using it to fight against 'waves of time' that threaten to make each life a freak of chance, rather than part of a meaningful pattern. The memories are often associated with a particular phrase and place. 'Clap-bread' takes Alice back to the county of her childhood and brings her ease of heart; the 'Oldham Weaver' song, whose tale of a past hardship gives Barton strength, comes from a Lancashire town by that name.[79] *Mary Barton* may uphold an ultimate faith in progress, but more striking are the many backward journeys (in thought) that enable characters to go on. The image of waves that erase memory—a natural rhythm—is countered by an effort of human consciousness to circle back at the very moment of trying to adapt to a new situation. The effort makes progress seem more a deliberate act of will, incorporating the past, than a simple reflex of nature.

Emotion, in *Mary Barton*, has its own rhythm that draws from the individual's past, and breaks into the legal process; it has the potential to free one, literally, from prison. It also has its own logic. Gould, summing up the desire for reconciliation among geologists of that period, writes of the two basic metaphors at work: 'time's arrow is the intelligibility of distinct and irreversible events, while time's cycle is the intelligibility of timeless order and lawlike structure. We must have both.'[80] Mary longs for a world outside the trajectory of the legal agenda, and finds it in the 'ramblings' of a sick woman, who talks of her past, and in her own recollection of her mother's voice: 'Old texts from the Bible that her mother used to read (or rather spell out) aloud, in the days of childhood, came up to her memory.'[81] They conjure up a sense of rest, a truth that exists somehow in tandem with the jarring process of the world around her. It is a recurring trope in *Mary Barton*: the act of memory, rather than locking characters into a past, can in fact help them adapt to the present. Adaptation is perhaps closer to the mark than 'progress' in describing the novel's prevailing mode of change.

If Gaskell's narrative strategies permit the use of scientific discourse, Kingsley invites it even more transparently, both in

[79] *Mary Barton*, 41, 220, 138–9, 345, 64, 66, 73.
[80] Gould, *Time's Arrow, Time's Cycle*, 15–6.
[81] *Mary Barton*, 273.

his novel and in his non-fiction. Of particular interest, here, is his understanding of embryology—the science of the embryonic stage of an organism. It may affect how we interpret his fiction of progress. It gave a twist to the widely held conviction that the growth and decay of the individual must somehow fit into a less tragic story for the race. His friend Bunsen in 1854 concluded: 'There is no finite life except unto death; no death except unto higher life. This formula is the solution of the great tragedy of human life.' He points to the origin of language as the 'most primitive and best established proof of this truth'; for 'Every language of which we know the history owes its origin to the decay and decomposition of another.' The history of language, like that of religion, 'constitutes the primordial history of mankind. An element of life, once established, cannot perish as to its principle; but its forms perish in order to bring on a higher development of that element.'[82] A similar idea was spreading in biological science. Kingsley, in his essay on 'natural theology', directs his reader's mind to what Huxley, Darwin, and Owen were saying about embryology.[83] J. W. Burrow remarks upon the impact of embryology on how the Victorians saw 'the relation between structural complexity and chronological sequence'.[84] The human in the uterus moves from a simple to a complex state, as if recapitulating evolutionary stages. This discovery reinforced a similar model constructed by philologists who argued that language, in both the child and the history of mankind, moved from a simple to a complex structure over time. Bunsen, for example, described the 'necessary' progress from inorganic to organic, and from unconscious to conscious forms of life; and insisted that the history of language showed a like progress, where the focus of meaning in an isolated word gave way to the importance of syntax.[85]

Kingsley's use of the autobiographic genre, in *Alton Locke*, is in line with such thinking. He argued, elsewhere, that each man bears the history of his race, each passing through the

---

[82] Bunsen, *Outlines of the Philosophy of Universal History*, i. 35.
[83] Charles Kingsley, 'The Natural Theology of the Future', in *Scientific Lectures and Essays*, 323.
[84] J. W. Burrow, *Evolution and Society* (Cambridge, 1966), 113.
[85] Bunsen, *Outlines of the Philosophy of Universal History*, i. 37; ii. 81.

intellectual growth through which the nation has passed.[86] He shared with Gaskell a Wordsworthian sense of the heart that is common to us all—transcending class, speech, location, and time, in spite of a growing complexity. Where he differs from Gaskell is in his sturdier equation between the direction of growth and a trust in progress.

It is not immediately visible. It contends with the novel's awareness of the role that circumstance plays in an individual's development. The coexistence—of necessary (simple to complex) growth and the accident of location—is key to the novel's apparent inconsistency. By an accident of birth, Alton gets thrown into a workplace where he learns coarseness and slang. If his real-life contemporary Thomas Cooper had not been 'tethered' to a cobbler's bench in youth, he would not have fallen 'a-thinking' as he did, and 'many words would have been left unsaid which, once spoken, working men are not likely to forget'. Crossthwaite despises the government for not protecting children from the degradation that causes them to run wild in the streets, 'vomiting forth slang, filth, and blasphemy'. The ugliness of their surroundings comes out in the speech. London markets send up 'odours as foul as the language of sellers and buyers'; the houses are 'brawling torrents of filth, and poverty, and sin'; while inside the British Museum library await books that might cleanse the wretched city if put to use by the rich.[87]

Recall, however, Kingsley's own mandate to 'work clear of Locke and return to Bacon'.[88] The novel only *seems* undecided in its model of progress, moving back and forth between accidental and linear paths of development. It does not portray a development from slang to standard English; but from the simple to the complex. The latter growth might contain, at every stage, a principle of good (of God's intent), while the former, though seeming a product of chance to the individual, warns society against letting fall its responsibility. It is the social, but not the primary factor. Mackaye instructs Alton: 'Is no the verra

[86] Charles Kingsley, 'On English Composition', in *Literary and General Lectures and Essays* (London, 1890), 234.

[87] *Alton Locke*, 28, 22, 108, 87.

[88] Letter dated 1854, quoted in *Charles Kingsley: Letters and Memories of His Life* (London, 1877), i. 380.

idea of the classic tragedy defined to be, man conquered by circumstance? Canna ye see it there? And the verra idea of the modern tragedy, man conquering circumstance?' He takes Alton to visit a poor family who, in their simplicity, have yet managed to avoid the city's filth; Lizzy, for instance, 'hasn't learnt to say bad words yet'. The Bible (often presented as a text for the poor and otherwise uneducated) gives Ellen words enough to make her a 'better preacher' than Mackaye, for all his background in the classics. There is no fixed relationship between education and progress. A labourer tells Alton: 'Why, when I was a boy, we never had no schooling. And now mine goes and learns singing and jobrafy, and ciphering, and sich like. Not that I sees no good in it. We was a sight better off in the old times, when there weren't no schooling. Schooling harn't made wages rise, nor preaching neither.' His language reveals to Alton 'a mind as ill-educated as discontented'. Compare both his language and temperament with those of Ellen, whose speech, heavily influenced by Scripture (with its 'old English' bias), is simple without deviating much from the norm, and who affects Alton with her bravery in hardship. The labourer may not see any benefit in his son's education; nor do the students at Cambridge offer much hope as the educated; but the culprit is not education, as a value, so much as the failure to direct it towards a selfless end. Note also that Kingsley never puts half-garbled speech in the mouths of those who trust in a final predominance of good. It takes Alton some time even to understand Mackaye— well-read and cynical—through an accent and vocabulary that grow more opaquely Scottish the more upset he becomes.

The idea of relative (or accidental) progress, then, suffers in Kingsley's use of language to convey the direction of the human race. Cycles are introduced to show that the animal part of our nature must be borne—and overcome—as we move towards higher levels of consciousness. Crossthwaite sees it as a sort of trial by fire, and compares Alton to a 'young bear' at the beginning of it: 'you'll find that a working man's training is like the Red Indian children's'. Most die in the flames. For the child of Alton's literate upbringing there were the 'old Jewish heroes', as well as the 'Reformation-martyrs', to look back (and up) to for a point of reference: 'I thought that these were old fairy tales, such as never need be realised again. I learnt otherwise in after years.' Children of rich parents, on the other hand, are favoured with the analogy of the Greek heroes. The sense of historical repetition, on different levels of resemblance, coincides with a biological (or evolutionary) element in the cycle of human nature: in Alton's dream he awakens as a baby ape, and, with a pool as a mirror, sees in his own face 'a melancholy, thoughtful countenance, with large projecting brow—it might have been a negro child's. And I felt stirring in me germs of a new and higher consciousness . . .'. Over the (dream) years he watches in himself 'the fearful degradation which goes on from youth to age in all the monkey race, especially in those which approach nearest to the human form'.[89] He implies that the awareness of growth and decay is pivotal to a rise of consciousness; that different races of people reveal stages towards that cognition. Valerie Shepherd argues that 'Interest in comparative, historical philology links logically with Victorian imperialism and the era's preoccupation with evolution.'[90] Kingsley, in his own life, liked to keep the stages in order. On a trip to Ireland he felt horrified at the peasants, and wrote in a letter home: 'To see white chimpanzees is dreadful; if they were black, one would not feel it so much.' Yet he found the Blacks of the Virgin Islands repulsive: the women worked 'amid screaming, chattering, and language of which, happily, we understood little or nothing'. Even the 'poet of the gang' dismayed him, for 'The tunes were . . . all barbaric'. Such 'brutality' came hard to one who tried 'to believe that all God's humans may be somewhen, somewhere, somehow, reformed into His likeness'.[91]

Trench, a fellow Christian, was writing of the 'evolution of languages' in 1855, and saw the 'speciation' of dialects as the effect of new environments upon a population that had 'been separated off from the main body' of a particular language group.[92] It sounds not unlike Darwin's report of finches on the

---

[89] *Alton Locke*, 89, 90, 122–3, 16, 50, 12–3, 341.
[90] Valerie Shepherd, *Language Variety and the Art of the Everyday* (London, 1990), 34.
[91] Susan Chitty, *The Beast and the Monk* (London, 1974), 209, 259–60.
[92] Trench, *English: Past and Present*, 95, 82–3. As a matter of interest, the 1992 edition of the *Oxford Companion to the English Language* maintains that 'Using a biological analogy, dialects can be described as the result of evolutionary speciation' (p. 290).

Galapagos Islands, where, separated from others of their species, their bills changed in size and shape to adapt to different foods. Kingsley, however, did not swerve towards a model of relative adaptation; rather, he used a triad of historical cycle, the growth and decay of the organism, and the image of a mirror to enhance the idea that a recapitulation of earlier stages is not only human, but a promise of better things to come. Leadership—the carrying of the torch—is bred in the bones of a few, whom others will mimic in time.

Alton Locke invests the poet-leader with a simple, standard English that is meant to reach back into the past (of which the stages bear witness in present *kinds* of people) while aspiring to a richer complexity, not of vocabulary, alone, but of form—a form both old and new. O'Flynn represents the false god. Crossthwaite once believed him to be that rare combination of 'gentleman' and 'thorough-going people's man', with his array of classical learning and his gunfire of 'cerebration', 'eclecticism', and 'mentation'. Alton responds with a meek 'It sounds very grand', but he later deflates the orator's balloon. The 'long gravelly sweeps' of a tidal shore reveal to Alton 'the poetry which lies in common things', and he envisages an age of artists and writers 'tending in that direction': 'from Crabbe and Burns and Wordsworth to Hood and Dickens, the great tide sets ever onward, outward, towards that which is common to the many, not that which is exclusive to the few—towards the likeness of Him who causes His rain to fall on the just and on the unjust'. The *language* of common things, we can infer, is a prose strongly influenced by biblical English, which Alton considers to be a Christianized variety of Old English. When Eleanor appears in his dream as a prophetess she speaks like a book in the Old Testament: 'You shall build cities, and they shall crumble . . .', she tells him; 'For out of Paradise you went, and unto Paradise you shall return . . .'. She denies the futility of the cycle by asserting a value of process: 'You went forth in ignorance and need—you shall return in science and wealth, philosophy and art.' New ideas demand a new vocabulary, but also a form essentially able to handle the additions—a simple base structure that can unfold into a complex design. *Alton Locke*, of the three novels treated here, is the most allegorical—adapting scientific terms to what Alton deems the earliest form of literature, the fairy-tale. His example of the Hebrew stories, as a precursor to his own tale, supports the idea that his autobiography in some way recapitulates the development of literate expression—both keeping the essence of the earliest form, and building onto it a higher degree of consciousness. It supports 'the righteous law of mingled development and renovation', Alton's own expression of the need to combine the arrow and the cycle.[93]

Bunsen's *Philosophy of Universal History* offers a clue to the vision of language at the bedrock of Kingsley's novel. Bunsen accounted for the uneven growth of human varieties by the different circumstances that 'more or less' cradled each:

there will be in some races a more continuous and organic evolution, retaining more of uninterrupted consciousness of the past; while others will tend rapidly towards a premature or conventional development; and others again will preserve the old state with inflexible tenacity. Thus one race will distinguish itself above all others by a full development from the inorganic to the organic formation. Although its language thus becomes in the course of ages the most perfect organic structure, that race will, by virtue of the harmonic development of all its parts toward perfection, preserve more of the ancient heirloom than other less harmoniously developed races.[94]

Bunsen spoke for all three novelists, in degrees of relevance: the ideal language did not shed its parts, but grew complex enough to incorporate them in a plane with modern, linguistic demands. The frailty of the world meant that no language could reach a summit and remain there; but the best might come close.

The novels bring rupture and continuity into play—with audible clashes—opting for a kind of reconciliation. Of the three, *Alton Locke* bears the closest resemblance to Müller's work; at least, it uses a similar motif, wherein bursts of change—often violent—support rather than invalidate a continuum of progress. A key to the paradox may be found in Carlyle's *Past and Present*. Carlyle, whose presence in Kingsley's novel has often been mentioned, asked of his reader:

---

[93] *Alton Locke*, 48, 98, 349–50, 138.
[94] Bunsen, *Outlines of the Philosophy of Universal History*, ii. 101–2, 108.

who taught thee to *speak*? From the day when two hairy-naked or fig-leaved Human Figures began, as uncomfortable dummies, anxious no longer to be dumb, but to impart themselves to one another; and endeavoured, with gaspings, gesturings, with unsyllabled cries, with painful pantomime and interjections, in a very unsuccessful manner,—up to the writing of this present copyright Book, which also is not very successful! Between that day and this, I say, there has been a pretty space of time; a pretty spell of work, which *somebody* has done![95]

Carlyle insists both upon a natural growth from ape to book, and upon the real moment of each creative act. He tries to convince us of the physical presence behind each stage of linguistic development. Carlyle's 'Great Man' theory of history is well known. Scott had followed Percy in a similar view of poetic development. What Kingsley brings most polemically into his novel is the image of the poet-hero as one both capable of error (it makes him human, as did Carlyle's 'not very successful' book) and part of an inevitable flow towards perfect understanding. Kingsley, in a gesture that is part theological and part scientific, writes in the voice of a 'flawed genius' to show that interruptions, while seeming to confute the notion of gradual change, in fact reveal the essence of change to be a realization of what is already inside. The ruptures are both superficial and necessary—as long as the 'nation' remains the best reflection of God's will.

Language, in *Alton Locke*, often serves as a fulcrum in the balance of moment and progress. In the tailor's garret, we hear two varieties of speech express a need to block out all feelings beyond the immediate; with different effect. Jemmy Downes (who torments Alton on his first day of work) sings a 'doggerel song' in Cockney. The words mock those who would plan (and be temperate) for the future, or 'the good of the nation'; far better to indulge in the 'baccy, beer, and gin' that make up the 'prime of a working-tailor's fortin' '. Alton, on the other hand, confesses that his own sole virtue '(if virtue it be) is the power of absorbing my whole heart and mind in the pursuit of the moment, however dull or trivial, if there be good reason why it should be pursued at all'. Standard English voices the mode of

---

[95] Thomas Carlyle, *Past and Present* (1843; Oxford, 1918), 116–17.

experience that holds within each event a teleological sight; Cockney lends itself to unconscious change.

Stagnation occurs on more than one social plane. Mackaye makes a bitter distinction between the words 'brothers' and 'brithren in Christ': 'Ask the preachers. Gin they meant brothers, they'd say brothers, be sure; but because they don't mean brothers at a', they say brithren—ye'll mind, brithren—to soun' antiquate, an' professional, an' perfunctory-like, for fear it should be owre real, an' practical, an' startling, an' a' that . . .'; Robert Burns, in contrast, knew the real meaning of brother-hood. The preachers use language to stall action. Crossthwaite uses the Bible to promote a different sort of inertia: 'Help yourselves and Heaven will help you.' He calls for a strike—an act of sitting still—and for 'combination' (of working people) to fly in the face of any law, social or natural, that lets the rich eat the poor. Combination, while more dynamic in spirit than what the preachers allow, would grind the system to a halt. Alton bypasses the need for a strike in his own vision of a future built on a constant flow of talk:

It is the cities, John, the cities, where the light dawns first—where man meets man, and spirit quickens spirit, and intercourse breeds know-ledge, and knowledge sympathy, and sympathy enthusiasm, combina-tion, power irresistible; while the agriculturalists remain ignorant, selfish, weak, because they are isolated from each other. Let the country go. The towns shall win the Charter for England! And then for social reform, sanitary reform, ædile reform, cheap food, interchange of free labour, liberty, equality, and brotherhood for ever!

Alton thus makes uneven development within a nation part of his argument for the link between intercourse and national progress. Brotherhood (Burns notwithstanding) is a forward-looking glimpse of England that includes the erudite (note 'ædile'!) in its vocabulary.

The novel stresses the value of the individual act in the process of transformation, even if each merely quickens a potential already there. The weakness of Chartism, Alton finds, is the tendency of its proponents to see man 'as the creature and puppet of circumstances—of the particular outward system, social or political, in which he happens to find himself'. Sudden events, collapses in time, parry the image of gradual, inevitable change. Alton observes with relief that 'the morals of the working-tailors, as well as of other classes of artisans, are rapidly improving', in part because of 'the wisdom and kindness of a few master-tailors'. God forbid we cite evolution as an excuse for apathy. Alton identifies his own literary fervour with abrupt social change: 'In the history of individuals, as well as in that of nations, there is often a period of sudden blossoming . . .'; the blossom may include a storm. His description of the city bears an inverted likeness to Müller's image of the frozen river of literary language, broken up by disturbances within: 'It was a dark, noisy, thunderous element, that London life; a troubled sea that cannot rest, casting up mire and dirt . . .'. Yet the older Alton, looking back, sees the danger of allowing too much dirt to rise to the surface, unfiltered. Sudden events are not to give way to agitated, unthinking response. They are to serve as upthrusts of revelation, where things that had been slowly developing appear on the surface. Recall the episode in *Mary Barton* when Mary, shocked by her own rejection of Jem, sees in a moment the love that had been growing in her all along, and the grief she must feel in a future without him. In Kingsley's novel, when Mackaye dies, Crossthwaite and Alton feel themselves 'trembling between two worlds': 'Even our passionate artisan-nature, so sensitive and voluble in general, in comparison with the cold reserve of the field-labourer and the gentleman, was hushed in silent awe between the thought of the past and the thought of the future.' Their sight, though hazy, is just clear enough to show them a looming evil, to augur the downfall of their movement.

The novel attests to the inadequacy of any system, in contrast with a more fluid reliance upon the spirit of God. The older Alton looks back with some chagrin on a time when he, like other Chartists, made an idol of Electoral Reform, hoping to gain a stronger voice in (he quotes Carlyle) 'the national palaver'. Parliament is too amoral a system to guide him, or anyone else. Nor does the Established Church offer trustworthy, spiritual help, with the exception of a few such men as Thomas Arnold. Clergymen, in general, rely upon empty creeds and forms to guarantee their right to lead; they betray 'in every tract, in every sermon, an ignorance of the doubts, the feelings, the very language of the masses'. Nor is the working-class mind able to heal the linguistic breach, as Alton demonstrates in his fiery burst of outrage at the Press—spreading evil words that will excite only the already excitable Chartist. Although the older Alton does not give a fully sympathetic portrait of the Dean, he accords with him on one main point. The Dean likens the 'true poet' to the 'rational Christian', who believes 'that inspiration is continual and orderly, that it reveals harmonious laws, not merely excites sudden emotions'. He scoffs at both the modern poet and the Quakers who suppose inspiration 'to be only extraordinary and paroxysmic'. His scorn foreshadows the distaste that soon turns Alton away from the style of O'Flynn, writer for the *Weekly Warwhoop*—a fitting vehicle of 'that perennial hurricane of plotting, railing, sneering, and bombast, in which he lived, never writing a line, on principle, till he had worked himself up into a passion'.[96]

The penultimate chapter of *Mary Barton* features a debate between Mr Carson and Job. Job, who once took pride in his familiarity with obscure terms and phrases, now defers in matters of eloquence to the businessman. He claims that the power-looms 'make a man's life like a lottery', but admits that they, like all inventions, are 'the gifts of God'. Time restores a sense of progress: Job is old enough 'to see that it is part of His plan to send suffering to bring out a higher good'. So is Mary. When she rejects Jem, the 'comparative peace' of her life gives way to 'the violence of her sobs'—an event of sudden change that turns out to be part of the gradual dawning of her love. Yet Gaskell's treatment of Mary, in comparison with that of Job, turns on a different angle. The narrator assumes we *all* share the girl's experience: 'For we have every one of us felt how a very few minutes of the months and years called life, will sometimes suffice to place all time past and future in an entirely new light . . .'. Such moments 'may change our character for life'.[97] Mr Carson, after all, is altered deeply by the unexpected murder of his son. The poor simply have fewer ways of blotting out misfortune. Mary feels the suddenness more than the overall direction, and the narrator gives more credence (by lending

[96] *Alton Locke*, 26–7, 267, 104, 303, 110, 27, 94, 320, 110, 192, 194, 164, 192.
[97] *Mary Barton*, 37–8, 457, 176.

voice) to her experience than to Job's philosophy of progress. In the lectures, William Gaskell claims that the Saxons invaded not in a flash, but had spread into England more slowly than historians once led us to think. He uses the invasion to illustrate the 'ordinary rule' of civilized languages overpowering the ruder ones.[98] *Mary Barton*, on the other hand, tends in its subjective detail to evoke the abruptness of change, and the emptiness of knowing that gradual change for the better happens outside the rim of most people's experience. These two phenomena are linked to social barriers of speech, which may in part explain the shift in emphasis from civil progress to divine.

A SUMMARY

The model of contrast between analogy and homology—central to debates in biology about the way to classify, and the role of inheritance—is useful in our study of language in nineteenth-century fiction, where tension pulls at the link between body and speech. We see a double image. Nature is shown to be a chaotic force; biology, akin to chance and eruptive change. Yet language, as our potential to emerge from the model of accident, is portrayed as a natural gift. 'False' leaders are the ones who use language artificially—as a tool apart from true intent. In *Mary Barton* we find an attempt to make a 'plain' speech that reflects autonomy rather than rhetoric; to distinguish between the use of language to express truth, and to manipulate. We are given to infer that language is a tool. Plain speech fits into the metaphor, as a deliberate mix of emotion and analysis.

The ability to translate implies that numerous tongues can convey one idea (on the basis of analogy); yet in all the fiction, here, there is reference to kin, province, or race. Genealogy is not far around the corner. Often, the plainest speech—closest to the truth—is aligned with traits that are inherited. In *Alton Locke*, a displacement of the family suggests that the lineage is racial. Scott and Gaskell tend to focus on influences closer to home. What all three share is a use of metaphor (in a mix that appears almost careless at times) to associate plain speech with

---

[98] William Gaskell, 'Two Lectures on the Lancashire Dialect', 362, 363.

an individual's choice to control events; with motives that take into account the well-being of the community. It makes the difference between a wise and a selfish use of language; between adaptation and badly understood teleology. Where metaphors blur—among nature, divine gifts, and ladders of speech—we can see an attempt to fit moral agency into a new model of progress that admits as much uncertainty about the future as the past. Plain speech is invoked as a safe bet. It checks logic—the abstract science of outcome—with past loyalties and desires. It ensures a sense of belonging, and choice.

Geology exploded the image of time in more than one way. The scale became larger, while the certainty of direction shrank. We see a change in the idea of latency: the germ does not imply a single expression, over time, but rather a whole set of possible responses that, because of time, may preclude one another. In the novels, our view of the future stops *in medias res*. We are asked to trust (with varying degrees of hopefulness) in those who draw from their own varieties of speech the elements that link inheritance (the nouns of home and country) with the ability for abstract thought—to put old elements to work in moments of unpredictable need.

The novels do not give in to the 'bogey of chance', but nor do they offer a clear organization—*Mary Barton* perhaps least of all. Two movements can be traced. The microscope is lifted back to 'prove' social chaos to be the product of our myopia. At the same time, interest in psychology was growing in the nineteenth century. Language often stole the focus. Speech inside the home gave clues to motive and development. The new science shared with geology the image of growth in layers; the idea that an individual form is evidence of a great sweep of development through time; the attempt, in such a scheme of recapitulation, to explain odd 'shapes'. The novels, with their pressure for change and acute sense of the peculiar, lend themselves to a study of how people tried (in the nineteenth century, at least) to fit idiosyncrasy into a model of progress—where speech may be more skill than identity. The 'mirror of growth', as a metaphor of language, in the fiction grew a troubled face.

4

Figures of Speech: Language and
the Family Dynamic

The palace and the castle may have come to us from the
Norman, but to the Saxon we owe far dearer names, the
home, the hearth, the house, the roof.[1]

(Trench)

SCIENTIFIC discourse added to linguistics the metaphors of
age, duration, and excavation. Huge sweeps of time seemed to
characterize the philologists' model of inquiry. And yet, within
this model, they took an interest in life on a much smaller
scale—in the home. Hensleigh Wedgwood, friend and cousin of
Gaskell, denied that modern words bore little reference to the
past; he recalled to readers a time when geology had seemed just
as futile—when 'our ancestors' thought it impossible 'to obtain
personal experience of the powers by which the surface of the
earth has been reduced to its present form'. Etymology would
prove to be no less thinkable than geology had done. The key,
available to us all, lay in 'the infant learning to speak'.[2] Not all
philologists agreed with his model—of childhood recapitulating
the history of language—but many drew upon metaphors of the
closest family ties. Analysis of 'Saxon English', in particular, lent
itself to the union of history, nation, and hearth. Two ends of a
pole—evolutionary and domestic—often collapsed into single
images.

One explanation is the anthropological bent of much of the
research. Vocabularies were noted more easily from objects of
daily life than from abstract ideas. A parallel was drawn
between the search for original language(s) and the study of

---

[1] Richard Chenevix Trench, *On the Study of Words* (London, 1851), 61.
[2] Hensleigh Wedgwood, *A Dictionary of English Etymology* (London, 1859),
pp. iv–v.

other, 'uncultivated' societies outside urban Britain. Hilary Henson writes of the related sciences, claiming that 'Accounts of primitive languages generally consisted of brief word-lists elicited from interpreters, or from sessions of pointing and asking for names.'[3] It is hard to point to ideas. Many linguists described both ancient and present speakers of 'primitive languages' as being without the ability to think in abstract terms. Such people, instead, needed the physical body of the mother, or the heat of the fire, or the cold feel of water, to link object and word. Language, for them, existed spatially; one could trust a word only as far as one could throw it.

Ironically, the Victorian period also saw a proliferation of books, articles, and pamphlets that 'named' the centre of cultivated life—the middle-class home. The home was sifted into minute parts, showing standards of taste in furniture, speech, food, and dress. Writers pointed to objects and intonations, saying 'good' or 'bad', turning the home into a set of 'rules by which individual personality became a social category'.[4] The idea of home, as the matrix of civil behaviour, coexisted with an interest in words that could look into the 'dark passages' of our primitive beginnings.[5]

Ideas about a child's development often got mixed with value-laden discourses on non-standard English speech—either from the past or in the present. Family, speech, and the very notion of development got conflated when, for example, linguists probed words that spoke of domestic relations. Wedgwood analysed the word 'husband' as follows: 'the element *band* is extant as a substantive word in the Scandinavian languages. The Icel. *bondi*, *husbondi*, Dan. *bonde*, *husbonde*, the master of the household, paterfamilias, colonus, ruricola, is commonly explained as from *buandi*, *boandi*, the active participle of *bua*, *bos*, to dwell, to till.'[6] His etymology looks disinterested

---

[3] Hilary Henson, 'Early British Anthropologists and Language', in Edwin Ardener (ed.), *Social Anthropology and Language* (London, 1971), 8.

[4] Andrew St George, *The Descent of Manners* (London, 1993), 105.

[5] John Cleland in 1766 described his job in etymology as 'illustrating dark passages in history'. Quoted from his book *The Way to Things by Words, and To Words by Things*, in Murray Cohen, *Sensible Words* (Baltimore, 1977), 134.

[6] Hensleigh Wedgwood, 'On False Etymologies', *Transactions of the Philological Society*, no. 6 (23 Mar. 1855), 63.

enough; but it is worth noting the use of family terms in a science (a nascent linguistics) that explored kinship as a metaphor of language. Attempts in philology (or comparative linguistics) to find universal principles of language used—as examples—words denoting private experience.

Novels fit into the pattern because, in the nineteenth century at least, much of their action occurs between walls. The usual form, of interpolating dialogue in narrative, merges with the novel's use of space: people in a room tend to speak to one another, not write. Speech took up a special domain of value. In 1859 James Hunt, speech therapist to the stuttering Charles Kingsley, contrasted written and spoken English; he noted 'a considerable difference with regard to the number of Teutonic and Romance terms used in our written and spoken language. In the former, one-half of the words will mostly be found to be of foreign extraction, whilst in the latter, three-fourths, at least, are home-grown'.[7] He thereby links domesticity, and a greater percentage of racial 'purity', with speech over the written word.

The 'Teutonic' languages often evoked the home. De Quincey, writing *On Wordsworth*, argued that lyricism and 'domestic affections' are the natural province of 'Saxon words'. Saxon was the 'aboriginal element'; it was 'the language of the nursery whether for rich or poor, in which great philological academy no toleration is given to words ending in "osity" or "ation".'[8] Few writers wanted a totally 'Saxon' language. Kingsley believed that 'Anglo-Saxon, (a female race) required impregnation by the great male race,—the Norse introduction of Northmen by Edward paving the way for the Conquest, &c.'[9] Dickens claimed that 'pure Teutonic' was spoken in England for 600 years—until 1066, when Norman French ('a sort of corrupt Latin') invaded. He predicted that the love of Latin, prevailing in Queen Anne's day, would soon give way to a love of books in 'Saxon-English'. Writers will come closest to 'all hearts with

---

[7] James Hunt, *A Manual of the Philosophy of Voice and Speech* (London, 1859), 221.

[8] Quoted in Richard Chenevix Trench, *English: Past and Present* (London, 1855), 21–2.

[9] From a letter dated 17 Apr. 1849, in *Charles Kingsley: His Letters and Memories of His Life* (London, 1877), i. 201.

words [i.e. Saxon] that are familiar in every home, and find their way even into the prattle of the nursery'.[10] Gaskell rebuked one of her daughters, Marianne, for allowing French to enter her closet. Marianne had written 'chemise' when she ought to have chosen 'the pretty simple *English* word'; for 'As Mrs. Davenport said the other day, "It is only washerwomen who call Shifts *chemises* now".' In a letter to a friend, Gaskell mocks the elaborate style of Johnson, with his non-Saxon words.[11]

Latin forms, not surprisingly, were often associated with men and the outside world. Diana Vernon, in *Rob Roy*, studies the classics, but Frank (the narrator) deems it a very masculine trait; yet it takes her away from her rather crude, hard-drinking 'family' of male cousins. In Gaskell's *Ruth*, the mother wants to learn Latin to be able to give it to her son, though she knows it will take him to a world beyond her. In 'Cousin Phillis', Paul tells his father why he cannot marry Phillis: he describes her as 'more like a man than a woman—she knows Latin and Greek'. The father answers, 'She'd forget 'em, if she'd a houseful of children.'[12] In Kingsley's *Westward Ho!* Frank writes letters to his father that are 'full of Latin quotations'; his mother, on the other hand, collects his 'diplomas and letters of recommendation, the Latin whereof she was always spelling over (although she understood not a word of it), in the hopes of finding, here and there, that precious *excellentissimus Noster Franciscus Leighius Anglus*, which was all in all to the mother's heart'.[13] Of the three authors, Kingsley offers the dichotomy with the lightest shade of doubt or parody.

George Eliot in 1856 saw a connection between women, domesticity, and national speech. In 'The Natural History of German Life' she describes a Slavonic race, called the Wends, living in Lusatia 'either scattered among the German population or in separate parishes'. They educated their children in the Slavonic language. Eliot writes of the cultural tension: 'German

[10] Charles Dickens, 'Saxon-English', in W. F. Bolton and D. Crystal (eds.), *The English Language 1858–1964* (London, 1969), 1–7.
[11] Elizabeth Gaskell, *Letters* (Manchester, 1966), nos. 117, 9.
[12] Elizabeth Gaskell, 'Cousin Phillis', in *Cousin Phillis and Other Tales* (Oxford, 1991), 291.
[13] Charles Kingsley, *Westward Ho!* (1855; London, 1906), 26.

education, German law and government, service in the standing army, and many other agencies, are in antagonism to [the Wends'] national exclusiveness; but the *wives* and *mothers* here, as elsewhere, are a conservative influence, and the habits temporarily laid aside in the outer world are recovered by the fireside.' Women hold onto the early language—the language spoken first in the home—in this case Slavonic. And yet the home is not impermeable; 'official' education can seep in. Eliot notes that in Hungary, for instance, it is the outdoor German colonists, the wandering reapers, who retain 'their old Saxon songs and manners', while the 'more cultivated' emigrants soon forget their own language and speak Hungarian instead. Cultivation mixes with settled life and a loss (or change) of national identity. A much smaller unit of identity, in conjunction with literacy, is formed: 'In the cultivated world each individual has his style of speaking and writing. But among the peasantry it is the race, the district, the province, that has its style; namely, its dialect, its phraseology, its proverbs and its songs, which belong alike to the entire body of the people.'[14]

In Eliot's novel *Adam Bede* we are invited to question the origin of a song. Did it come from one mind or many? 'There is a stamp of unity, of individual genius, upon it, which inclines me to the former hypothesis . . .', says the narrator, adding, however, that 'this unity may rather have arisen from that consensus of many minds which was a condition of primitive thought, foreign to our modern consciousness'.[15] In essay and novel, Eliot sees the modern (cultivated) self as more self-enclosed than its predecessor. For the peasantry, the home is where the culture and dialect of 'the entire body of the people' is orally handed down; for the cultivated, it reinforces a singularity of style—often in a written form. It is not the home itself, then, that retains or adjusts language. More accurately, it is the mixture of cultural pressures that determines how (and in how many ways) the home will be of influence. Eliot presented a model of living dialects holding fragments of ancestral memory—

[14] George Eliot, 'The Natural History of German Life', in *Essays of George Eliot* (London, 1968), 275.
[15] George Eliot, *Adam Bede* (1859; New York, 1965), 531.

the 'consensus of many minds'. At the same time, there was a growing interest among Victorians in how words spoke of the *individual's* past; in how they related to an individual's psychological growth, creating a unique style—an idiom. Ideas were forming on speech as an access to psychological history—a history that shaped itself primarily in the home. The novels, here, contain moments of language (or dialect) acquisition revealing how each writer connected images of domesticity and the 'body of the people' to an understanding of character development. Horace Churchill, in Maria Edgeworth's *Helen*, tells the ladies that 'the language of every country is, to a certain degree, evidence, record, history of his character and manners'.[16] Character may be individual or national. Scott, a fan of Edgeworth's writing, claimed in his own *Minstrelsy* that the poetry of a nation depends on the character of its people, events, and the character of the language.[17] James Hunt, decades later, collapsed the scale: 'the history of the origin and growth of the English idiom, is the history of England. Language may, therefore, without much impropriety, be called the *psychogram of man's inward nature*.'[18] Usually 'idiom' refers to a person's unique form of speech or writing; Hunt uses it, here, synonymously with 'language', imagining a single matrix of individual and collective identity.

Stefan Collini writes at length on the idea and value of character in the nineteenth century.[19] The point to be made here is the departure from eighteenth-century struggles for a universal language that would erase difference. George Eliot asks her reader to suppose the globalizing scheme had worked; to imagine

that you have a language which has no uncertainty, no whims of idiom, no cumbrous forms, no fitful shimmer of many-hued significance, no hoary archaism 'familiar with forgotten years'—a potent de-odorized

---

[16] Maria Edgeworth, *Helen* (1834; London, 1987), 135.
[17] Walter Scott, *The Minstrelsy of the Scottish Border* (1802–3; Edinburgh, 1850), i. 11.
[18] Hunt, *A Manual of the Philosophy of Voice and Speech*, 203.
[19] Stefan Collini, *Public Moralists* (Oxford, 1993), throughout.

and non-resonant language, which effects the purpose of communication as perfectly and rapidly as algebraic signs. Your language may be a perfect medium of expression to science, but will never express *life*, which is a great deal more than science.

For Eliot, though, it was not enough simply to record variations. She lauded Dickens for his precise rendering of 'idiom and manners', but complained that he fails to give us 'psychological character'.[20] The goal was to connect speech with emotion and motive. In many nineteenth-century novels, the idea of character merges with a uniqueness of speech; childhood memory was often used to put a response to events into a pattern of identity. In the works cited here, at least, the sound of a voice or the utterance of a word, apart from syntax, re-create for the character a past that gives the present more meaning. The character's action is shown to be founded upon a previous emotional complex involved with a particular form of speech.

In the eighteenth century Rousseau had argued for the primacy of the home in a child's development, and for the link between his first encounter with language and his relation to the people around him: 'If the voice of blood is not strengthened by habit and care, it is extinguished in the first years, and the heart dies, so to speak, before being born.' Characters differ because of their linguistic environment: 'Minds are formed by languages; the thoughts take on the colour of the idioms.' The 'most important' education, the first, 'belongs incontestably to women'.[21] In the mid-nineteenth century F. D. Maurice called the family the matrix of character.[22] He wrote of the 'primitive language' of infancy, which 'bears witness to hidden springs in ourselves, to hidden springs in our *neighbours*'.[23] His idea of character, though, flows into a concept of the underlying 'springs' of the nation. Like many popular linguists of the day, Maurice drew large circles of identity around patterns of speech; yet connections were being made, none the less, between idioms and factors that affected a person's unique development. Only, they can seldom be disentangled from national terms.

---

[20] Eliot, 'The Natural History of German Life', 287–8, 271.
[21] Jean-Jacques Rousseau, *Émile* (Harmondsworth, 1979), 46–7, 109, 37.
[22] F. D. Maurice, 'Social Morality', in *Social Morality* (London, 1893), 9–10.
[23] F. D. Maurice, 'Language', in *Social Morality*, 134.

Alexander Bain, a Victorian psychologist known to George Eliot, defined the ear as a 'matrix for holding together our recollections of language'. His theory of 'the acquisition of the Mother Tongue' is similar to John Locke's. Bain held that 'we remember much sooner the names of things that impress us, than the names of indifferent things'. That is why our first language is the most evocative:

In acquiring Foreign Languages by the usual methods, we have more of the purely verbal than in the mother tongue. We do not usually connect the names of a foreign language with the objects, but with the names already learnt. We may connect sound with sound, as when we are taught orally, articulation with articulation, or mark with mark in the eye. Thus 'domus' and 'house' may be associated as two sounds, two articulations, or two sights.

In the mother tongue, by contrast, 'house' is a complex of known objects and relations. But memories are a mix of 'pure ideas of the actions and scenes themselves' and 'verbal descriptions' (whether or not these are told); so even the once palpable 'house' of childhood comes to us through language. The difference is one of immediacy. It is easier to hear an utterance in our first language, 'even when very faintly pronounced', than in our second: 'The same contrast is observed between a familiar voice and the voice of a stranger. . . . The more thoroughly accustomed the mental system is to an impression, the lighter the touch needed to make it present at any moment.'[24]

Questions of mind and body, and what made the link, came into even the more pragmatic writings on speech. James Hunt treated Kingsley for a stammer. His *Manual of the Philosophy of Voice and Speech* is appropriately named. It sets practical medical advice next to theories of language variation and descent. He dedicates the work to Kingsley: 'It will ever be to me a source of the greatest satisfaction that I have been instrumental in enabling you more freely to give *vivâ voce* expression to those noble thoughts which breathe in all your writings.' His book makes physiology indispensable to language. He calls the nervous system 'that part of our organism which connects body

---

[24] Alexander Bain, *The Senses and the Intellect* (London, 1855), 475, 432, 433, 447, 460.

and mind'. He cites the linguist Steinthal, who wrote *Ursprung der Sprache* in 1851, and who 'conceives that mind and body were originally so dependent on each other, that all the mental emotions found their echo in the body, especially in the respiratory and vocal organs'. Hunt believed that the echo still occurs in the child and savage—just as it had in 'the primitive man'. The modern, civilized adult operates less by instinct, and is able to 'subdue his vocal organs [to] form articulate sounds' that designate objects and their relations outside himself. A parrot, by contrast, only mimics. It learns by rote and does not really *speak*, because thought precedes speech.[25] Neither instinct nor mimicry, Hunt implies, is rational thought.

Locke, too, had insisted that 'some, not only Children, but Men, speak several Words, no otherwise than Parrots do'—not because they know the meaning, but because they are 'accustomed to those Sounds'.[26] If Robinson Crusoe had caught a parrot, as he wished, and had taught it to speak to him, it would have given him but the echo of his own thoughts.[27] The image of the parrot comes up in several of the novels, here, to suggest words that are empty of thought. Mimicry had a place in society none the less. Lady Cuxhaven, in Gaskell's *Wives and Daughters*, wants to bring up a French girl with her own daughters in order 'that they might get a good accent early'. Accent alone (not French ideas) was a mark of class. Cynthia, who studied French in Boulogne, laughs 'at Molly's earnest endeavours to imitate the French accent in which the former had been reading a page of Voltaire'.[28] In 1834 an anonymous guide to etiquette stated that 'The moment a Woman speaks, you can tell whether you are listening to a lady or not. The tone of voice, the accent, the use of peculiar phrases . . .'.[29] Inquiry into the content of what is said, in *Wives and Daughters*, is sometimes less urgent than acquiring a habit of sound. Mimicry of tone

---

[25] Hunt, *A Manual of the Philosophy of Voice and Speech*, iii, 33, 171, 132.
[26] John Locke, *An Essay Concerning Human Understanding* (1690; Oxford, 1975), 408.
[27] Daniel Defoe, *The Life and Adventures of Robinson Crusoe* (1719; Harmondsworth, 1972), 122.
[28] Elizabeth Gaskell, *Wives and Daughters* (1864; Oxford, 1991), 19, 329.
[29] *Etiquette, Social Ethics, and the Courtesies of Society* (1834), quoted in L. C. Mugglestone, 'Ladylike Accents', in *Notes & Queries*, 235 (Mar. 1990), 5.

could affect *development*, and thus be seen as a cause, not just a gauge. Collini mentions Bain, among other popular mid-Victorian psychologists and physiologists, who 'toyed with the notion that habit could modify or leave a deposit in the nervous system itself'.[30] Registers of speech depended not just on class and region, but on the time (duration and the speaker's age) of acquisition as well. For all the links made to physiology, books and manuals on voice tended to focus on the ability to change the way we sound. It is hard to rebuild our flesh and organs.

St George writes of the Victorian fascination with the art of conversation: 'it represented an area of private life open to the dictates of self-improvement which was also an area of public life where progress could be tested against contemporaries'.[31] Armstrong, too, believes that domestic fiction and conduct books transformed fantasies of 'self-production' into a social sphere.[32] There was ambivalence in the project to pin down speech, even in the home, in spite of all the cries for a standard; as if, for speech to be useful in itself, there had to be a forever elusive 'right' way to talk.

If the voices around us, in childhood, prompted our own vocal development, and if speech grew with character, was character then determined by our childhood home? How does the tension between individual and family identity arise? Murray Cohen's study of linguistics in England shows that by the end of the eighteenth century linguists 'understand language to be the means of communicating the intentions and feelings of speakers to hearers'.[33] The link between idiom and motive got formed among writings on psychology. J. S. Mill wrote that 'every individual is surrounded by circumstances different from those of every other individual; every nation or generation of mankind from every other nation or generation: and none of these differences are without their influence in forming a different type of character'. Language was 'the depository of the accumulated body of experience'. It followed patterns of

---

[30] Collini, *Public Moralists*, 98.
[31] St George, *The Descent of Manners*, 64–5.
[32] Nancy Armstrong, *Desire and Domestic Fiction* (New York, 1987), 164.
[33] Cohen, *Sensible Words*, 135–6.

inheritance. Our creation of meaning, then, was in relation to a lexicon of the past generation.[34] Mill put individual expression—and, by implication, needs—into a framework of limited response.

By the mid-1860s, though, Müller was lecturing: 'Even we, in this literary age, and at a distance of thousands of years from those early fathers of language, do not speak at home as we speak in public.'[35] We can see nineteenth-century fiction dealing with the split in two ways. Speech that is particular to home life is in some cases made part of the dynamic that forms a character's motives and emotions. In others, the gap itself plays a greater role in the formation of desire.

The dilemma of wanting to promote a 'language of the nursery', while yet urging the need for development and a measure of progress, can be illustrated in two works by Bain, published over twenty years apart. In *An English Grammar* (1863) he defines 'Anglo-Saxon' as a slightly misleading term, and quotes Müller to show the abundance of English words derived from 'a Latin source'. Anglo-Saxon gave us 'the names connected with kindred, home, domestic life, and the strong natural feelings and their expression'. Psychology, though, requires some articulation of how these feelings relate to the unique self, and Bain contends that 'the Saxon vocabulary' has little to offer in that respect: 'the great mass of words for the mental operations are of classical origin'.[36] In a later book, he puts the case more strongly, referring to 'superstition about keeping to Saxon'. Not only would it be impossible to write in 'pure Saxon'; it would also be self-limiting. Some Norman French words, after all, 'were adopted as universal household words; being, in fact, incorporated with the old vocabulary'.[37]

Bain's growing sense of the need to include a Latin-based vocabulary puts a few of the novels' idiosyncrasies into a clearer light. The 'mother tongue', in all of them, is seen as a way of getting into a character's formative self; into the basic structure,

---

[34] John Stuart Mill, *A System of Logic* (1843; Toronto, 1974), books IV–VI, pp. 864, 869, 685.

[35] Max Müller, *Lectures on the Science of Language* (1861; London, 1871), i. 63.

[36] Alexander Bain, *An English Grammar* (London, 1863), 120, 128, 129.

[37] Alexander Bain, *On Teaching English* (London, 1887), 4, 1–2.

almost, of his or her development. At the same time, language is presented as a *measure* of thought, revealing by its different forms the presence or lack of intelligence. The marriage that Kingsley envisioned, between Saxon and Latin, draws language and character into a model of domesticity, while implying that the history of English (and England) gives the modern speaker a better way of expressing a more civilized origin.

THE FICTION

Scott would not have read Bain prior to writing *The Heart of Midlothian*. But he might have encountered similar ideas. Thomas Sheridan in 1781 claimed that 'there is not an act of the mind, an exertion of the fancy, or emotion of the heart, which have not annexed to them their peculiar tone and notes of the voice, by which they are to be expressed'.[38] Tone of voice, in Scott's novel, reveals in Madge her national identity: 'A voice was heard to sing in one of those wild and monotonous strains so common in Scotland . . .'. Yet it also reveals a state of mind: Madge's mother, half-crazed throughout, screams for her child 'at the highest pitch of her cracked and mistuned voice'. These examples are of static associations; Madge's Scottishness and her mother's wildness do not change in the course of the novel. But Sheridan wrote of a person's *range* of vocal performance, which complicates identity. Scott understood. Reuben Butler, who loves Jeanie Deans, is the local scholar. Jeanie speaks in Scots, Reuben in standard English. Yet, strong feelings—of pride (in his own knowledge of Latin) and exasperation (at Saddletree's ignorance)—affect his voice: ' "Then, what the *deevil* d'ye take the nominative and the dative cases to be?" said Butler, hastily, and surprised at once out of his decency of expression and accuracy of pronunciation.'

Scott was also aware of the rhetoric of tone—the use of sound to persuade. Jeanie feels she must go to London herself to beg for her sister's life: 'writing winna do it—a letter canna look, and pray, and beg, and beseech, as the human voice can do to the human heart. A letter's like the music that the ladies have for

---

[38] Quoted from Sheridan's *Rhetorical Grammar*, in Cohen, *Sensible Words*, 108.

their spinets—naething but black scores, compared to the same played or sung. It's word of mouth maun do it, or naething, Reuben.'[39]

The human voice can play a variation on a theme, and not just state it baldly. It affects the heart directly, unlike the score that must be translated into feeling. It is as if Jeanie were anticipating the ideas of Charles Lunn, who in the early 1870s defined words as metaphors that 'mean nothing in themselves'. They do not have a physical impact. There is a great difference between the word 'sun' and the feel of warmth; the mind has to make a connection. '[B]ut a beautiful sound of voice appeals direct to the emotions'.[40] Lunn, like Bain, refers to the music not *in* speech, but in contradistinction to it. The sound of the voice, not the words, affect the heart. Jeanie's drawing-room analogy, by contrast, brings into play both manner *and* content.

Effie, Jeanie's sister, adapts her speech, and especially her writing, to meet the new codes of her husband's world; and yet the change simply draws upon a quality that had always been there in her childhood. Margaret Hale, in Gaskell's *North and South*, learns new words in a new city, but how much of her self is truly changed by the experience? A look at her various duties gives an answer: 'She had planned other employments for herself: a letter to Edith, a good piece of Dante, a visit to the Higginses.'[41] Each task involves a linguistic variant, dating from three separate episodes in her life. The juxtaposition of diverse elements, like a trick by Alexander Pope, suggests a singleness of character in all her duties, with a touch of humour (unbeknownst to her) at her deafness to any incongruity. Ayacanora (in Kingsley's *Westward Ho!*) learns English (again), but in a model of rehabilitation that undermines our impression of radical change.

Most nineteenth-century novels, however, put a much slighter amount of adaptation (if any) into the speech itself. Even novels depicting a character's growth (*Alton Locke*, for example) seldom alter the way a character speaks from beginning to end,

---

[39] Walter Scott, *The Heart of Midlothian* (1818; Oxford, 1982), 156, 185, 51, 267.
[40] Charles Lunn, *The Philosophy of Voice* (London, 1874), 37.
[41] Elizabeth Gaskell, *North and South* (1854–5; Oxford, 1982), 75.

despite the introduction of new influences. An exception is Eliot's *The Mill on the Floss*. The adult Tullivers speak in a Warwickshire dialect. So do the various aunts and uncles. The two children, Maggie and Tom, come into the novel speaking a language close to their parents'—though with fewer marks of dialect. By the middle, however, they have adopted standard English. The adults do not change at all. What does this suggest? Have the parents gone past the age of 'pliant' minds and vocal organs? Unlike *The Heart of Midlothian*, Eliot's novel shows in fine detail the children's acquisition of new forms of language. Each has a different lesson to learn, in accord with social expectations. Tom, at King's Lorton, discovers that 'life, complicated not only with the Latin grammar but with a new standard of English pronunciation, was a very difficult business, made all the more obscure by a thick mist of bashfulness'. Language comes at him like a hurdle; he brings to it his own psychological complex; later, we see two traits—a new dialect and a new confidence—emerge together, with only a hint of cause and effect. The status he achieves is both a part of and larger than himself: 'Tom's ear and tongue had become accustomed to a great many words and phrases which are understood to be signs of an educated condition . . .'. The narrator could hardly have made a more cautious (or ironic) choice of words. Maggie, on the other hand, 'had only been to school a year at St. Ogg's, and had so few books that she sometimes read the dictionary'. Her propensity—to study—is already there when she looks at a scarcity of resources. Like Tom, she *responds to* her linguistic environment; in both cases, we must assume that the beginnings (though not the whole) of character-formation took place near birth. Different predispositions meet different opportunities. Maggie has to fight against the lexicon of romance. A lover's attentions 'summon a little of the too-ready, traitorous tenderness into a woman's eyes, compelled as she is in her girlish time to learn her life-lessons in very trivial language'.[42] The novel stirs up many times the bitter-sweet bond between the affections of the heart and the codes of

---

[42] George Eliot, *The Mill on the Floss* (1860; Oxford, 1980), 117–18, 133–4, 98, 368.

society, until the two get blended together, and it is hard to know what a character really wants or intends.

Eliot's reference to 'a woman's eyes' and 'language' may be read in the context of a Victorian mixture of physiology and psychology. Bain compared the voice to the eye and the ear, 'in both which a diminutive amount of muscular substance is the seat of a powerful sensibility'. Bain, like Eliot, implied that children bring to language—even to the mother tongue—a complex of feelings: 'Intense feelings affect the whole of the moving organs, but all organs are not equally moved. The parts first acted on by any feeling are the features and the respiratory and vocal organs, which are therefore by pre-eminence the organs of *expression*, some of them, indeed, serving hardly for any other purpose.'[43] The structure of the body makes language the natural expression of feeling. It is a neat idea. The novels, however, make it harder for us to assume a linear sequence. Schor, discussing *Mary Barton*, argues that the problem with Gaskell's reliance upon 'maternal wisdom' is that it requires children who 'have a language to ask for only the simplest needs'.[44] The point remains that they *do* ask. For the rest of the chapter I will look at how novels bring to the level of commentary a link between language variation and feelings and intentions; how a character, by slipping among varieties, may actively manipulate events by affecting emotions; how rhetoric fits into a model that puts a family dynamic anterior to speech.

' "Donna thee sit up, mother," said Adam, in a gentle tone. He had worked off his anger now, and whenever he wished to be especially kind to his mother, he fell into his strongest native accent and dialect, with which at other times his speech was less deeply tinged.'[45] The narrator of *Adam Bede*, Eliot's first novel (1859), gives an explanation of Adam's speech that shows voice to reflect both mood and intention. The word 'fell' might suggest some lack of deliberate choice. But the fact that he 'wished' to be kind indicates that Adam knows in advance the effect of his words and tone. Anger against his father, and remorse for its expression, motivate him to speak more closely

[43] Bain, *The Senses and the Intellect*, 311.
[44] Hilary M. Schor, *Scheherezade in the Marketplace* (New York, 1992), 36.
[45] Eliot, *Adam Bede*, 41.

the language of his parents. His movements to and from the house become a motif throughout.

Scott, at the start of the century, made such choices less explicit. Often the word 'choice' can hardly be used. His narrators, at any rate, seldom bring it to light. What one often does find is a combination of voice, effect, and ancestral origin. In *Old Mortality*, for example, a battle arises between the royalists (whose Catholicism is linked, beyond the family, to feudalism) and the Dissenters (whose ties—and breaks—occur on a more domestic level). Women and children of the anti-royalist side gather to watch: 'Like the females of the ancient German tribes, the shrill cries which they raised, when they beheld the glittering ranks of their enemies appear on the brow of the opposing eminence, acted as an incentive to their relatives to fight to the last in defence of that which was dearest to them.' Family bonds are associated with cries that go back to a German ancestry; both motivate action. The object of protection—'that which was dearest to them'—is left suitably vague; religious freedom and love for individuals (not a creed) are part of a Saxon (as opposed to Roman) heritage. The word 'shrill' to define their cries, however, slightly dehumanizes them. The women do not appear conscious of what their voices mean to the narrator.

Also to the battle come the Highland clans. They are summoned to the royalist side, but they represent no loyalty, in this particular role, to either creed or family. Their loose position is in part ascribed to their linguistic isolation. The Catholics, on the other hand, like Lady Margaret and Major Bellenden, share with many of the insurgents a Lowland Scots tongue. Ancestry collides with deliberate intent. Bellenden complains that he would rather be 'hacking at fellows with foreign faces and outlandish language. It's a hard thing to hear a hamely Scotch tongue cry quarter, and be obliged to cut him down just the same as if he called out *misericordé* . . .'. His loyalty to Scots (the people *and* the language) is represented as being out of his control—closer to emotion than will. He slips into Scots when talking of his fears of old age, just as Lady Margaret does when she is frightened.[46]

---

[46] Walter Scott, *The Tale of Old Mortality* (1816; Edinburgh, 1993), 131, 98.

Emma Letley, though, refers to Lady Margaret as a 'linguistic manipulator'.[47] The novel does, in fact, contain a degree of 'consciousness' about the effects of language upon other people. Bothwell, for instance, enters the presence of Lady Margaret: 'His language, as well as his manner, seemed also to be refined for the time and occasion . . .'. His verbal dexterity comes from his having 'sometimes kept company much better suited to his ancestry than to his present situation of life'.[48] Again, though, it is as if his ancestry catches up with him, linguistically. The phrase 'seemed also to be refined' does not suggest much mental activity. Lady Margaret may talk in Scots to her servant, and standard English to others, but often there is little to connect the change to any motive. It seems more a reflection of mood.

The Heart of Midlothian provides a more elaborate, thematic arrangement for an inquiry into emotion and will. It associates tone of voice with one of the most basic of human instincts—maternal protection. The instinct is problematized by the verdict of child murder. It also complicates the model of language as the expression of feeling. We may very well question its reliability, or at least its subtlety, as a lens into motive, since we are presented with two voices (one innocent and one guilty) that evoke the same emotion.

Meg breaks into the courtroom: ' "I tell ye," raising her termagant voice, "I want my bairn! is na that braid Scots?" ' She speaks with a voice of nature rather than reason, but it persuades the magistrate well enough. Effie's trial offers a parallel: ' "Not guilty of my poor bairn's death," said Effie Deans, in an accent corresponding in plaintive softness of tone to the beauty of her features, and which was not heard by the audience without emotion.' Her dialect, like Meg's, appeals directly to the heart. Her lawyer testifies to the accuracy of her tone: ' "My Lords," said he, "in that piteous cry you heard the eloquence of maternal affection, far surpassing the force of my poor words—Rachel weeping for her children! Nature herself bears testimony in favour of the tenderness and acuteness of the prisoner's parental feelings. I will not dishonour her plea by

---

[47] Emma Letley, 'Language and Nineteenth-Century Scottish Fiction', in Douglas Gifford (ed.), *The History of Scottish Literature* (Aberdeen, 1988), iii. 332.
[48] *Old Mortality*, 77.

adding a word more.'[49] The 'eloquence of maternal affection' needs no logic of syntax; it can be felt in a single cry. Hunt wrote of the cry as 'the universal language of animal creation. It is purely instinctive, being independent of all experience.' It allows for difference only on the level of species.[50] The novel's plot, however, calls for a much finer tool of distinction. It turns out that Meg stole Effie's child in order to secure protection for her own 'bairn', Madge. When she dies her mind is 'at once a chaos of guilt, rage, and apprehension for her daughter's future safety; that instinctive feeling of parental anxiety which she had in common with the she-wolf and lioness, being the last shade of kindly affection that occupied a breast equally savage.' The same instinct, in two separate women, got imbricated in very different motives. The association of tone with instinct, then, tells us very little by itself.

The novel, as a whole, gives us reason to doubt a link of consistent meaning between nature and speech. The Duke, ignorant of Lady Staunton's true identity, notes in her voice a resemblance to Jeanie's. He explains: 'She is a Scotchwoman, and speaks with a Scotch accent, and now and then a provincial word drops out so prettily, that it is quite Doric . . .'. His deductions, however, begin to escape the truth. From what little he has been told he concludes that Jeanie's sister 'speaks that pure court-Scotch, which was common in my younger days; but it is so generally disused now, that it sounds like a different dialect, entirely distinct from our modern *patois*.' Jeanie muses on 'how the most correct judges of life and manners can be imposed on by their own preconceptions'. The Duke, knowing Effie only in an upper-class circle, cannot imagine that she comes from the Gorbals or the Cowgate. His false knowledge of family connection deafens him to the signal of accent in the other sister's voice. If nature created a vocal bond, society renders it meaningless.

There is room to question how much nature on its own *does* accomplish, even apart from any reading of its signs. Effie meets her son for the first time. His hair is 'twisted and matted like the *glibbe* of the ancient wild Irish'; his eyes are 'keen and sparkling;

---

[49] *The Heart of Midlothian*, 184, 217, 222.
[50] Hunt, *A Manual of the Philosophy of Voice and Speech*, 126.

his gesture free and noble, like that of all savages'. His name, Whistler, evokes sound without meaning. His looks, even, mark his isolation from breeding, and 'Jeanie tried in vain to trace the likeness of either of his very handsome parents.' He is not cut off linguistically, however. He uses Jeanie's tongue to trick her into releasing him. Character, it seems, emerges from family ties (unknown to Whistler) rather than language. Jeanie, trusting in the family bond, cannot imagine he will break her trust—much less kill his own father. He finally ends up among a tribe of wild Indians; and it can only be presumed that he 'lived and died after the manner of that savage people, with whom his previous habits had well fitted him to associate'. Effie's retreat to a convent, in light of Scott's representation of the Catholic Church, suggests a failure to keep in touch any longer with her kin, in spite of her hard-won dexterity of manner and style.

Her acquisition of new forms—linguistic and sartorial—lead to the break with her family. Just as Whistler's ability to speak to Jeanie does not guarantee shared values, so does Effie's learning stand apart from the entrance to her sister's emotional life. Jeanie can use only the Scots dialect, even in writing, but her feelings are none the less deep. Effie goes through five different expressions of emotion in as many minutes, giving way to 'a natural excessive vivacity of temper, which no one, however, knew better how to restrain under the rules of artificial breeding'.[51] Her facility to adapt to new rules fits her changeability. Lukács claims that in Scott's novels the lines of political demarcation cut through the tightest circles of human relationship.[52] The rift between the sisters may reflect their culture, but not because voice is a clear window to character. Other, more broadly social factors have to be taken into consideration. 'It is well known', assures the narrator, 'that much, both of what is good and bad in the Scottish national character, arises out of the intimacy of their family con-nexions.'[53] Whistler and Jeanie both speak a dialect that, for many, is the language of domestic warmth; but Whistler uses this 'reflection' to destroy the family he never had. Thus, while

---

[51] *The Heart of Midlothian*, 486, 459, 480, 504–7.
[52] Georg Lukács, *The Historical Novel* (London, 1962), 41.
[53] *The Heart of Midlothian*, 115.

forms of speech may be used by the narrator to illustrate, and by characters to alter the dynamics of kin, it is the commentary *on* their use (rather than a trust in simple reflections) that enable us to make a link between emotion and will. Voice alone is a weak gauge.

Scott's novel is evidence of a contemporary interest in formations of mental and moral qualities—where language was seen to be a mirror *and* a cause. 'Since language is the exponent of character, it is necessary to refer to its abuse, as if it does not in all cases show a vulgar and pretentious mind, it is apt to render it so.'[54] This quotation, from *The Habits of Good Society* (1859), proves that the dual nature of language had sunk into public discourse (or, at least, its etiquette manuals) by mid-century. Two years later Bain wrote *On the Study of Character*, and justified it by saying, 'There is nothing more certain, than that the discriminating knowledge of individual character is a primary condition of much of the social improvement that the present age is panting for.' To promote this end, he recommended a study of the will, through introspection and the observation of other minds—'children and animals especially'.[55] Part of Bain's book appeared in a magazine, *Fraser's*, that also published Kingsley's work. Kingsley, the most vocal of the novelists about social improvement, also 'journalized' the most about the mental differences between man and animal. Strangely, though, as Eliot insisted, his novels do not seem to be 'psychological'. Tones of voice and dialect reveal origin and, sometimes, destiny. But thematic emphasis upon the latter undermines the image of home as a matrix of personal growth.

The 'familiar voice' is often that of a parent or sibling. In Gaskell's *Mary Barton* the heroine is roused from a stupor of grief by the tones of her cousin Esther, whom she mistakes for her dead mother. Hilary Schor refers to the evocative power of such '*sounds* of memory'.[56] These sounds remind *us* of the mother who instilled in Mary the impulsive compassion that

---

[54] St George, *The Descent of Manners*, 76.
[55] Alexander Bain, *On the Study of Character* (London, 1861), pp. v, 29–30.
[56] Schor, *Scheherezade in the Marketplace*, 34.

drives Mary to rescue Jem. The voice also jars against Mary's coolness towards Esther, reminding us of the father's more judgemental influence. Another potent confluence of memory and language occurs in *The Heart of Midlothian*. Effie stands on trial for child-murder. A simple lie, spoken by her sister Jeanie, would have freed her. Jeanie cannot bring herself to lie; instead, she walks barefoot to London to beg mercy before Queen Caroline. A pardon comes, but Effie must leave Scotland. Years later she returns, under the name of Lady Staunton. Her looks and manner fit the role of a nobleman's wife. She greets her sister in disguise, and learns that Jeanie has named her daughter Femie. Both 'Femie' and 'Effie' derive from Euphemia. Jeanie's choice *almost* to give her daughter the sister's name reflects two things: a desire to remember her sister, and an escape from Effie's shame. Words can evoke both pleasure and pain. Lady Staunton hears Jeanie call to her daughter, and comments on the variation: ' "I thought the ordinary Scottish contraction of the name had been Effie," replied the stranger, in a tone which went to Jeanie's heart; for in that single word there was more of her sister—more of *lang syne* ideas—than in all the reminiscences which her own heart had anticipated, or the features and manner of the stranger had suggested.'[57]

Scott uses memory, evoked by a Scottish word, to juxtapose the essence of a character (unchanging and recognizable through disguise) with the changes wrought by circumstance. Jeanie's departure from the dialect norm, in naming her child, gets meaning from her family bonds. After all, household intimacy is at the source of the plot. The law reasoned that Effie would have told Jeanie of her pregnancy, if innocent. Effie's failure to do so, and Jeanie's refusal to lie (her father's moral influence), motivated the journey. The idea of 'Effie' includes many contradictory feelings that result in linguistic and geographic exile. At the same time, the word makes Jeanie feel involved once again. It is a record not so much of difference, between the present and the past, as of a cycle that incorporates change.

Jenny Uglow, comparing Gaskell's *Cranford* with Eliot's *Silas Marner*, says that both novels touch 'the tenderest spots of memory and [bring] the single, the odd and the wanderer into

[57] *The Heart of Midlothian*, 473.

the circle of family and community'.[58] Again, there is an image of circle, drawn by memory. But the image is too neat. In *Cranford*, for example, Miss Matty uses the word 'hoaxing'. She then apologizes to Mary, for it 'is not a pretty word', and tells her not to repeat it: 'I don't know how it slipped out of my mouth, except it was that I was thinking of poor Peter, and it was always his expression.'[59] Peter is Miss Matty's brother, an exile from home because he angered their father. Miss Matty is conscious of a social code: on the one hand, 'hoaxing' conjures up a much-loved family member; on the other, it threatens to put Miss Matty beyond the family pale. She hopes Mary will not tell her father, 'for I should not like him to think that I was not choice in my language, after living with such a woman as Deborah'. Miss Matty fears paternal disdain; she saw where it landed her brother. She holds up Deborah (the child who most closely imitated the father, and Dr Johnson) as a standard, putting her sister on a higher level of verbal influence than their mother. On the smallest level of community—the family—occur divisions of language that complicate the idea of bringing the wanderer back into the circle. Bain in 1859 might have been describing family dynamics: 'Language being instrumental in guiding our operations, we form connexions in our mind between the various phases of an operation and the language of direction, approbation, or disapprobation therewith.'[60] In *Cranford*, idiosyncratic language triggers memory and shows how a family past—the dynamics of approval—influenced the acts that now make the circle uneven.

Wives and Daughters may be termed the most psychological of Gaskell's novels, in its overt examination of how families motivate choice. We watch, for example, as Osborne's French wife, Aimée, inadvertently widens the rift between her husband and his French-hating father. At Osborne's death she comes into the Hamley household, and nearly dies. Mr Gibson, the local doctor, tries to revive her: 'Before she lost this faint consciousness, which was habit or instinct rather than thought, Mr Gibson spoke to her in French. The child's one word of

[58] Jenny Uglow, *Elizabeth Gaskell* (1993; London, 1994), 298.
[59] Elizabeth Gaskell, *Cranford* (1853; London, 1972), 50.
[60] Alexander Bain, *The Emotions and the Will* (London, 1859), 396.

"maman" had given him this clue. It was the language sure to be most intelligible to her dulled brain; and as it happened,—only Mr Gibson did not think of that—it was the language in which she had been commanded, and had learnt to obey.' Several points can be made. Mr Gibson speaks in French because, as Bain suggested, he knows it is easier to understand the speech of one's childhood. He does not (we are told) use language deliberately to manipulate Aimée. Obedience is the fortunate effect. The clause ('only Mr Gibson did not think of that') makes him both wise and innocent. Yet elsewhere in the novel, language is central to his control over Molly, his own daughter. She has to struggle with him to get French lessons; she reads his face like a book to gauge his moods, and, unlike her new stepmother, knows his looks 'as well as she knew her alphabet'. He may be unconscious of his power, but he exerts it none the less. It hovers close to Molly's linguistic achievements. He decides to marry in order to protect her from unwanted suitors. Her grief, as a result, provokes Ralph to stir her curiosity in books, gaining her entry into scientific discourse (another realm, in the novel at least, of male approval). Curiously, Molly does not speak with her father's accent, even though he is her sole parent. It makes thematic sense: while most of her crises of growth involve fears of losing his love, her actions bear reference to a wider, English-sounding community. Yet, if the child does not imitate her parent, language still involves moments of powerful emotion that get triggered, later on, by a chance phrase or tone.

Gibson's control, deliberate or not, appears all the more godlike because of the blank of his own background. Only rumours exist. The narrator does not tell. The townsfolk assume, because of his black hair and Scottish accent, that he is 'the illegitimate son of a Scotch duke, by a Frenchwoman'. Curiously, his speech is derived from the father, his looks from the mother. On occasion he slips into Scots: 'He's "no blate," as they used to say in Scotland . . .'. But he refers to an impersonal past, not to his own origin. It means nothing, psychologically.[61] Unlike Mary Barton, he does not start up at the ghost of his

---

[61] *Wives and Daughters*, 608–9, 32, 185, 28, 253.

father when he hears a dialect word. Lacking Mr Gibson's memories, we see his ideas as already formed, as they would appear to his daughter: unquestionable.

Most novels, of course, offer a range of detail. Not all characters appear 'round'; some are just props. But in Kingsley's *Westward Ho!* there is one who suddenly gains a past, like the evaporation of amnesia, towards the end of the book. Ayacanora, the daughter of an Englishman, grew up among a tribe in the West Indies, where Amyas Leigh and his Devonshire crew find her in the role of warrior-prophetess. For the tribe she is almost a totem, a song of reassurance or foreboding. They look to her for glimpses into the future, not the past. Stripped of her function, among the English sailors, she also loses her adult status: 'For the warrior-prophetess of the Omaguas soon became, to all appearance, nothing but a very naughty child . . .'. A child is what Amyas dubs her, as she tries to mimic the talk of his men. She is, however, close to his age; if she seems infantile to him, it is because she lacks the character that memories of his own culture would have instilled in her. But these memories are soon to be restored—or put where they 'ought' to have been, had she grown up among the English.

The first clue to her childhood is a Devonshire ballad, sung by Salvation Yeo in 'the true nasal twang': 'And it befell also that Ayacanora, as she stood by Amyas's side, watching the men, and trying to make out their chat, heard it, and started; and then, half to herself, took up the strain, and sang it over again, word for word, in the very same tune and tone.' The sound turns Yeo 'deadly pale'. While Ayacanora's face did not recall the little girl he once knew, her voice does—just as Devonshire speech enables the crew to recognize Lucy Passmore in the wraith that emerges from the Spanish Inquisition. In both cases, the dialect is associated with painful events. Amyas asks, 'do you recollect, Ayacanora—do you recollect—what shall I say? anything that happened when you were a little girl?' After a while she replies, 'Trees—great trees like the Magdelena— always nothing but trees—wild and bad everything. Ayacanora won't talk about that.' Her use of 'monkey-cups' excites Yeo's suspicion that she really is the 'little maid' he searches for. He and his mates had once helped her to drink from these flowers

among the trees, and had taught her the word.[62] Spoken again,
after many years, it recalls the love that once prompted their aid.

Adam Bede's narrator believes that the smallest signs of love
are 'like those little words, "light" and "music," stirring the
long-winding fibres of your memory, and enriching your present
with your most precious past'. That is why the 'finest language'
is made up of 'unimposing words'.[63] It could be a supplement to
Wordsworth's 'Preface to *Lyrical Ballads*'. Here is the language
of 'real life'—not a local dialect (for the most part Amyas's men
speak in standard English) but a simple vocabulary, unlike the
elegant language that Frank Leigh was wont to use, and Amyas
to mock. But Wordsworth knew that some recollections hurt. In
the 'Preface' he advocates a language 'closely resembling that of
real life' (not identical to it). Such words, because linked to the
'deeper passions', will always evoke a 'painful feeling'. He
argues that the pain can be tempered by the pleasure we derive
from metre.[64] Ayacanora finds it hard to remember the past—
the brutal death of her father and his men. Amyas's probing
disturbs her: 'She lifted up her eyes suddenly to his, with a look
of imploring agony, as if beseeching him to spare her. The death
of a whole old life, the birth of a whole new life, was struggling
in that beautiful face, choking in that magnificent throat . . .'. It
is as if she chokes on the palpability of words. She no longer
sings.

It is not until the end of the book that she combines her new–
old speech with music. Amyas's love produces the effect: 'her
voice rose up within that happy home'. Her song bears his
thoughts 'back to the Paradise of the West, in the wake of the
heroes who from that time forth sailed out to colonize another
and a vaster England, to the heaven-prospered cry of Westward-
Ho!' The blend of music and speech erases the hell that was
mixed with Amyas's experience; it revises the past, and
guarantees a rosy future. The narrator, from the very start, had
asserted that his subject was suited to an epic, not a novel.
Ayacanor's song is his epic of nationalist pride. Her words do

[62] *Westward Ho!*, 487, 493, 494.
[63] *Adam Bede*, 504.
[64] William Wordsworth, 'Preface to Lyrical Ballads', in *William Wordsworth*
(Oxford, 1984), 611.

not only gain access to memory; they make it into something new and better. The 'happy home', then, is a space of recognition (Mrs Leigh's 'divine instinct' hears her son's voice from an impossible distance) and of re-creation.[65]

Voice got much attention in the nineteenth century, and in many forms—from singing manuals to books on physiology. Ideas about different registers of speech (among them dialects) connected the physical construction of the throat to emotions that prompt action. 'Many forms of cadence prevail in the world,' wrote Bain in 1855. Cadences differed from country to country, province to province. They had an individual, physical tone as well: 'As a rule we drink in the cadences most suitable to the natural march of our own vocal organs, or most fascinating to our senses.' Bain defines cadence as 'something more than accent', for it differs 'far more among the different inhabitants of the same province, than accent does'. Cadence might be part of a dialect, intersecting region. Other factors entered in: 'Vocal organization, mental character, and education modify the cadence of the voice to very different tunes.'[66] The novels illustrate this configuration. Mrs Hale, for example, in Gaskell's *North and South*, refuses to learn the new vocabulary that Margaret offers. She objects on the level not of meaning but of sound. 'I don't believe you know what a knobstick is,' accuses Margaret. The mother answers, 'Not I child. I only know it has a very vulgar sound; and I don't want to hear you using it.'[67] Her dismay involves sound, class ('knobstick' is factory slang), and mental character—indicating, as in her objection to Mr Hale's reading aloud, a reluctance to expand her social and linguistic worlds. Her use of the word 'child' reinforces the domestic sphere of her reaction.

The usual pattern, in the novels, is for a character to acquire language at home (between walls more or less permeable) before speaking in the world at large. The order of presentation may be reversed, but the pattern is implied. *Westward Ho!* departs from

[65] *Westward Ho!*, 497, 591, 503.
[66] Bain, *The Senses and the Intellect*, 434–5, 473.
[67] *North and South*, 237.

it in several ways. The characters do not appear, often, to speak the dialect of their parents. This would make sense in the mid- to late nineteenth century, when children were recorded often to speak in a tongue unlike their parents'.[68] In the sixteenth century of *Westward Ho!* it makes less sense. Kingsley probably did not want to put all of the dialogue into dialect. More significant, I think, is the fact that much of the learning in his novel occurs outside the home. Amyas, for instance, acquires Spanish and Indian on his voyages. We never see it happen. Ayacanora learns (and readopts) English in the forest among the sailors. But then, as the narrator explains, distances were greater and letters scarcer in the sixteenth century. It was also a parlous time: 'those were the days in which wives and mothers had learned (as they have learned once more, sweet souls!) to walk by faith and not by sight for those they love'.[69] Homes were but a temporary refuge for their sons.

George Eliot, in a review, sees *Westward Ho!* as a refreshing change (though she did not much favour Kingsley on the whole): 'After courses of "psychological" novels (very excellent things in their way), where life seems made up of talking and journalizing, and men are judged almost entirely on "carpet consideration", we are ready to welcome a stirring historical romance . . .'. She later adds, however, that his characters are simplistic.[70] The novel actually does contain a lot of 'talking and journalizing', but Eliot's intention seems to have been to contrast it with the drawing-room sort of romance. Most of it happens outdoors. It is as if the novel, to be 'psychological', needs at least *some* action on the carpet.

Amyas was, however, educated at home—or close by. As a child he read the Psalms with his mother. He and his brother (who studied abroad) speak a different register, we are told. Amyas 'talked, like Raleigh, Grenvil, and other low persons, with a broad Devonshire accent; and was in many other respects so very ignorant a youth, that any pert monitor in a national school might have had a hearty laugh at him'. Since most of the

---

[68] Tony Crowley, *The Politics of Discourse* (Basingstoke, 1989), 158–60.
[69] *Westward Ho!*, 230.
[70] George Eliot, 'Westward Ho! and Constance Herbert', in *Essays of George Eliot*, 125, 127.

dialogue occurs in standard English, we have to imagine the accent. Frank, supposedly, speaks the English of royalty. Amyas says that Frank speaks like a book; elsewhere, though, Will Cary makes the same comment about Amyas. In fact, there is no obvious difference of language between them. We know that Amyas read *fewer* books—the Bible and Prayer Book, and works on King Arthur, the West Indies, and 'The Cruelties of the Spaniards'. Their influence upon him is pretty clear. When he comes back from the sea, blinded, he sits in the bay-window where he had read the books as a boy: 'He put out his hand and felt for them; there they lay side by side, just as they had lain twenty years before.' He has returned, both different and unchanged, to the woman who once read him the Psalms.

Mrs Leigh, his mother, enables other people to change, but speaks in a tone that never does. It is apotheosis, not physiology. Though her parents came from Yorkshire, she appears to speak standard English. Her 'silver voice' is 'low, dreamy, like the far-off chimes of angels' bells from out the highest heaven'. Her 'divine instinct', with relation to her son's voice, has been mentioned. She appears already made, for she 'was, and had been from her youth, one of those noble old English church-women, without superstition, and without severity, who are among the fairest features of that heroic time'. When she and Amyas meet, after his years at sea, the 'sailors, 'prentices, and coarse harbour-women were hushed into holy silence, and made a ring round the mother and the son'.[71] Her lack of superstition and severity is a lesson to Amyas, who displays both. But he cannot learn until he is ready. Bain wrote (of the voice) that 'the natural flexibility or variety of the organs must be coupled with delicacy of the ear for articulate effects in order to make rapid progress'.[72] Mrs Leigh's voice—often too subtle to be heard— does not 'appear' much until the end, when Amyas's blindness makes him both more attuned to divine influence, and bound to the home.

Frank and Amyas represent two kinds of education; but when they meet at home their mother unites them in chivalry. Tension evaporates at the angel's touch. Scott and Gaskell, in comparison,

[71] *Westward Ho!*, 9, 8, 589, 590, 21, 504.
[72] Bain, *The Senses and the Intellect*, 431.

give more problematic (and interesting) representations of language acquisition. Their novels contain moments of friction in the home at entry points of writing and speech.

My focus has been upon speech, because the home tends to abet dialogue rather than written communication. Families did keep in touch by letter. Elizabeth Gaskell wrote almost daily—often to her daughters. By mid-century the circle of home, at least figuratively, had widened in potential if not in fact. David Vincent notes that the arrival of letters in a working-class home was in the early century a 'rare event', until postal rates came down. Nor did the lower cost guarantee a letter, since many could not write. Houses often contained a range of literacy—except in the middle classes, where writing had become standard. Across England, the number of weddings that could boast a signature from every party (instead of a cross) in the register, did not reach 50 per cent until 1879.[73] Literacy brought perhaps the most obvious infiltration of new kinds of language.

Scott grew up where (and when) people were expected to speak more than one dialect. Perhaps that is why domestic tensions in *The Heart of Midlothian* pull tightest across the written word. Literacy had stronger affiliations with the outside world. Butler leaves home to study, and it renders him almost useless on his grandmother's farm: 'While studying the *pons asinorum* in Euclid, he suffered every *cuddie* upon the common to trespass upon a large field of pease belonging to the Laird . . .'. Latin and Scots occupy different spaces. Butler *by himself* cannot make them overlap. When he marries Jeanie, the split moves to another level: her father, Davie Deans, does not suffer Latin gladly. Butler's erudite quotations goad him. He insists upon his own Latin-free wisdom, and Butler is 'not pleased, as a man and a scholar, to be always dictated to by his unlettered father-in-law'. Jeanie, in some ways, bridges the gap. Butler teaches her to write (with partial success), and a few of her letters appear—written in Scots. She does not 'rival Butler in learning', but then nor does literacy unsuit her for domestic duties. She returns to her dairy where the cows 'acknowledged her presence by lowing, turning round their broad and decent

---

[73] David Vincent, *Literacy and Popular Culture* (Cambridge, 1989), 41, 43, 23.

brows when they heard her well-known "Pruh, my leddy— pruh, my woman," and, by various indications, known only to those who have studied the habits of the milky mothers, showing sensible pleasure as she approached to caress them in their turn.' Mutual learning is here: the cows know her voice, and she their 'mute' language. There is maternal warmth. Gaskell wrote of a like moment in *Sylvia's Lovers*, where Sylvia speaks the language of the dairy with an ease she does not feel among books. The cows are Jeanie's 'charges'—mothers and children at once.

Jeanie's 'family' suggests that differences of language do not, in themselves, cause tension. They can strengthen bonds. Jeanie draws Butler into a circle of mutual instruction. He teaches her to write; she teaches him the language of her father. On the brink of her journey, she asks him to write to her father of her plan:

for, God help me, I have neither head nor hand for lang letters at ony time, forby now; and I trust him entirely to you, and I trust you will soon be permitted to see him. And, Reuben, when ye do win to the speech o' him, mind a' the auld man's bits o' ways, for Jeanie's sake; and dinna speak o' Latin or English terms to him, for he's o' the auld warld, and downa bide to be fashed wi' them, though I daresay he may be wrang.

Jeanie's idea of family includes several kinds of speech, and little judgement. Even if her father is wrong, she implies, his taste is to be indulged. The important thing is to reach through to the other, no matter what the style.

Effie, her sister, is another story. Her moment of acquisition occurs in a few pages, between two letters—one ill-spelt, the other quite elegant. Within four years (absent to the reader) Effie transforms herself from a poor student to a lady of culture. Yet the change is not fundamental: 'Jeanie's humility readily allowed that Effie had always, when she chose it, been smarter at her book than she herself was . . .'. Effie was a latent, if unexpressed, scholar. Her buried talent blooms in her new 'home' with George Staunton. But that home is in exile, and not at all like the picture of Jeanie's dairy. 'Love, or fear, or necessity, however, had proved an able school-mistress, and completely supplied all her deficiencies.' The Staunton family— whom we do not see at home, and whose son runs wild on the heath—is not a model of natural speech. Rather, standard English gets pumped into Effie to make her presentable, if never exact in her pronunciation. A strange twist occurs in the pattern of transmission: Effie's own son does not learn the standard (in literacy or speech) but when Effie sends money to Jeanie, the latter puts it aside for the education of her own children.[74]

Vincent shows how the entry of literacy into a household often brought a loss of influence to its female members.[75] It occurs in *Helen*, the novel (by Edgeworth) that foreshadows *Wives and Daughters*. Lady Davenant is a great politician, says Mr Collingwood: 'and female politicians, with their heads full of the affairs of Europe, cannot have time to think of the affairs of their families'. Lady Davenant explains her passion. She once read a line in *The Rambler*: 'No life pleasing to God that is not useful to men'. She saw it as a call to enter a man's world, against her mother's will. That one sentence, then, 'did more than all my mother's entreaties could effect'.[76] Gaskell's *North and South* gives further support to Vincent's claim. The Thornton house, where Mrs Thornton is at least her son's equal in power, contains·very few books. She derides his study of Latin and Greek, which he ends up dropping. The Hale house, on the other hand, is strewn with books of all kinds. Mrs Hale experiences her husband's scholarship as a tyranny; she dislikes it when he reads to her, and never accepts his choice to teach. In both cases, the women are antagonists to literature. Margaret Hale, who adopts her father's taste, is a much more powerful figure than her mother—who fades into death. Yet literacy itself does not threaten Mrs Hale. Margaret teases her with 'knob-stick'—a word she picked up by ear. Speech can make just as forceful an entry into the home, though it lacks the tangibility of a book; and book-learning, in other works by Gaskell (notably *Ruth*), can actually bring a mother and child closer together.

Speech may indeed have been felt as the greater threat. The eighteenth century saw a rise of ideas about language acquisition in children, with such theorists as Priestley and Monboddo: in the eighteenth century 'the child is "discovered" linguistically,

---

[74] *Heart of Midlothian*, 84, 448–9, 434, 269, 455.
[75] Vincent, *Literacy and Popular Culture*, 180.
[76] Edgeworth, *Helen*, 11, 63.

as well as in other ways'.[77] Earlier still, Locke had warned of the impressionability of children, which made them open to 'the Superstition of a Nurse, or the Authority of an old Woman'. They might absorb any doctrine, 'for white Paper receives any Characters'.[78] Notwithstanding the choice of metaphor, Locke elsewhere states that children acquire language best through 'constant Conversation'. If a second language is desired, it must be taught early, 'that the yet pliant Organs of Speech might be accustomed to a due formation of those Sounds'. Locke offers as proof the fact that 'we so often see a *French*-Woman teach an *English*-Girl to speak and read French perfectly in a Year or Two, without any Rule of Grammar, or any thing else but prattling to her'.[79] The effect of mere prattling, especially in the presence of a nurse or servant, could be disastrous for the child, if the quality was poor. Bain made similar points (with less alarm) in 1855: 'Our ear for articulation is formed in the first instance on the voices around us; we identify with ease a letter or a word as pronounced by those; in fact, the casual peculiarities of their manner become as it were fused with our sense of the articulations themselves. A child born in Yorkshire acquires an ear for the vowels and consonants of the alphabet as sounded in Yorkshire.'[80] By the mid-nineteenth century it was pretty much accepted that young minds most readily absorbed language—in sound, shape, and vocabulary. As Hunt avers coolly: 'It appears to be admitted on all sides that articulated language is not like natural language, derived from nature, *i.e.* it is *not instinctive*, but *acquired*; and common observation teaches us that children learn to speak by imitation.'[81] Older people had more difficulty. That is why speech might have been perceived as the greater threat in the household. Children could easily pick up scraps of dialect (at school, in the streets, in the factory) that sounded foreign—or, in Mrs Hale's case, 'vulgar'—to their elders. Locke saw potential for harm in older women; older women, like Mrs Hale, might have viewed it

[77] Cohen, *Sensible Words*, 125.
[78] Locke, *An Essay Concerning Human Understanding*, 81.
[79] John Locke, *Some Thoughts Concerning Education* (1693; Oxford, 1989), 216, 218. [80] Bain, *The Senses and the Intellect*, 471.
[81] Hunt, *A Manual of the Philosophy of Voice and Speech*, 163.

differently—fearing instead the pliability of their children's minds.

Disdain for 'silly lady novelists' did not alter the fact that women played a great role in the teaching of children. Middle-class children, at least, spent their most formative years among older sisters, nurses, governesses, mothers, and other female kin. Morag Shiach complains that histories of education in the nineteenth century give little information about how girls and women fit in.[82] I suspect she means formal education. Linda Colley reveals that by the year 1800 over 70 per cent of English peers (male, of course) attended only four public schools. Their removal from home, in so centralized a fashion, created an association (linguistic and otherwise) with class rather than family.[83] It may be compared to working-class behaviour, as Patrick Joyce describes it: 'Home life and family affairs were indeed a staple of literature in which barriers of gender seem to have been as little marked as those of status within the working class. The private arena was as important as the public: dialect recitation at home and among neighbours was common practice among the northern working classes.'[84] Joyce implies an involvement of women, at least thematically, in the transfer of a dialect-spoken culture. Because it occurred informally, however, it is hard to trace. Did women recite?

Victorians did, however, write a lot about, and for, female students of the middle classes. Their home was a site of learning that flowed both ways. Nancy Armstrong mentions the abundance of books published during the century for the instruction of women at home.[85] Harriet Martineau, in *Household Education*, confutes the idea that public schools held a central place in English society. Martineau 'points out that important citizens—Sir Isaac Newton, Elizabeth Fry, even Queen Victoria herself—were educated at home'. Women were not to be simply fitted into the picture: 'Rather than locate

---

[82] Morag Shiach, *Discourse on Popular Culture* (Stanford, Calif., 1989), 79.

[83] Linda Colley, *Britons* (New Haven, 1992), 167.

[84] Patrick Joyce, 'The People's English', in Peter Burke and Roy Porter (eds.), *Language, Self, and Society* (Oxford, 1991), 164.

[85] Armstrong, *Desire and Domestic Fiction*, 63.

feminine influence within the domestic sphere, [Martineau] radically locates *education itself* within that sphere.'[86] In Edgeworth's *Helen* the absence of a maternal figure puts both girls in social peril. Gaskell's letters to her daughters show determination to keep her hand in their education, even though she felt sure of the quality of their schools. Her eldest, Marianne, took upon herself the instruction of her youngest sisters. Sophie, in 'Mr Harrison's Confessions', teaches her brother the alphabet.[87] It was a family affair. Gaskell had been coached in languages by her own father.[88] Her husband, William, concerned himself with the children's spelling: 'a trifle too phonetic, and we must try to reform it'.[89] Kingsley's father had taught him Latin.[90]

Men, of course, took part in handing down language to their children; but in the novels, where men affect or respond to a child's acquisition, a greater strain appears in the family dynamic. Those are the moments when children want to break away—through language. Molly, in *Wives and Daughters*, spends the evening by accident with a family of higher status than her own. A lady speaks to her in French: 'I'm only Molly Gibson, ma'am,' she admits, to explain her failure to understand. When her father comes to fetch her, he teases her about her enlarged circle of influence: 'I expected to find you so polite and ceremonious, that I read a few chapters of *Sir Charles Grandison*, in order to bring myself up to concert pitch.' Molly's rift from her father, when he announces his engagement to Clare, is given terms of linguistic uncertainty: 'She did not answer. She could not tell what words to use.' She fears the outcome of her own rage, and is silenced: 'It was as if the piece of solid ground on which she stood had broken from the shore, and she was drifting out to the infinite sea alone.' She drifts to another ground of language that exchanges, but does not

[86] Linda H. Peterson, 'Harriet Martineau's *Household Education*', in Patrick Scott and Pauline Fletcher (eds.), *Culture and Education in Victorian England* (Lewisburg, Pa., 1990), 190–1.

[87] Elizabeth Gaskell, 'Mr Harrison's Confessions', in *My Lady Ludlow* (Oxford, 1989), 361.

[88] Uglow, *Elizabeth Gaskell*, 41.

[89] Barbara Brill, *William Gaskell* (Manchester, 1984), 45.

[90] Robert Bernard Martin, *The Dust of Combat* (London, 1959), 23.

destroy, her father's link between language and control. Ralph
translates scientific texts for her into a speech she understands—
both to please her *and* to subdue her rebellion. Molly later
impresses a man of science (a lord, no less) with her dinner-party
talk on biology. Clare sees the new jargon as a husband-catching
device, but for Molly it serves, more immediately, as a way of
breaking from an old, insupportable dynamic.

Fathers do not always feel in control. Squire Hamley accuses
his son Osborne of having 'a bit of the *mounseer* about him,
which he caught with being so fond of going off to the
Continent, instead of coming back to his good old English
home'.[91] If style of speech drew upon literary and national
standards, it also played a role in family dynamics—as the focus
of attachment and jealousy. Gaskell gives her characters a
glimmering idea of how changes in speech alter relationships
and, consequently, the self; voice permeates memory, and is part
of the environment that creates personality, but it does not
totally undermine freedom. Male figures in her novels who try
to alter the speech of their children create an environment of
departure; the child searches for a new voice, albeit in a world
that can offer a limited array of new social ties.

Social demands on language, for ever-changing signals of
identity, made the grammar-book too rigid to be of much use.
Sometimes knowledge of the most demotic forms takes a central
role in the manipulation of speech. *Wives and Daughters* plays
upon the fear of manipulation. No single register of speech
guarantees immunity from others. People who converse 'well'
can be hurt, in dialogue, by coarser tones. Schor finds a source
for Gaskell's novel in *The Tatler* and *The Spectator*: 'just as we
can find the roots of the novel in conversation manuals and
guidance books, organized talk and story transformed into
narrative, so here Molly's "heroine-ship" grows out of gossip,
the novel only a step away from "dirt on a girl's name" '.[92]
Molly, drawn into a new circle of friends, grows apart
linguistically from the 'dear old' Miss Brownings. She notices
(with shame) 'the coarser and louder tones in which they spoke,

[91] *Wives and Daughters*, 19, 25, 114, 316–17.
[92] Schor, *Scheherezade in the Marketplace*, 201.

the provincialism of their pronunciation, the absence of interest in things, and their greediness of details about persons'.[93] The Brownings' very accent is associated with the gossip that almost ruins Molly—in the sight of the townsfolk *and* of her father. Molly's inability to find the right language for her 'indiscretion' (much like the plot in *Helen*) puts her in danger. It takes the patronage of the slang-conversant Lady Harriet to restore her reputation. Collini observes the paradox of character: that, while 'character-testing' in the nineteenth century took place in private, it required public recognition for it to become 'an ascribed quality'.[94] It is the case with Molly. Her worth, in our eyes, comes from her silence about the true reason behind her meetings with Preston. She almost martyrs herself, socially, in order to destroy letters that would have torn the cover from her new mother and sister. Because of her silence, her story gets told in 'coarser and louder tones' than she would have used. Ironically, it protects those who try to correct her own verbal impurities. But the novel suggests that 'character' can be lost if silence—the refusal or inability to speak on all levels of discourse—goes unheard. 'Household harmony'—the goal of Mr Gibson—obscures the key to his daughter's motives. Thus, while *The Heart of Midlothian* creates an ideal home out of several kinds of speech, where each member accommodates the other's idiom, the society in *Wives and Daughters* makes it advantageous for *each* character to be 'at home' in as many idioms (and dialects) as possible. Mrs Hamley's standard of conversation is so high, and her sphere so limited, that she fades out of the social world into death. The novel suggests that its own form—of commentary around the speeches and silences— is needed to replace a lost trust in pure dialogue as a signal of intent. Commentary reminds us that speech can be taken many ways.

Westward Ho! gives us a picture of what it would be like if there were no family units. In the moors of Devon live the Gubbings— a wild, almost inhuman race. The narrator quotes Fuller, to show he has done his anthropological research: 'They live in cots (rather holes than houses) like swine, having all in common,

---

[93] *Wives and Daughters*, 153.   [94] Collini, *Public Moralists*, 106.

multiplied without marriage into many hundreds. Their language is the dross of the dregs of the vulgar Devonian; and the more learned a man is, the worse he can understand them.' Let this be a lesson to communists and advocates of free love. It contrasts vividly with the domestic paradise surrounding Mrs Leigh. The degradation of home parallels that of language; clarity—of articulation and possession—is nowhere to be found. Kingsley, sharing in a widespread fear of Catholicism, made the Gubbings vulnerable to the propaganda of Catholic priests—venting his scorn of a religion that asks any man to be celibate. On the other end of the scale, in the Leigh household, Ayacanora uses her most punctilious English just when she and Mrs Leigh begin calling each other mother and daughter. Rose represents another—incomplete—kind of home: 'Poor little Rose! Had she but had a mother!' The girl, whose father looked to the seas for his fortune, becomes attracted to the Spaniard that Amyas keeps for ransom. The Don's 'measured voice, with a foreign accent, thrilled through her'. We are invited, to some extent, to blame her susceptibility upon a lack of maternal guidance. If her trust in Lucy Passmore is unwise, it seems natural enough that she should look for a mother-figure to fill the empty space. For most of the novel, however, her own motivations are overshadowed by the figure she becomes to the Devon sailors. Rose becomes a ship, a symbol of England's chivalry and empire.

England, in *Westward Ho!*, stands for the holiest kind of union between man and woman—the apotheosis of the home. Ayacanora immediately allies herself with the English. To her tribe she cries out, 'I am a daughter of the Sun; I am white; I am a companion for Englishmen! But you! your mothers were Guahibas, and ate mud; and your fathers—they were howling apes! Let them sing to you! I shall go to the white men, and never sing you to sleep any more . . .'. In other words, she gives up the role of mother among men of bestial origins to become a proper, English daughter. Mrs Leigh is rather like the sun around which the household moves.

For the most part, we are given little familial evidence to explain Ayacanora's drive to become an English girl—apart from the fact of her English blood and earliest memories. But her reacquisition of the language and manners becomes a focus of hidden intentions—if only hidden from the characters. Ayacanora, for example, does not need Amyas to teach her English. Yet she insists upon making him a schoolmaster. The two seem to be the only ones on board oblivious to (or hiding from) erotic potential. But it triggers their actions. Amyas, repelled by her Spanish blood, uses her plea for English manners to push her away—insisting upon unprecedented formality. To his mother he introduces Ayacanora as 'a poor wild Indian girl—my daughter, I call her', insisting upon barriers that do not really exist in order to hide the one that does. He knows his hatred is wrong, though it stems from the love he felt for his brother, and the guilt surrounding Frank's death. The spaces between emotion and will in the novel often involve gaps of speech, and the effort to move across them.

The effort, however, is so unidirectional that it leaves the realm of psychology for nationalism. Ayacanora acts out of a basic need for love and a 'real' home, but her motives are clearly guided by a nation's culture and intentions.[95] Kingsley seems less concerned with the causes behind individual patterns of behaviour, than with shunting these patterns into England's biography. It is interesting that Eliot marked both Kingsley and Dickens for a failure to create believable (i.e. psychological) characters. Recall Dickens's belief that writers would soon 'find their way even into the prattle of the nursery'—not that they would imitate the language of infants, but that infants would take up the Saxon words spoken *to* them.[96]

Kingsley, then, did not follow the kind of thinking that made Bain, in the mid-century, characterize the 'voluntary command of speech' as an adhesion of word ('oral, or vocal, or both') with 'the select stream of cerebral power flowing to the articulating members'. The last requirement is 'a motive urgency, of the nature demanded by the will, in order to consummate the act'.[97] The body and the needs of the heart combine. Schor says that misunderstanding is eroticized in *North and South*.[98] In *all* of Gaskell's works, gaps of language are both felt and used to

---

[95] *Westward Ho!*, 267, 77, 238, 422, 488, 505.
[96] Trench, *English: Past and Present*, 21–2; Dickens, 'Saxon-English', 1–7.
[97] Bain, *The Emotions and the Will*, 395–6.
[98] Schor, *Scheherezade in the Marketplace*, 128.

mend gaps of relationship. *Wives and Daughters* can be read as a novel of motivations that arise from unmet emotional needs and transform the linguistic landscape. The source of longing does not often match, exactly, the solution. But language is used to find one.

Armstrong, commenting on nineteenth-century sociologists, protests that in citing the home as the matrix of all problems they lose sight of the varied political influences at work in each individual.[99] Not all Victorians put the two approaches—domestic and political—at odds. F. D. Maurice, whom Gaskell dubbed the most influential man of their time, lectured on how the family dynamic extended into the society at large. He spoke of the parent–child relation as 'the primary fact of my existence. I can contemplate no other facts apart from it.'[100] The strength of the Anglo-Saxons, he implied, lay in their reverence for 'the relations of father and child, of husband and wife'.[101] The future held the promise of not reverence but analysis: 'Families and houses appear very considerable items in our most recent books; their effect for good or for evil upon the course of events in every land, is admitted with greater clearness just as our observations become more exact.'[102] The relationships in Gaskell's novels do clearly alter a character's behaviour, both drawing upon a political context and recognizing change within.

Squire Hamley, in *Wives and Daughters*, exemplifies how dialect can reveal a social code influencing a father's bond with his children. *His* father, in a fit of malice towards Oxford, sent him to a 'petty provincial school'. He did not lose his local dialect. Mrs Hamley explains his hatred of 'college slang': 'he has never been there you know'. He refers to the 'freemasonry' of 'all you public schoolboys' as his reason for not inviting his sons' friends to their home: '. . . I'll have no one here at the Hall who will look down on a Hamley of Hamley, even if he only

[99] Armstrong, *Desire and Domestic Fiction*, 172, 24.

[100] F. D. Maurice, 'Domestic Morality: Parents and Children', in *Social Morality*, 21.

[101] F. D. Maurice, 'On Books', in *The Friendship of Books and Other Lectures* (London, 1893), 50.

[102] Maurice, 'Domestic Morality', 60.

knows how to make a cross instead of write his name'. The Squire's sense of linguistic exclusion affects his family: 'and perhaps the jealousy and *mauvais honte* that this inferiority had called out long ago, extended itself in some measure to the feelings he entertained towards his sons'. The narrator's use of the French phrase is appropriate here. The Squire, most alienated from Osborne (who speaks the most 'correct' English), also detests the French. But he later warms to Osborne's French wife, Aimée, who speaks only 'broken English'.[103] It is as if his sympathy for her verbal loneliness, and his interest in the French-speaking child, overcome his national prejudice.

A SUMMARY

The Heart of Midlothian complicates the parallel of nation and home-speech by giving us, in one family, a wide range of linguistic pattern—from Whistler to Effie. Language, in Scott's novel, has less to do with birth than with a sense of how the character adapts to local needs—reflecting, at the same time, different stages of civilization. It is in some ways a departure from other works by Scott. *Guy Mannering*, for example, with its motif of a stolen child (who appears later, origin unknown), allows the character to prove (through actions and speech) a kind of civilization that had been there all along. In *Westward Ho!*, an erasure of memory performs the same trick. Ayacanora relearns her mother tongue, and sheds the features of a more primitive (superstitious) society.

In *Wives and Daughters* we find the most commentary on how a conscious use of language fits into the idea that the self (desires, fears, and motives) emerges through the home. Gaskell, of the three, gives her characters more 'awareness' of the effects of different kinds of speech. Rhetoric, as a concept, struggles with the motif of biology. Mr Gibson's unknown origin, for example, gives his manipulation of language a more potent effect, because it would be hard for someone else to access *his* language of obedience, or use it to control him. The extent to which biology determines the self is a question that Gaskell

[103] *Wives and Daughters*, 40, 85, 261, 259.

explores—though not to Eliot's fullness, perhaps. While Kingsley finds a transcendent voice—the song of Ayacanora or the 'silvery' tones of Mrs Leigh—to conflate home and English history, Gaskell puts conflict at both levels. Within the home, and in the society at large, characters (Molly, in particular) learn new uses of language *and* struggle against it to better define who they want to be, and whom they want to avoid. There is no transcendence. In this, Gaskell is closer to Scott. What she more heavily underlines, and what is lost a little in Scott's mockery of the pedant, is the use of other, more 'learned' (Latin-influenced) varieties to give a new perspective, at least, on the struggle; to lessen the sense of being trapped by four walls, and to offer new kinds of belonging. Her novel reduces a tension between the idea of 'character'—as a fixed personality and style of speech— and the plot of individual growth.

The novels bring into dynamic foreground the problem— invoked by other prose writings—of how to fit the idea of 'homely' speech, at the hearth, into the model of a progressive nation. The hope of permanence, in the idea of language as a storehouse of memory (national and individual), is in conflict with the metaphor of language as a tool that can be used to change a static, no longer viable phase. The 'domestic' novels locate the riddle in a gap between the voices of narrator and character; the former being (among other things) a mode of telling us the *tone* of speech.

The question 'What makes us human?' takes a curious form. The idea that each person's true, unique nature is felt in the tone of voice (not in the accent or the vocabulary) is suspiciously close to the non-linguistic cry that we share with other species, the emphasis falling on sound rather than syntax. Emotions are the field of psychology: ironically, the latter comes to be seen as both a vessel and prompt for the rhetoric—the artful use of words—to part us from the determinism of both our bodies and the social circle into which we are born. Where Kingsley shifts the focus to national growth, he slips into the rubric of a biological motif. Where the novelists draw attention to language in the family, and the individual's response, we find rather a new way of looking at emotion. It is not just a sign of an earlier phase of development. Emotion becomes, rather, a turning-point in each life, with a power of recurrence that affords many moments of change. At the same time the bond between language and memory attaches our emotion to a knowledge of social effect; to the realization that our survival is oftentimes more in the hands of art than of biology.

Concluding Remarks

THE 'Advertisement' to Scott's *The Antiquary* may seem an odd way to end, given its function as a preface to his novel. Yet it acts, here, as a reminder of the main structures of thought—the metaphors—that have informed my work throughout. Scott tells us that his latest novel is the third in 'a series of fictitious narratives' set in three periods: his father's generation, his own youth, and the most recent decade. In the latter two, especially, he has

> sought my principle personages in the class of society who are the last to feel the influence of that general polish which assimilates to each other the manners of different nations. Among the same class I have placed some of the scenes, in which I have endeavoured to illustrate the operation of the higher and more violent passions; both because the lower orders are less restrained by the habit of suppressing their feelings, and because I agree with Mr Wordsworth, that they seldom fail to express them in the strongest and most powerful language. This is, I think, peculiarly the case with the peasantry of my own country, a class with whom I have long been familiar. The antique force and simplicity of their language often tinctured with the oriental eloquence of Scripture, in the mouths of those of an elevated understanding, give pathos to their grief, and dignity to their resentment.[1]

Scott, Gaskell, and Kingsley each wanted to give an articulate voice (not just a cry) to those whose words were seldom read. I have not been trying to debunk a myth of good intentions. My plan was to fit statements about language, and the mix of dialect and standard English in fiction, among metaphors of change and identity.

Scott's 'Advertisement' tells a big tale. It implies that characters, in dialogue with each other, can 'illustrate the operation' of passions that affect us all; and that were felt in the past. It assumes a value in the juxtaposition of difference, unlike the 'general polish' that erases barriers between the élite of all

---

[1] Walter Scott, *The Antiquary* (1816; Edinburgh, 1995), 3.

nations. It approves of the mixture of 'antique' and 'oriental' languages—the former associated with 'force', the latter with 'eloquence'. Finally, it makes a distinction between the acts of 'narration' and of recording 'manners'.

Each of the three novelists was influenced by Wordsworth; each was conscious of the problem of prose—of 'plain English'— and of telling how things really are. Adam Smith, whom Gaskell admired, had described it as a difference between Latin and English. Latin, with its complicated structure of conjugations and declensions, allowed for a prettier sound, but did not lend itself to clear understanding. English, with its much simpler structure, had an untidy appearance and a harsher sound, but offered the best medium for communication. Smith concluded that English was the result of nations mixing, 'either by conquest or migration'. Latin implied the insularity of child-hood.[2] Hugh Blair (whose lectures caused Charlotte Brontë to cry, she was given so much to read[3]) supported Smith: 'The Latin order is more animated; the English, more clear and distinct.' Where English lost in aesthetics, it gained in virtue, for 'Speech is the great instrument by which man becomes beneficial to man . . .'. He believed that human reason 'is not the effort or ability of one, so much as it is the result of the reason of many, arising from lights mutually communicated, in consequence of discourse and writing'.[4] The novel creates a matrix for both. Efforts to include non-standard speech and writing in the nineteenth-century novel, and the apology (as in Scott's 'Advertisement') for a change in aesthetic, can be seen both in a radical light, and as an attempt to mount reason above dangerous emotions.

Openings for discourse are more available to a complex, literate society than to people who must be in earshot to communicate. If sheer bulk of response is a sign of worth, then words among the literate have the best chance of accumulating social value. If nationalist movements, as Gerald Newman claims, invoke both

---

[2] Adam Smith, 'Considerations Concerning the First Formation of Languages', in *The Theory of Moral Sentiments*, 6th edn. (London, 1790), 446–7.

[3] Elizabeth Gaskell, *The Life of Charlotte Brontë* (1857; London, 1985), 133.

[4] Hugh Blair, *Lectures on Rhetoric and* Belles Lettres (Basel, 1801), i. 138, 1. Blair began these lectures at Edinburgh in 1759.

'uncorrupted' and 'scholarly' discourses,[5] then the movement towards the standardization of *writing* in nineteenth-century Britain can be seen as a way of turning private goals of importance—of audience—into a national purpose. Belief in language as a tool gave people hope; treatment of language as an object, detached from roots of physical origin, weakened (without destroying) their identity with a language of childhood and region. Nationalization of the written standard promised a wider sphere of influence (power) while it put earlier, pre-literate forms in a museum. This last point is significant. Many 'dialect' novels of the period featured the gap between 'past' (oral, native, insular) and 'present' (literate, willed, national) in order to invoke, for public use, the energy of private dreams.

The interest in idiosyncrasies of speech, and how they reflected the nation's past, did not lead to high tolerance for private matters of taste in the present. Each novelist mocked (however gently) the pursuit of language for art's sake alone—putting it in conflict with unmet, basic needs. The plot of *Rob Roy*, for example, stems from Frank's unwillingness to learn the jargon of commerce; his lack of attention to 'the mysteries of agio, tariffs, tare, and tret'. He admits that he is turning away from the stuff of life; that commerce 'is to the general commonwealth of the civilized world what the daily intercourse of ordinary life is to private society, or rather, what air and food are to our bodies'.[6] He puts the language of commerce on a level with that of 'ordinary life'; the 'civilized world' is linked to 'private society' in his analogy, yet he cannot bring himself to join in the palaver. It is not to his taste. A lot of damage ensues from so personal a whim.

Gaskell more persistently questioned the aesthetic value of language, in spite of her own preferences. She may have disparaged Cockney, for example, and have felt the advantage of a good teacher of English pronunciation, but she also made fun of the 'grand Johnsonian sentence'.[7] In her fiction she puts forward, tentatively, the idea that usefulness could take over as

---

[5] Gerald Newman, *The Rise of English Nationalism* (London, 1987), 111.
[6] Walter Scott, *Rob Roy* (1817; London, 1995), 11–13.
[7] Letters dated Aug. 1848 and Sept. 1852, in Elizabeth Gaskell, *Letters* (Manchester, 1966), 83, 200.

the arbiter of taste. In *Ruth* the 'musical voice' of the Welsh-speaking Mrs Hughes 'sounded as soft as Russian or Italian'. Ruth studies none of these languages; instead, she gets up at dawn to read Latin, to promote her son's career. Mr Benson picks up his Welsh grammar 'and tried again to master the ever-puzzling rules for the mutation of letters', but his thoughts turn instead to the 'life-in-death' enigma of a young woman. The book avails him little: he talks with such grammatical correctness, and poor pronunciation, that the Welsh beg him to speak English.[8]

Ruth does not promote Latin as the better language, intrinsically. It can hardly be the higher form of art, if music may be deemed (as Keats believed) close to a pure aesthetic, and of value for its own sake. Latin wins in the context of a use that is local in time and place. It gets rather different treatment in *North and South*, where the systematic study of languages is at odds with commerce. In the town of Milton, 'To use a Scotch word, every thing looked more "purposelike".' The hard-working Scots, not the pages of Virgil, become the reference-point. Margaret (the heroine) denies the vulgarity of the move. She says to Thornton (himself caught between factory jargon and a desire to read the Classics): 'though "knobstick" has not a very pretty sound, is it not expressive? Could I do without it, in speaking of the thing it represents? If using local words is vulgar, I was very vulgar in the Forest,—was I not, mamma?' Not only does she upset a model (much alive in Gaskell's time) that values rural dialects above urban; she also sets a notion of expressiveness against that of what sounds pretty—a rather subtle distinction, as both are based on sensory impact, giving usefulness a weight in the balance.[9]

Kingsley, in *Two Years Ago*, ridicules the 'modern meaning' of genius as 'a person who can say prettier things than his neighbours'. Tom, the hero of the novel, speaks both standard English and (now and then) his 'native Berkshire' dialect, with its own grammar. For all his education, he can still win in a 'word-battle of slang'. Naylor, a Cambridge man, is a first-rate

---

[8] Elizabeth Gaskell, *Ruth* (1853; Oxford, 1985), 99, 177, 105–6, 111.
[9] Elizabeth Gaskell, *North and South* (1854–5; Oxford, 1982), 58, 238.

Classics scholar, but his retention of a 'slang vocabulary' makes
him 'the dread of all bargees from Newnham pool to Upwar'.
He sings a Wessex song, in dialect, to deride the façade of
learning. The narrator—holding up the Shelleyesque Vavasour
as an example—scorns the practice of 'mere word-painting', on
the principle that a focus on beauty alone takes away from true
inventiveness of thought: 'Manner, in short, has taken the place
of matter.'[10]

Kingsley's novel seems to polarize artificial and true language,
in a Wordsworthian gesture to which all three of the novelists
could relate. Scott, too, had warned of the dangers of affecta-
tion, in the court, and drew a line between fashionable and best.
He looked back to the linguistic vogue of the Elizabethan
period, and saw it imitating 'the barbarous rules of the ancient
Anglo-Saxons, the merit of whose poems consisted, not in the
ideas, but in the quaint arrangement of the words, and the
regular recurrence of some favourite sound or letter'. He feared
(again, like Wordsworth) that the metaphysical poets had
destroyed the nation's 'taste for simplicity'. He urged its
recovery.[11] *Rob Roy* presses forward the belief that Scotland, as
part of Britain, was shaping its future not primarily in the court
(English or Scottish) but in commercial expansion: forces in the
market—the mode of competition—effect changes in language,
and vice versa. Frank fears he will lose his 'elegant accomplish-
ments' among his 'ourang-outang' cousins, but the greater
danger is that Rashleigh (the diabolically clever one) will so
adroitly take up the 'language of Lombard Street' that he will
use it to undermine the business interests of Frank's father. The
'language' of commerce demands not only a use of jargon, but
also a 'common' touch, inimical to the romantic hero. Frank, as
narrator, must divide himself in order for us to get the point: he
both worries about losing his own elegance, and muses that the
'polished' world at times allows 'exterior grace and manner' to
'supply mental deficiency'.[12]

---

[10] Charles Kingsley, *Two Years Ago* (London, 1893), 55, 100, 117, 315, 354,
144.
[11] Walter Scott, 'The Life of Dryden', in *The Works of John Dryden* (London,
1808), 9–10, 12.
[12] *Rob Roy*, 125, 89, 114, 47.

All three novelists evoke the danger of putting too high a value on an art, or tool, that can be picked up by anyone, with no way of screening the intent of the user. Gaskell and Kingsley hold up 'plain speech' as the most transparent (and trustworthy) medium. Yet, as a mixture of fragments of languages, open to identification, it can be reproduced at will, and is hardly a safe mirror of the soul.

Tensions in the fiction—between models of purity and hybridization, of static perfection and unregulated growth, of fact and narrative—become clearer when read amid commentary (both in the fiction and out) about the development and variety of languages. Nineteenth-century writers of fiction *and* non-fiction put moments of creation in coexistence with the image of steady growth. Shifts in the use of language, among authors, point in one of two directions: a willingness to surrender characters to change; or a desire to have their speech mirror, and re-establish, the necessary progress of nation or race. Plain English, as a presence of measure alone, ratified the image of growth as opposed to simple mutation. Where it appeared as an arbitrary standard, as it does most often in Gaskell's fiction, it took on a different value: it became a means of drawing private goals into the shape of the community. It focused the will on a double vision of progress, where the development of the self implies a blind spot to how the story ends; where a lack of perfect clarity—of imitative structure—fits us for an unexpected world.

Bibliography

PRIMARY SOURCES

Published Material

ARNOLD, MATTHEW, 'The Literary Influence of Academies', in *Arnold's Lectures and Essays in Criticism*, ed. R. H. Super (Ann Arbor, Mich., 1962), 232–57.

—— 'On the Study of Celtic Literature', in *Arnold's Lectures and Essays in Criticism*, ed. R. H. Super (Ann Arbor, Mich., 1962), 291–386.

ARNOLD, THOMAS, *Introductory Lectures on Modern History* (Oxford, 1842).

AXON, WILLIAM E. A., *Folk Song and Folk-Speech of Lancashire: on the Ballads and Songs of the County Palatine, With Notes on the Dialect in which Many of them Are Written, And an Appendix on Lancashire Folk-Lore* (Manchester, 1870).

BAIN, ALEXANDER, *An English Grammar* (London, 1863).

—— *The Emotions and the Will* (London, 1859).

—— *On the Study of Character, Including an Estimate of Phrenology* (London, 1861).

—— *On Teaching English: with Detailed Examples, and an Enquiry into the Definition of Poetry* (London, 1887).

—— *The Senses and the Intellect* (London, 1855).

BARNES, WILLIAM, *Early England and the Saxon-English; with Some Notes on the Father Stock of the Saxon-English, the Frisians* (London, 1869).

—— *Tiw; or, a View of the Roots and Stems of the English as a Teutonic Tongue* (London, 1862).

BLAIR, HUGH, *Lectures on Rhetoric and Belles Lettres*, 2 vols. (Basel, 1801).

BUNSEN, CHRISTIAN CHARLES JOSIAS, *Outlines of the Philosophy of Universal History, Applied to Language and Religion*, 2 vols. (London, 1854).

CAMDEN, WILLIAM, 'Prologue to his Translation of *Eneydos* (1490)', in W. F. Bolton (ed.), *The English Language: Essays by English and American Men of Letters 1490–1839* (London, 1973), 1–4.

CARLYLE, THOMAS, 'Corn-Law Rhymes', in *English and Other Critical Essays* (London, 1967), 142–64.

CARLYLE, THOMAS, 'On History', in *English and Other Critical Essays* (London, 1967), 80–90.

—— *Past and Present*, ed. A. M. D. Hughes (1843; Oxford, 1918).

DARWIN, CHARLES, *The Descent of Man* (1871; New York, 1874).

DAVIES, JOHN, 'On the Races of Lancashire, as indicated by the Local Names and the Dialect of the County', *Transactions of the Philological Society*, no. 13 (1855), 210–84.

—— 'On the Connexion of the Keltic With the Teutonic Languages, and Especially With the Anglo-Saxon', *Transactions of the Philological Society* (1857), 39–93.

DEFOE, DANIEL, *The Life and Adventures of Robinson Crusoe*, ed. Angus Ross (1719; Harmondsworth, 1972).

DE QUINCEY, THOMAS, 'The English Language', *Blackwood's* (Apr. 1839); repr. in W. F. Bolton (ed.), *The English Language: Essays by English and American Men of Letters 1490–1839*, (London, 1973), 198–213.

—— 'On Wordsworth's Poetry', *Tait's Edinburgh Magazine* (1845); repr. in *De Quincey as Critic*, ed. John E. Jordan (London, 1973), 397–424.

DICKENS, CHARLES, 'Saxon-English', in W. F. Bolton and D. Crystal (eds.), *The English Language 1858–1964* (London, 1969), 1–7.

DOUGLAS, JANET M., *The Life and Selections from the Correspondence of William Whewell, D.D., Late Master of Trinity College, Cambridge* (London, 1881).

DRYDEN, JOHN, 'Defence of the Epilogue', in W. F. Bolton (ed.), *The English Language: Essays by English and American Men of Letters 1490–1839* (London, 1973), 55–69.

EDGEWORTH, MARIA, *Helen* (1834; London, 1987).

—— *Letters from England 1813–1844*, ed. Christina Colvin (London, 1971).

—— and R. L., *Essays on Practical Education*, 2 vols. (London, 1815).

ELIOT, GEORGE, *Adam Bede*, ed. Gordon S. Haight (1859; New York, 1965).

—— *The Mill on the Floss*, ed. Gordon S. Haight (1860; Oxford, 1980).

—— 'The Natural History of German Life', *Westminster Review* (July 1856); repr. in *Essays of George Eliot*, ed. Thomas Pinney (London, 1968), 266–99.

—— 'Westward Ho! and Constance Herbert', in *Essays of George Eliot*, ed. Thomas Pinney (London, 1968), 123–36.

FERGUSON, ADAM, *An Essay on the History of Civil Society* (Edinburgh, 1767).

FREEMAN, EDWARD AUGUSTUS, 'Race and Language', *Contemporary Review* (1877); repr. in Michael D. Biddiss (ed.), *Images of Race* (Leicester, 1979), 205–35.

—— *A Dark Night's Work and Other Stories*, ed. Suzanne Lewis (Oxford, 1992).

GASKELL, ELIZABETH, *Cousin Phillis and Other Tales*, ed. Angus Easson (Oxford, 1991).

—— *Cranford*, ed. Elizabeth Porges Watson (1853; London, 1972).

—— *The Letters of Mrs Gaskell*, ed. J. A. V. Chapple and Arthur Pollard (Manchester, 1966).

—— *The Life of Charlotte Brontë*, ed. Alan Shelston (1857; London, 1985).

—— *Lizzie Leigh, The Grey Woman, and Other Tales* (London, 1913).

—— *Mary Barton: A Tale of Manchester Life*, ed. Stephen Gill (1848; Harmondsworth, 1976).

—— *My Lady Ludlow and Other Stories*, ed. Edgar Wright (Oxford, 1989).

—— *North and South*, ed. Angus Easson (1854–5; Oxford, 1982).

—— *Ruth*, ed. Alan Shelston (1853; Oxford, 1985).

—— *Sylvia's Lovers*, ed. Andrew Sanders (1863; Oxford, 1982).

—— *Wives and Daughters*, ed. Angus Easson (1864; Oxford, 1991).

GASKELL, WILLIAM, 'Two Lectures on the Lancashire Dialect', in *Mary Barton: A Tale of Manchester Life*, ed. Angus Easson (1854; Halifax, 1993), 361–91.

HERDER, JOHANN GOTTFRIED, 'Essay on the Origin of Language', trans. Alexander Gode, in *On the Origin of Language* (New York, 1966), 87–166.

HUNT, JAMES, *A Manual of the Philosophy of Voice and Speech, Especially in Relation to the English Language and the Art of Public Speaking* (London, 1859).

JOHNSON, SAMUEL, 'Preface to a Dictionary of the English Language' (1755), in W. F. Bolton (ed.), *The English Language: Essays by English and American Men of Letters 1490–1839* (London, 1973), 129–56.

KINGSLEY, CHARLES, *Alton Locke: Tailor and Poet, an Autobiography*, ed. Elizabeth A. Cripps (1850; Oxford, 1987).

—— *Charles Kingsley: Letters and Memories of His Life*, ed. Frances Kingsley, 2 vols. (London, 1877).

—— *Hereward the Wake, 'Last of the English'* (1866; London, 1881).

—— *Hypatia; or, New Foes With an Old Face* (1853; London, 1882).

—— *Literary and General Lectures and Essays* (London, 1890).

—— *The Roman and the Teuton: a Series of Lectures delivered before the University of Cambridge* (Cambridge, 1864).

KINGSLEY, CHARLES, *Scientific Lectures and Essays* (London, 1885).
—— *Two Years Ago* (London, 1893).
—— *Westward Ho! or, The Voyages and Adventures of Sir Amyas Leigh, Knight, of Burrough, in the County of Devon, in the Reign of Her Most Glorious Majesty Queen Elizabeth* (1855; London, 1906).
—— *Yeast* (1848; Dover, 1994).
LOCKE, JOHN, *An Essay Concerning Human Understanding*, ed. Peter H. Nidditch (1690; Oxford, 1975).
—— *Some Thoughts Concerning Education*, ed. John W. and Jean S. Yolton (1693; Oxford, 1989).
LUNN, CHARLES, *The Philosophy of Voice: Showing the Right and Wrong Action of Voice in Speech and Song* (London, 1874).
LYELL, CHARLES, *The Geological Evidences of the Antiquity of Man, with Remarks on Theories of The Origin of Species by Variation* (London, 1863).
—— *Principles of Geology, or the Modern Changes of the earth and its Inhabitants, Considered as Illustrative of Geology*, 2 vols. (1830–3; London, 1872).
MACAULAY, THOMAS BABBINGTON, 'Lord Bacon', in *Critical and Historical Essays Contributed to the 'Edinburgh Review'*, ed. F. C. Montague, 3 vols., vol. ii. (London, 1903), 115–239.
MAURICE, F. D., *The Friendship of Books and Other Lectures*, ed. T. Hughes (London, 1893).
—— *Social Morality: Twenty-one Lectures* (London, 1893).
MILL, JOHN STUART, *A System of Logic Ratiocinative and Inductive: Being a Connected View of the Principles of Evidence and the Methods of Scientific Investigation*, ed. J. M. Robson, books IV–VI (1843; Toronto, 1974).
MÜLLER, GEORGINA ADELAIDE, *The Life and Letters of the Right Honourable Friedrich Max Müller*, (ed.) 2 vols. (London, 1902).
MÜLLER, MAX, *Lectures on the Science of Language*, 2 vols. (1861; London, 1871).
—— *On the Stratification of Language* (London, 1868).
NEWMAN, FRANCIS W., 'The English Language as Spoken and Written', *The Contemporary Review* (Mar. 1878), 689–706.
—— *Orthöepy: or, A Simple Mode of Accenting English, For the Advantage of Foreigners, and of All Learners* (London, 1869).
PERCY, THOMAS, *Reliques of Ancient English Poetry. Consisting of Old Heroic Ballads, Songs, and Other Pieces of our Earlier Poets, Together with Some few of Later Date*, 3 vols. (1764; London, 1794).
PHILOLOGICAL SOCIETY, *Proposal for the Publication of a New English Dictionary* (London, 1859).

PRIESTLEY, JOSEPH, *A Course of Lectures on the Theory of Language and Universal Grammar* (Warrington, 1762).

ROUSSEAU, JEAN-JACQUES, *Émile, or on Education*, trans. Allan Bloom (Harmondsworth, 1979).

RUSHTON, WILLIAM LOWES, and MORLEY, HENRY, 'Saxon-English', in W. F. Bolton and D. Crystal (eds.), *The English Language: Essays by Linguists and Men of Letters 1858–1964*, 2 vols., vol. ii (London, 1969), 1–7.

SAYCE, A. H., *A Lecture on the Study of Comparative Philology, Delivered November 13, 1876* (Oxford, 1876).

SCHLEGEL, FRIEDRICH VON, *The Philosophy of Life, and Philosophy of Language, in a Course of Lectures*, trans. A. J. W. Morrison (London, 1847).

SCHLEICHER, AUGUST, *Darwinism Tested by the Science of Language*, trans. Alex V. W. Bikkers (London, 1869); trans. Alex V. W. Bikkers from *Die Darwinsche Theorie und die Sprachwissenschaft, offenes Sendschreiben an E. Häckel* (1852).

SCHUYLER, EUGENE, *Review of Wedgwood's English Etymology* (Andover, 1862).

SCOTT, WALTER, *The Abbot*, ed. Andrew Lang (1820; London, 1900).

—— *The Antiquary*, ed. David Hewitt (1816; Edinburgh, 1995).

—— *The Bride of Lammermoor*, ed. Fiona Robertson (1819; Oxford, 1991).

—— *Guy Mannering; or, the Astrologer*, ed. Andrew Lang (1815; London, 1905).

—— *The Heart of Midlothian*, ed. Claire Lamont (1818; Oxford, 1982).

—— *Ivanhoe*, ed. Andrew Lang (1819; London, 1904).

—— *The Journal of Sir Walter Scott*, ed. W. E. K. Anderson (London, 1972).

—— 'The Life of Dryden', in *The Works of John Dryden*, ed. Walter Scott, 18 vols., vol. i (London, 1808), 1–470.

—— *The Minstrelsy of the Scottish Border*, ed. J. G. Lockhart, 4 vols. (1802–3; Edinburgh, 1850).

—— *The Monastery*, ed. Andrew Lang (1820; London, 1901).

—— *The Pirate*, ed. Andrew Lang (1822; London, 1901).

—— *Redgauntlet*, ed. Andrew Lang (1824; London, 1901).

—— *Rob Roy*, ed. John Sutherland (1817; London, 1995).

—— *The Tale of Old Mortality*, ed. Douglas Mack (1816; Edinburgh, 1993).

—— *Waverley*, ed. Andrew Hook (1814; Hammondsworth, 1988).

SMITH, ADAM, 'Considerations Concerning the First Formation

of Languages, and the Different Genius of original and compounded languages', in *The Theory of Moral Sentiments; or, an Essay towards an Analysis of the Principles by which Men naturally judge concerning the Conduct and Character, first of their Neighbours, and afterwards of themselves. To which is added, A Dissertation on the Origin of Languages*, 6th edn., 2 vols., vol. ii (London, 1790).

—— *Lectures on Rhetoric and* Belles Lettres, ed. J. C. Bryce (Oxford, 1983).

SWIFT, JONATHAN, *A Proposal for Correcting, Improving and Ascertaining the English Tongue in a Letter to the Most Honourable Robert Earl of Oxford and Mortimer, Lord High Treasurer of Great Britain* (London, 1712).

TRENCH, RICHARD CHENEVIX, *English: Past and Present— Five Lectures* (London, 1855).

—— *On the Study of Words: Five Lectures Addressed to the Pupils at the Diocesan Training School, Winchester* (London, 1851).

WEDGWOOD, HENSLEIGH, *A Dictionary of English Etymology* (London, 1859).

—— 'On False Etymologies', *Transactions of the Philological Society*, no. 6 (23 Mar. 1855), 62–72.

—— *On the Origin of Language* (London, 1866).

WORDSWORTH, WILLIAM, 'Preface to Lyrical Ballads, with Pastoral and Other Poems (1802)', in *William Wordsworth*, ed. Stephen Gill (Oxford, 1984), 595–615.

Unpublished Material

Letters to Elizabeth and William Gaskell, John Rylands University Library of Manchester, Eng. MS 731/7–1. Reproduced by courtesy of the Director and University Librarian.

MARTIN, ROBERT BERNARD, 'An Edition of the Correspondence and Private Papers of Charles Kingsley 1819–1856', D.Phil. thesis, Oxford, 1950, Bodleian Library, Bodl. MS B.Litt. 2. 374.

SECONDARY SOURCES

AARSLEFF, HANS, *The Study of Language in England 1780–1860* (Minneapolis, 1983).

ARMSTRONG, NANCY, *Desire and Domestic Fiction: A Political History of the Novel* (New York, 1987).

AXON, WILLIAM E. A., 'George Eliot's Use of Dialect', in Gordon S. Haight (ed.), *A Century of George Eliot Criticism* (1880; London, 1966), 132–6.

BAKHTIN, M. M., *The Dialogic Imagination: Four Essays*, ed. Michael Holquist, trans. Caryl Emerson and Michael Holquist (Austin, Tex., 1981).

BANTON, MICHAEL, *The Idea of Race* (London, 1977).

BEER, GILLIAN, 'Carlyle and *Mary Barton*: Problems of Utterance', in Francis Barker *et al.* (eds.), *1848: The Sociology of Literature: Proceedings of the Essex Conference on the Sociology of Literature July 1977* (Colchester, 1978), 242–55.

—— *Darwin's Plots: Evolutionary Narrative in Darwin, George Eliot and Nineteenth-Century Fiction* (London, 1983).

BLAKE, N. F., *Non-Standard Language in English Literature* (London, 1981).

BOWLER, PETER J., *The Invention of Progress: The Victorians and the Past* (Oxford, 1989).

BRILL, BARBARA, *William Gaskell: 1805–1884* (Manchester, 1984).

BURROW, J. W., *Evolution and Society: A Study in Victorian Social Theory* (London, 1966).

—— 'The Uses of Philology in Victorian England', in Robert Robson (ed.), *Ideas and Institutions of Victorian Britain* (London, 1967), 180–204.

CHAPMAN, RAYMOND, *Forms of Speech in Victorian Fiction* (London, 1994).

CHITTY, SUSAN, *The Beast and the Monk: A Life of Charles Kingsley* (London, 1974).

COHEN, MURRAY, *Sensible Words: Linguistic Practice in England 1640–1785* (Baltimore, 1977).

COLLEY, LINDA, *Britons: Forging the Nation 1707–1837* (New Haven, 1992).

COLLIN, DOROTHY W., *The Composition of Mrs. Gaskell's 'North and South'* (Manchester, 1971).

COLLINI, STEFAN, *Public Moralists: Political Thought and Intellectual Life in Britain* (Oxford, 1993).

COLLOMS, BRENDA, *Charles Kingsley: The Lion of Eversley* (London, 1975).

CRAWFORD, ROBERT, *Devolving English Literature* (Oxford, 1992).

CROWLEY, TONY, *The Politics of Discourse: The Standard Language Question in British Cultural Debates* (Basingstoke, 1989).

DEAN, DAVID R., ' "Through Science to Despair": Geology and the Victorians', in James Paradis and Thomas Postlewait (eds.), *Victorian Science and Victorian Values: Literary Perspectives* (New Brunswick, NJ, 1985), 111–36.

DE MARIA, ROBERT, JR., *Johnson's 'Dictionary' and the Language of Learning* (Oxford, 1986).

DESMOND, ADRIAN, and MOORE, JAMES, *Darwin* (London, 1992).

DONALDSON, WILLIAM, 'Popular Literature: The Press, the People, and the Vernacular Revival', in Douglas Gifford (ed.), *The History of Scottish Literature*, 4 vols., vol. iii. (Aberdeen, 1988), 203–15.

DOWLING, LINDA, *Language and Decadence in the Victorian Fin de Siècle* (Princeton, 1986).

EASSON, ANGUS, *Elizabeth Gaskell* (London, 1979).

—— *Elizabeth Gaskell: The Critical Heritage* (London, 1991).

—— *Elizabeth Gaskell and the Novel of Local Pride* (Manchester, 1985).

ELIOT, GEORGE, 'Westward Ho! and Constance Herbert', *Westminster Review* (July 1855), in Thomas Pinney (ed.), *Essays of George Eliot* (London, 1968), 123–36.

FLEISHMAN, AVROM, *The English Historical Novel: Walter Scott to Virginia Woolf* (Baltimore, 1971).

FOUCAULT, MICHEL, *The Order of Things: An Archaeology of the Human Sciences* (1970; New York, 1994); trans. from the French, *Les Mots et les choses: Une archéologie des sciences humaines* (Paris, 1966).

GÉRIN, WINIFRED, *Elizabeth Gaskell: A Biography* (London, 1976).

GILL, STEPHEN, 'Price's Patent Candles: New Light on *North and South*', *Review of English Studies: A Quarterly Journal of English Literature and English Language*, NS 27 (1976), 313–21.

GILMOUR, ROBIN, 'Regional and Provincial in Victorian Literature', in R. P. Draper (ed.), *The Literature of Region and Nation* (Basingstoke, 1989), 51–60.

GOULD, STEPHEN JAY, *Time's Arrow, Time's Cycle: Myth and Metaphor in the Discovery of Geological Time* (London, 1991).

HAYDEN, JOHN O., *Scott: The Critical Heritage* (London, 1970).

HENSON, HILARY, 'Early British Anthropologists and Language', in Edwin Ardener (ed.), *Social Anthropology and Language* (London, 1971).

HEWITT, DAVID, 'Scoticisms and Cultural Conflict', in R. P. Draper (ed.), *The Literature of Region and Nation* (Basingstoke, 1989), 125–35.

HOPKINS, A. B., *Elizabeth Gaskell: Her Life and Work* (London, 1952).

HORSMAN, ALAN, *The Victorian Novel* (Oxford, 1990).

INGHAM, PATRICIA, 'Dialect as "Realism": *Hard Times* and the Industrial Novel', *Review of English Studies*, 37 (Nov. 1986), 518–27.

—— 'Dialect in the Novels of Hardy and George Eliot', in George Watson (ed.), *Literary English since Shakespeare* (London, 1970), 347–63.

JAMES, LOUIS, *Fiction for the Working Man 1830–1850: A Study of the Literature Produced for the Working Classes in Early Victorian Urban England* (London, 1963).

JOHNSON, EDGAR, *Sir Walter Scott: The Great Unknown*, 2 vols. (London, 1970).

JONES, BERNARD, 'William Barnes on Lindley Murray's English Grammar', *English Studies: A Journal of English Language and Literature*, 64 (1993), 30–5.

JOYCE, PATRICK, 'The People's English: Language and Class in England *c.*1840–1920', in Peter Burke and Roy Porter (eds.), *Language, Self, and Society: A Social History of Language* (Oxford, 1991), 154–90.

KLIGER, SAMUEL, *The Goths in England: A Study in Seventeenth and Eighteenth Century Thought* (Cambridge, 1952).

LASS, ROGER, *The Shape of English: Structure and History* (London, 1987).

LEITH, DICK, *A Social History of English* (London, 1992).

LEONARD, STERLING ANDRUS, *The Doctrine of Correctness in English Usage 1700–1800* (New York, 1962).

LEOPOLD, JOAN, 'Anthropological Perspectives on the Origin of Language Debate in the Nineteenth Century: Edward B. Tylor and Charles Darwin', in Joachim Gessinger and Wolfert von Rahden (eds.), *Theorien vom Ursprung der Sprache*, 2 vols., vol. ii (Berlin, 1989), 151–76.

LETLEY, EMMA, 'Language and Nineteenth-Century Scottish Fiction', in Douglas Gifford (ed.), *The History of Scottish Literature*, 4 vols. (Aberdeen, 1988), iii. 321–36.

LEVITT, JOHN, 'William Gaskell and the Lancashire Dialect', *Journal of the Lancashire Dialect Society*, no. 31 (Jan. 1982), 36–42.

LUKÁCS, GEORG, *The Historical Novel*, trans. Hannah and Stanley Mitchell (London, 1962).

MCARTHUR, TOM (ed.), *The Oxford Companion to the English Language* (Oxford, 1992).

MARTIN, ROBERT BERNARD, *The Dust of Combat: A Life of Charles Kingsley* (London, 1959).

MATTHEWS, WILLIAM, *Cockney Past and Present: A Short History of the Dialect of London* (London, 1938).

MELCHERS, GUNNEL, 'Mrs. Gaskell and Dialect', in Mats Ryden and Lennart A. Björk (eds.), *Studies in English Philology, Linguistics and Literature Presented to Alarik Rynell* (Stockholm, 1978), 112–24.

MUGGLESTONE, L. C., 'Ladylike Accents: Female Pronunciation and Perceptions of Prestige in Nineteenth-Century England', *Notes & Queries*, 235 (Mar. 1990), 44–52.

MUGGLESTONE, L. C., *'Talking Proper': The Rise of Accent as a Social Symbol* (Oxford, 1995).

MURISON, DAVID, 'Two Languages in Scott', in A. Norman Jeffares (ed.), *Scott's Mind and Art* (Edinburgh, 1969), 206–29.

NERLICH, BRIGITTE, 'The Evolution of the Concept of "Linguistic Evolution" in the Nineteenth and Twentieth Century', *Lingua*, 77/2 (1989), 101–12.

NEWMAN, GERALD, *The Rise of English Nationalism: A Cultural History 1740–1830* (London, 1987).

PAGE, NORMAN, *Speech in the English Novel* (Basingstoke, 1988).

PETERSON, LINDA H., 'Harriet Martineau's *Household Education*: Revising the Feminine Tradition', in Patrick Scott and Pauline Fletcher (eds.), *Culture and Education in Victorian England* (Lewisburg, Pa., 1990), 183–94.

PETYT, K. M., *The Study of Dialect: An Introduction to Dialectology* (London, 1980).

ROBBINS, KEITH, *Nineteenth-Century Britain: Integration and Diversity* (Oxford, 1988).

ROBINS, R. H., *A Short History of Linguistics* (New York, 1990).

RUPKE, NICOLAAS A., *The Great Chain of History: William Buckland and the English School of Geology 1814–1849* (Oxford, 1983).

ST GEORGE, ANDREW, *The Descent of Manners: Etiquette, Rules and the Victorians* (London, 1993).

SANDERS, ANDREW, *The Victorian Historical Novel 1840–1880* (London, 1978).

SCHOR, HILARY M., *Scheherezade in the Marketplace: Elizabeth Gaskell and the Victorian Novel* (New York, 1992).

SHARPS, JOHN GEOFFREY, *Mrs. Gaskell's Observation and Invention: A Study of her Non-Biographic Works* (Fontwell, 1970).

SHAW, HARRY E., 'Scott's "Daemon" and the Voices of Historical Narration', *Journal of English and Germanic Philology*, 88/1 (Jan. 1989), 21–33.

SHEPHERD, VALERIE, *Language Variety and the Art of the Everyday* (London, 1990).

SHIACH, MORAG, *Discourse on Popular Culture: Class, Gender and History in Cultural Analysis 1730 to the Present* (Stanford, Calif., 1989).

SMITH, OLIVIA, *The Politics of Language 1791–1819* (Oxford, 1984).

SMITH, SHEILA M., *The Other Nation: The Poor in English Novels of the 1840s and 1850s* (New York, 1980).

SUTHERLAND, JOHN, *The Life of Walter Scott: A Critical Biography* (Oxford, 1995).

TAYLOR, DENNIS, *Hardy's Literary Language and Victorian Philology* (Oxford, 1993).

TOOLAN, MICHAEL, 'The Significations of Representing Dialect in Writing', in Mike Short (ed.), *Language and Literature: Journal of the Poetics and Linguistics Association*, 1/1: 29–46.

TULLOCH, GRAHAM, *The Language of Walter Scott: A Study of his Scottish and Period Language* (London, 1980).

UGLOW, JENNY, *Elizabeth Gaskell: A Habit of Stories* (1993; London, 1994).

VICINUS, MARTHA, *The Industrial Muse: A Study of Nineteenth Century British Working-Class Literature* (London, 1974).

VINCENT, DAVID, *Literacy and Popular Culture: England 1750–1914* (Cambridge, 1989).

WAKELIN, MARTYN, *The Archaeology of English* (London, 1988).

WHEELER, MICHAEL, *The Art of Allusion in Victorian Fiction* (London, 1970).

—— 'Mrs. Gaskell's Reading, and the Gaskell Sale Catalogue in Manchester Central Library', *Notes & Queries*, 24 (1977), 25–30.

WILT, JUDITH, *Secret Leaves: The Novels of Sir Walter Scott* (Chicago, 1985).

WRIGHT, EDGAR, *Mrs. Gaskell: The Basis for Reassessment* (London, 1965).

Index